AUTHORS IN THE CLASSROOM

A Transformative Education Process

Alma Flor Ada
University of San Francisco

F. Isabel Campoy

With the collaboration of
Rosalma Zubizarreta

PEARSON

Boston | New York | San Francisco
Mexico City | Montreal | Toronto | London | Madrid | Munich | Paris
Hong Kong | Singapore | Tokyo | Cape Town | Sydney

Series Editor: Aurora Martínez Ramos
Series Editorial Assistant: Katie Freddoso
Senior Marketing Manager: Elizabeth Fogarty
Senior Production Editor: Annette Pagliaro
Editorial Production: Omegatype Typography, Inc.
Composition Buyer: Linda Cox
Manufacturing Buyer: Andrew Turso
Cover Administrator: Joel Gendron
Electronic Composition: Omegatype Typography, Inc.
Interior Design: Carol Somberg

For related titles and support materials, visit our online catalog at www.ablongman.com.

Between the time Website information is gathered and then published, it is not unusual for some sites to have closed. Also, the transcription of URLs can result in typographical errors. The publisher would appreciate notification where these errors occur so that they may be corrected in subsequent editions.

Library of Congress Cataloging-in-Publication Data

Ada, Alma Flor.
    Authors in the classroom : a transformative education process
Alma Flor Ada and F. Isabel Campoy, with the collaboration of Rosalma Zubizarreta.
        p. cm.
    Includes bibliographical references.
    ISBN 0-205-35139-5 (alk. paper)
    1. English language–Composition and exercises–Study and teaching (Elementary) 2.
Creative writing (Elementary education) 3. Children's literature–Authorship. 4.
Authorship–Collaboration. 5. Education–Parent participation. I. Campoy, F. Isabel. II.
Zubizarreta-Ada, Rosalma. III. Title.

LB1576 .A385 2004
372.62'3–dc21

                                                                                    2002038325

Printed in the United States of America

10 9 8 7 6 5 4 3 2 1   08 07 06 05 04 03

TO THE GREAT TEACHERS WHO CONTINUE TO LIGHT THE PATH:

Félix Varela

José de la Luz y Caballero

José Martí

María Montessori

Escuela Libre de Enseñanza

Celestine Freinet

Maestro Romualdo

Rosa Sensat

Sylvia Ashton Warner

Dolores Salvador Méndez

Paulo Freire

We would like to express our gratitude to all of the teachers who promote equality and justice in their classrooms. Among the many educators from whom we have learned, we would especially like to acknowledge:

Josie Arce, Elvira Armas, Kristin Brown, Elena Catena, Linda Christiansen, Gladys Cruz, Louise Derman-Sparks, Sylvia Dorta-Duque de Reyes, Maxine Green, Diana Hernandez, bell hooks, Herbert Kohl, Stephen Krashen, Enid Lee, Raimundo Lida, Donaldo Macedo, Deborah Menkart, Toni de Miranda, Sonia Nieto, Carmen Perez-Hogan, Bob Petersen, Rosa María Peyrellade, Mary Poplin, Jackie Reza, Lourdes Rovira, Rosalia Salinas, Ricki Sherover-Marcuse, Ira Shor, Tove Skutnabb-Kangas, Nancy Jean Smith, Shelley Spiegel-Coleman, Francesco Tanucci, Rita Tenorio, Catherine Walsh, Joan Wink, Lilly Wong-Fillmore.

AND TO OUR FIRST AND MOST CONSTANT TEACHERS

Alma Lafuente Salvador and Modesto Ada Rey

María Coronado Guerrero and Juan Diego Campoy Coronado

CONTENTS

chapter 2

AUTHORS IN THE CLASSROOM   30

chapter 3

THE ROLE OF DIALOGUE IN THE CLASSROOM   41

part **II**

A TRANSFORMATIVE PROCESS   49

unit **1**

AFFIRMING SELF   50

unit **2**

RECOGNIZING HUMAN QUALITIES   78

u n i t *3*

STRENGTHENING SELF-IDENTITY   100

u n i t   **4**

BUILDING COMMUNITIES   120

u n i t   **5**

THE POWER OF TRANSFORMATION   138

u n i t   6

UNDERSTANDING THE PAST, CREATING THE FUTURE   157

unit 9

DEVELOPING RELATIONSHIPS

u n i t **10**

FROM YESTERDAY TO TOMORROW   234

ACKNOWLEDGMENTS

Our most sincere gratitude to all teachers, their students, and the parents of their students who have graciously granted permission for the inclusion of their self-published books in this text. You are a wonderful example of the power of voice; may others soon follow in your footsteps.

A heartfelt thank you to all the participants in our courses, seminars, workshops, and presentations with whom this process was developed. May you soon open the door of authorship to others.

Thank you to Marianne Halpin for her assistance on the development of the list of recommended books. You are a beautiful example as a librarian, as a lover of children and books, and as a friend.

Thank you to Aurora Martínez, Acquisitions Editor at Allyn and Bacon, who nurtured the development of this book, and Karla Walsh and the team of Omegatype Typography, Inc., who gently and effectively guided the manuscript to its present book format.

For their careful revision of the manuscript of this book and their valuable insights, we would like to recognize and express our gratitude to:

Elsa Auerbach, University of Massachusetts, Boston
Jim Cummins, OISI, University of Toronto
Stephen Krashen, University of Southern California
María E. Torres-Guzmán, Teachers College, Columbia University

INTRODUCTION

As authors of numerous books, we are well aware of the privilege inherent in being published. It can bring about recognition, acceptance, and admiration. We are also aware that this privilege is enjoyed by too few people in the world, even in the wealthiest of societies. Technology has given us the means to print, decorate, duplicate, and disseminate our writing, yet few feel free to avail themselves of this opportunity.

Many years ago, as a very young classroom teacher in Lima, Perú, Alma Flor read the writings of Celestine Freinet (1969, 1973, 1974). His dream of establishing a publishing house in every classroom deeply resonated in her imagination. From that day on, her students not only wrote but also published, even if publishing meant tedious hours spent cutting old mimeograph stencils and manually cranking a decrepit machine, and even if the product came out rather blurry on poor-quality paper. Her students were authors, and their fascination with the power of words increased daily.

When Alma Flor Ada came to the United States in the 1970s, she had also been inspired by the seminal work of Paulo Freire (1970, 1982) and his tenet that education consisted of the development of voice. Finding ditto machines in every school, sometimes in every classroom, seemed like a magical promise. How much easier it was to write or type on a ditto master than on cumbersome mimeograph stencils, and how much more appealing were the copies! Filled with expectation, she thought these machines would revolutionize schools, making every classroom a prolific publishing house where numerous books written by students and teachers would be produced.

But the dream was far from reality. Most of us are sadly aware that, rather than serving as a liberating force, ditto machines were generally put to nefarious use, as the source of endless worksheets that flooded students' desks, drowning out their creativity.

Other forms of low-cost technology have been equally misused or ignored, when instead they might provide wonderful opportunities for recording and sharing students' voices and lives. Cameras, cassette recorders, overhead transparencies—all could be powerful vehicles for highlighting and celebrating students' lives. Now we are in the

1

midst of a new technological revolution. Computers could indeed transform every classroom into a publishing house. But for this to take place, students first need to discover the motivation to write; they need to understand the power that developing their thoughts and ideas in writing can bring.

Meanwhile, Isabel Campoy, who had been writing and publishing for many years, became an acquisitions editor. As such, she identified educators with excellent pedagogical practices and encouraged them to write professional books. Sometimes she had to begin by convincing these educators of their own abilities. Her many years as an editor convinced her of the possibility of awakening the author within.

Eventually, Alma Flor and Isabel joined forces to create the process we have named "Authors in the Classroom." Having experienced in our own lives the pain and the glory of writing, as well as the power of writing for content and meaning in addition to form, we wanted to share the benefits of daring to write with others. After having presented this process in numerous courses and workshops over the last ten years, we decided to write this book so that anyone who wishes to do so may embark on this journey. For the writing process, we enlisted the help of Rosalma Zubizarreta, Alma Flor's daughter. In addition to having been a classroom teacher, Rosalma has translated children's books, produced educational materials, and worked in educational reform. In particular, her work in facilitating dialogue and exploring diversity issues inform the first three chapters of this book.

In our workshops, we have witnessed with pain the fear that many teachers have of writing and of sharing their writing. To understand this difficulty, consider the contradictions between what is expected of teachers and the education and support they receive (Ada, 1987). Most teacher education programs neglect the development of strong writing abilities and confidence as a writer. Writing is approached as a well-structured set of rules and regulations concerning choice of words, appropriate grammar, punctuation, and tone. But rarely is it presented as a vehicle for reflecting on who we are, nor as a possibility for expressing ourselves forcefully, without fear of judgment. Although vocal by necessity in front of their students, too many teachers fear speaking up or speaking out. Too many valuable thoughts go unheard, too many rich teaching experiences are withheld, too many profound reflections are silenced.

It is inappropriate to expect teachers to develop in their students skills with which they are not confident themselves. Providing teachers with techniques on how to teach writing does not seem to have produced sufficient or effective writing in the classroom. In our experience, helping teachers discover for themselves the power of authorship does indeed generate the enthusiasm for writing that can transform the way in which students and families relate to the teacher, to the act of learning, and to the discovery of their own voices.

This book is about the need for and the power of awakening teachers' voices so that they are in a better position to inspire their students to write. Furthermore, we have seen the authorship process help teachers connect more deeply with their students' families, creating a bridge between the academic climate of the classroom and the home culture (Ada & Campoy, 1998c; Ada & Zubizarreta, 2001.) We know that developing voice in teachers and students promotes classrooms in which individuality is heard, diversity is respected, and independent thinking and creativity are fostered (hooks, 1994; Walsh, 1991b). When parents are included in this process, the benefits increase tremendously.

When we encourage teachers, students, and parents to empower themselves as authors, we are providing opportunities to listen to and record numerous voices that have gone unheard, lives about which no one has ever written. We are also reaffirming parents' role as educators by inviting them to partake directly of the benefits of print and books, and of the value of recording, reproducing, and disseminating their experiences.

We speak of celebrating human experience not from a naïve perspective that ignores the pain, contradictions, and oppression revealed by many of the voices we hear. To the contrary, we honor these revelations as starting points for reflection on the part of both reader and writer. Putting life experiences into words is the beginning of listening to those who have been ignored or unseen, and it can be the first step toward a process of liberation.

Our intent is to develop greater awareness of the power of teachers', students', and parents' voices, as well as to provide practical tools for encouraging the development of voice. One of the most effective ways to do this is to share the writings of other teachers so that members of the educational community can read one another's books and become inspired by one another's life experiences and reflections.

Many manuals, courses, workshops, and seminars are devoted to teaching the art of writing to people of all ages (Graves, 1982; Marzán, 1997). That is not our goal. We leave the teaching of mechanics, revision, editing, and style to other venues. This book deals instead with freeing the spirit, unlocking the fears that have stopped too many people from exploring their own expression. We present here an effective process for awakening the silenced author. It is an invitation to reclaim the voices that have been ignored, unheard, or silenced, and to discover the power that those voices can bring to our educational discourse.

We encourage a process of self-publishing, not to deter anyone from pursuing professional publishing at a later time, but in order to not be constrained by the restrictions of that world. For those who seek information on professional publishing opportunities, we provide some suggestions and references at the end of the book.

The themes and structures we include in the teaching units have all been developed for our courses and workshops. They are intended to facilitate the creation of books focused on content and meaning. They are effective insofar as they can be presented during the course of one session and produce immediate results. This is not to disregard the significance of revision and editing nor the satisfaction of creating a well-developed product. But all that can come in due time, once the fear of writing has been dispelled, once the authenticity of one's own experiences has been revealed, once the ownership of one's own history has been established.

Over the years, the Authors in the Classroom process has deepened through the efforts of countless teachers who have chosen to make this work their own and to explore, extend, and improvise on the basic structures we have offered. By taking the risk of writing their own stories and making their own books to share with their students and the students' families, they have chosen to serve as a model for students and families to begin writing and reflecting on their own lives.

As you encounter their work in these pages, we hope that you too will experience how writing can transform us into authors, from followers of other people's agendas to shapers of our own ideas. And that is just the beginning, for we hope you will also experience how writing can offer inspiration and leadership to our communities. Instead of being individuals who ignore or fear one another, we can become community members who share one another's stories, embrace one another's pain, and rejoice in one another's happiness. By sharing our stories with one another, we can start feeling powerful enough to take on the work of making our neighborhoods a better place to live and our world one of well-being and justice for all.

✦ CONTENT AND USE OF THIS BOOK ✦

STRUCTURE

The success of the Authors in the Classroom model does not depend only on a step-by-step procedure, but also on philosophical and humanistic foundations:

- ◆ The conviction that, as human beings, we possess an intrinsic equal value, and that our opinions, experiences, and feelings deserve to be heard
- ◆ The creation of a supportive classroom environment in which students feel welcome and safe in sharing their thoughts and their writing
- ◆ The willingness of teachers to share their own writing with students and parents and thus serve as both model and source of inspiration for others
- ◆ The commitment to this process as a three-pronged approach, remembering that all three groups of voices—teacher, students, and parents or relatives—are critical to its success

Furthermore, the process is supported and enhanced by the following educational practices:

- ◆ Inviting students to interactively explore a broad range of high-quality literature that can serve as both models and sources of inspiration
- ◆ Selecting books and questions for dialogue that encourage reflection
- ◆ Using dialogue as a way to prepare for writing, further the reflective process, and build community
- ◆ Creating a classroom community in which equality, justice, and peace are explored in both thought and action

Given the importance of these foundations, we have devoted the first section of this book to developing these concepts further, before proceeding to the teaching units in the second half of the book.

Chapter 1 begins with the principles of Transformative Education, our own philosophy of education which is a synthesis of various existing approaches. It continues with a more in-depth exploration of Anti-Bias education, one of the key elements of Transformative Education. Since Anti-Bias work is best understood experientially, this chapter includes a series of reflective journal activities that can be completed individually by educators.

Chapter 2 presents some rationale and background for the Authors in the Classroom model. To help teachers better implement this model, we have included a chapter on dialogue. Chapter 3 explores the importance of dialogue as a precursor to writing, as a tool with which to include all parents and families, especially those with limited schooling experience, and as a way of creating a supportive classroom community.

Chapter 3 begins with a description of the Creative Literacy process (Ada, 1988, 1991, 2003; Ada & Campoy, 1998a), a transformative education approach designed to encourage reflection by engaging in dialogue with the text. This four-stage process begins by inviting readers or listeners to interpret the content of the text. Next, students are invited to explore their emotional responses to the text, as well as to contrast the information from the text with their own personal experiences. This leads to a critical analysis of the ethical and social implications of the text and its consequences for the values of justice, equity, and peace. In the final stage of the dialogue, students are invited to reconsider the role of protagonist in their own lives, in light of the insights derived through interaction with the text. Also included in Chapter 3 are suggested guidelines for facilitating dialogue in the classroom.

The second half of this book consists of ten teaching units that are applicable to students of all ages. Each unit includes several authoring projects organized around a unifying theme drawn from everyday life. The unit begins with a brief reflection on the theme, followed by the objectives to be covered in the unit.

Because reading is the best preparation for writing, the writing activities are introduced with a reading experience. In lessons 2 through 9, the reading experience includes the Creative Literacy process. After the shared reading and discussion of a text, the units proceed to the authoring process. We begin with a section on "Teachers as Authors" that invites teachers to follow a step-by-step process for creating their own books. In the next two sections, "Students as Authors and Protagonists" and "Parents as Educators and Authors," suggestions are given to assist teachers in leading students and parents through the writing process. Each of these sections includes various examples of books created by teachers, students, and parents. These examples demonstrate diverse approaches to the authoring process. At the end of each unit is a section that consists solely of additional examples of books authored by teachers, students, and parents.

When working with your students, you may want to offer them the opportunity to explore a variety of books related to the theme of the unit and/or to the particular literary structures introduced in the unit. Therefore, we have included a list of additional books for children and adolescents at the end of each unit.

Unit 1 is much more extensive and detailed than the rest of the units because it introduces the process for the first time. However, because each unit is self-sufficient, the rest of the units can be explored in a different sequence than the one proposed here.

Units 2 through 9 begin with the Creative Literacy process as a means of engaging students in dialogue with a text. Because the Authors in the Classroom program is based on modeling, we have included some selections of our own writing as possible texts to introduce each unit. Of course, the Creative Literacy Dialogue process can be applied to any book of your choosing.

The heart of each unit, as described earlier, consists of a series of activities to help teachers create their own books on the given theme, as well as to assist teachers in guiding students and parents through the process. Of course, teachers can apply and extend this process to themes other than the ones we have included here. What we offer are the themes that have emerged in our own practice, ranging from self-discovery and exploring one's past to recognizing one's talents and building community. The common thread in each unit is finding strength in the past and in the present to enable us to move creatively into the future.

Finally, the book includes the brief section "Extending Authorship beyond the Classroom," and we've also included a list of recommended books for children and young adults, as well as a bibliography of sources cited and suggested readings.

ON USING THIS BOOK

Authors in the Classroom, the approach presented here, is not restricted to any specific type of student, to any specific language, nor to any specific age level. It has been used with kindergartners and with doctoral students, in monolingual as well as bilingual settings, using the first or the second language, from Arizona to Hungary, from New York to Micronesia. Because it addresses each individual's need to express his or her own voice, as well as to recognize and honor the communities of which they are a member, the process can be adjusted to the age and sophistication of the participants. Although the texts generated will vary depending on the context, the process of creating each poem or book is designed to result in reflection and empowerment.

To Develop Authorship in Your Students and Their Families

If your goal is to encourage the development of your own voice as well as the voices of your students and their families, we encourage you to follow the steps included for each unit. The suggested process can be outlined as follows:

- Gather as many high-quality books as possible on the selected topic and/or the given literary structure. A starter list is included, and the public or school librarian may be able to help identify others.
- Introduce the books to the students. Read to them and with them. Talk about the books. Invite the students to share the books with their families, or find another way to share the books with parents and family members.
- Talk with your students about the theme of the unit. The suggestions in Chapter 3 can be helpful for introducing your students to dialogue.
- Choose one of the books (or use one of the texts we have included here) to use as a basis for the Creative Literacy process, an in-depth conversation around a story or poem.
- Follow the suggestions we have included for creating your own book. Use the examples of other teachers' books for inspiration.
- Share your book with your students and their families. Talk with them about what it has meant to you to author this book, and offer any insights you may have experienced along the way.
- Invite the students and their families to create their own books.

- Design a way for students to share their work and their creative processes with one another.
- Find a way to share parents' thoughts and the books they have created in the classroom and in the school at large.
- Celebrate everyone's authorship. This includes celebrating the learning that has taken place along the way and the original experiences that gave rise to the books, as well as the finished products.

Repeat the process with a new topic. Each time you do so, you add depth to your collective experience and to your shared reflections.

To Join the World of Authors

If you are not presently in the classroom, or if you would like to work on developing your own creativity, you may want to focus on the "Unveiling the Authors Within" section of each unit and the "Teachers as Authors" subsections. It may also be helpful to work through the material on oppression and liberation in the first chapter of Part I, as these activities can facilitate the awakening of a personal voice.

Almost every example in this book was created by a teacher (or by a student or family member as a result of a teacher's example and encouragement). Clearly, *Authors in the Classroom* is addressed to teachers, yet anyone wishing to participate in the world of authors could follow the process we have described here and discover the richness of authorship. This can be done individually, with a partner, or with a group of friends. We invite you to join us in the adventure of awakening the author within.

I

THEORETICAL PRINCIPLES

TRANSFORMATIVE EDUCATION

❖ UNDERLYING PRINCIPLES ❖

Educators teach from a set of beliefs about human nature and the learning process. Regardless of whether we consciously ascribe to an educational philosophy, every choice we make in the classroom, every decision we make, and even the way we frame and make sense of our experiences is profoundly influenced by our beliefs.

Some of our beliefs may be consciously held and the product of ongoing reflection. Others might be experienced as an inarticulate "knowing" that has been shaped by our experience or that responds to our intuition. And there are others of which we may not be aware at all until we discover them in the process of analyzing our own behavior in order to develop greater self-understanding.

The process of growth is not easy, as it usually involves the awareness of some degree of tension between the conscious goals to which we aspire and the deeply held, often unconscious beliefs that are manifested in our actions. None of us is able to fully live out the ideals we hold. At the same time, the more clearly we can articulate our ideals, the stronger our sense of direction will be. It will also help us participate more actively in our own evolution as long as we remain willing to recognize and explore our own limitations. It is in this spirit that we share with you some of the principles of our own educational philosophy.

The set of interrelated principles that we call Transformative Education serves as a way of thinking about the world and understanding relationships between teachers, students, and families. It is also a tool with which we can continually examine and learn from our own experience and practice and thus further our own growth. In this sense, the goal of Transformative Education can be understood as inner transformation, as well as facilitating transformation in students' lives and in the life of society as a whole.

Instead of being seen as something "extra," Transformative Education is best understood as a tool to renew and further the goals that teachers already hold. In working with teachers throughout the world, we discovered that the following goals are shared by a vast majority of teachers. Again and again, teachers have expressed the desire that their students:

◆ Become lifelong learners
◆ Develop a love of reading
◆ Feel pride in their cultural heritage, including their home language
◆ Appreciate and respect their families and their teachers
◆ Value all forms of life
◆ Develop a sense of responsibility toward nature and the planet they inhabit
◆ Respect others and ask to be respected
◆ Learn to find peaceful resolutions to conflicts and promote harmony
◆ Be compassionate, just, and generous
◆ Develop all of their talents, including their creativity and artistic abilities
◆ Enjoy beauty in all its manifestations
◆ Understand their potential to contribute to and improve society

Ultimately, the value of Transformative Education lies in how it can help teachers and students realize their own goals.

We are defining Transformative Education as an integrated synthesis of theoretical principles from various disciplines. Some of the disciplines that inform our perspective on Transformative Education are listed below, along with key insights from each discipline. At the same time, we need to keep in mind that we are describing not just an intellectual point of view, but also a social stand on issues concerning equity, inclusion, justice, and peace, a stand born out of a deep and unconditional respect for all human beings and all forms of life. For us, the authors of this book, the following principles shape not only our professional work but also our personal, social, and political beliefs and values:

◆ Constructivist Theory

Human beings are beings of knowledge.

All of us are naturally engaged in a continuing process of making sense of the world around us, and we have an intrinsic desire to learn, to grow, and to develop new skills. Teaching is more effective when it connects with and supports this inherent tendency. To help students develop their potential to learn and to make meaning of the world around them is to foster their humanness (Vygotsky, 1962, 1978; Freire, 1985; Ferreiro & Gómez Palacio, 1986; Smith, 1995).

◆ Feminist/Womanist Theory

Human beings are beings of love and caring.

All of us learn better when we feel safe and respected, when we feel good about ourselves, when we have positive connections to others, and when we have a sense of belonging to a community. The ability to relate well to others is a learned skill, and environments that foster growth in human relationships also encourage academic growth. To foster our ability to love and care for ourselves and others is to foster the human essence (Gilligan, 1982; hooks, 1984, 1989, 1994; Pinkola-Estés, 1997; Lorde, 1984).

◆ Aesthetics

Human beings are intrinsically drawn to beauty.

Throughout the world, many of the artifacts created by intact cultures convey a sense of beauty. Whether baskets or clay pots, canoes or clothing, they show that human beings have a need to make things that are not merely useful but also beautiful. And all cultures create their own music, dance, song, and poetry.

Offering students an aesthetic environment, inviting them to participate in aesthetic experiences, and encouraging their creativity are fundamental aspects of nurturing their spirits (Greene, 1995, 1996, 1998).

◆ Critical Theory

Human beings are the sole constructors of social reality. As such, we are responsible for participating in its ongoing creation and improvement.

Social reality is not a product of nature but of human beings. As such, it is imperfect. And we as human beings have the responsibility to constantly improve that which we have created. We have the ability to see both what is and what ought to be. To live ethically is to participate in the conscious transformation of our social reality, to move toward greater equity, inclusion, justice, and peace.

The fact that some social evils—such as war, conquest, colonization, slavery, hate crimes, and poverty—have existed for a long time in many parts of the world does not justify inaction. We do not use the fact that we do not have wings, or that most human beings in history never had the opportunity to fly, to argue that therefore it is not possible for human beings to fly. There is no reason why creating equitable social and economic systems should be less feasible for our species as a whole than flying to the moon (Adorno & Horkheimer, 1972; Marcuse, 1968, 1977; Gramsci, 1971; Freire, 1970, 1982; Habermas, 1981; Giroux, 1983).

◆ Multiculturalism

The Earth is diverse by its very nature. Human beings are as diverse as the reality of this planet.

On this planet there is not *one* kind of tree but instead many different kinds. None could claim to be *the* tree. There is not *one* kind of flower but instead an enormous variety, not *one* type of insect but instead an extraordinary number of types of insects.

We all need to learn to think in terms of diversity. Although the dominant group in a society may create an image of the "norm," in truth only a tiny percentage of people fit within that narrow range. When we look at the reality of the vast majority of us, there is no real "norm" in any true mathematical sense. We are all unique, different from one another in our own ways. Only by recognizing, understanding, respecting, and celebrating diversity will we be able to create equity, inclusion, justice, and peace (Nieto, 1992, 1999; Takaki, 1993; Delpit, 1995).

◆ Anti-Bias Education

To become fully human, we must unlearn prejudice and bias and become one another's allies.

Prejudice and biases have been prevalent throughout human history. Most cultures are ethnocentric and promote a view of others who are different as lesser and/or threatening. Although no child is born prejudiced, most social groups teach their children at a very young age to distrust those who are different and to look on those who are less privileged as inferior and/or dangerous. Therefore, many people grow up unaware of their own personal biases and unconscious of the systemic biases embodied in social structures. Institutional bias creates injustice and encourages a climate that leads to violence against other human beings.

Being human implies being able to feel a sense of connection to all the members of our own species. To become more fully human, we need to unlearn prejudice and biases and learn to become one another's allies (Sherover-Marcuse, 1981; Derman-Sparks et al., 1989; Derman-Sparks & Phillops, 1997; Delpit, 1995; Lee, Menkhart, & Okazawa-Rey, 1997; Tatum, 1997; Reza, 2002).

◆ Critical Pedagogy

Throughout the world, most forms of public education promote the domestication and colonization of the human mind in order to maintain the status quo.

There are often discrepancies between, on the one hand, the school's stated goals and the goals held by individual teachers and, on the other hand, the effects produced by the way in which schools and education are structured. Becoming aware of these discrepancies and calling attention to them is the first step we need to take. Although it is generally not possible to completely resolve the contradictions inherent in these situations, bringing them into consciousness is an educational process in its own right. Naming the problem is the first step toward action (Freire, 1970, 1997; Freire & Macedo, 1987; Poplin & Weeres, 1992; Shor & Freire, 1987; Walsh, 1991a, 1991b, 1996; Wink, 1997).

◆ Bilingual Education

Language is one of the strongest elements in our self-definition, as well as one of the most significant elements of a culture.

Identification with the mother tongue begins before birth. When children are made to feel ashamed of their home language, the effects are far reaching, affecting relationships with parents, community, culture, and self. No one should be asked to reject his or her mother tongue in order to benefit from learning other languages. The rejection of the mother tongue frequently results in internalizing shame about one's own identity as well as the identity of parents and ancestors. Knowing two languages can benefit self and others, and should not be a privilege of the elite but something accessible to all children. Although it is often said that knowing two languages makes a person twice as valuable, we like to stress that knowing two or more languages provides greater opportunities to work on behalf of humanity (Ada, 1997a, 1997b; Ada & Campoy, 1999b, 1998c; Baker, 1997; Brisk, M., 1998; Brisk & Homington, 2002; Cummins, 1996, 2000; Fishman, 1972, 1976, 1989, 1996; Krashen, 1984, 1993, 1999; Skutnabb-Kangas, 2000; Skutnabb-Kangas, Phillipson, & Rannut, 1994; Wong-Filmore, 1991).

In a transformative pedagogy, all of these components work together to help us understand ourselves, one another, and the world in which we live. Equally important, they help develop our capacity to take action in a creative manner, allowing us to offer our individual contributions in a way that enhances the well-being of our communities and our world.

The process of transformative pedagogy relies on reawakening and connecting with the inherent desire to learn, creating loving and caring relationships and environments, and the strength of the arts. It addresses all of the various aspects of intelligence and strengthens critical and reflective abilities through practices that are interactive, creative, and joyful.

Transformative Education recognizes diversity as essential to life and fosters respect for all forms of diversity (gender, sexual preference, culture, religion, ethnicity, physical appearance and health, age, and beliefs). Home and community are seen as integral parts of the students' lives as well as valuable sources of knowledge. Practitioners of transformative pedagogy recognize the prevalence of biases and prejudice, and acknowledge the need to unlearn racist practices and assumptions as an essential ingredient for the creation of a just society and a peaceful world.

Finally, Transformative Education recognizes the importance of voice, the need for education to foster the critical consciousness that leads to speaking one's personal and social truth. Voice takes special force when words are not only spoken but also written.

All the principles outlined here inform the Authors in the Classroom process described in this book. Reading and writing are approached from a *constructivist* perspective, which incorporates the students' individual experiences and collectively creates new knowledge. The Creative Literacy process encourages the critical reflection toward the attainment of a just society espoused by *critical theory*. A key element of the work is the creation of a safe, nurturing, and supportive environment, which promotes listening to everyone, inspired by *feminist/womanist* thought. The process of developing and empowering voice is fundamental to *critical pedagogy*.

The use of literature and the emphasis on creativity are *aesthetic* manifestations. The books recommended for children and adolescents are *multicultural*, written by authors who represent a plurality of views and realities. This respect for diversity is also present in the *multicultural/Anti-Bias orientation* of the Creative Literacy process.

Finally, many of the examples presented are *bilingual*, or have been translated from languages other than English, demonstrating that creativity can happen in any language. Teachers using this book are encouraged at all times to access the home language of the students and parents and validate its use. All of these principles are embodied in each of the units of Part II.

In the rest of this chapter, we take a closer look at oppression and liberation, basic elements of Anti-Bias education, and key elements in the process of reclaiming of one's own voice.

❖ OPPRESSION AND LIBERATION: A CLOSER LOOK ❖

The Transformative Education journey described in this book, through the process of encouraging authorship in the classroom and in the home, begins with the freedom of our own voices. This is why it is essential to discover and transform the restrictions that may have been placed on our voices.

One of the key understandings of anti-bias work is that all of us are oppressed whenever anyone is oppressed. Any time we witness or participate silently in the oppression of others, our own sense of humanity is diminished and our joyful, creative voice is silenced. Of course, whenever we ourselves experience oppression and do not have any allies who can offer us support and affirmation, we also are silenced, especially when we are young and vulnerable.

Social injustice could not be maintained for long if we were not all conditioned in various ways to accept it. Part of that conditioning includes learning to distance ourselves from the pain of our initial encounters with injustice, encounters that occurred when we were still very open and sensitive as children. As we learn to avoid certain areas of our experience, our thinking narrows and becomes distorted. To increase our ability to think clearly about these issues, we need to be willing to reconnect with our own early experiences. Although we may encounter some painful feelings in the process, we are also regaining our capacity to feel a deeper sense of joy and connection with ourselves and others.

The process of liberation basic to anti-bias work is an ongoing one, and what we offer here is only an introduction. Also, this process is best explored experientially and collectively, so that we can learn from one another's personal experiences as well as our own. Despite the limitations imposed by the format of a book, we believe this work is essential to include here. Therefore, we have provided some simple questions for you to work with while you read this material as an invitation to relate these concepts to your own personal experience. Although working these materials with others can greatly enrich the experience, if that is not possible we encourage you to go through them on your own at your own pace.

One simple yet effective way to support yourself in this journey is to write your thoughts, memories, and feelings in a private journal as you read the rest of this chapter. If you are working with a partner or a small group, you may choose to share parts of your journal with one another from time to time. It is also fine if you prefer to keep your journal private.

In addition to using your journal to respond to the questions for personal exploration at the end of each section, we encourage you to stop and write down at any point the feelings, memories, or reflections that arise during your reading. In fact, you may wish to take some time right now to begin your journal writing.

What do you think may be difficult about this process?

What fears or hopes come up for you as you finish reading this page?

✤ UNDERSTANDING OPPRESSION ✤

DIFFERENCE AND OPPRESSION

Oppression is clearly a long-standing problem in human society, and various explanations can be offered for its origins. Without arriving at any final conclusions, we can observe that people's natural tendency to bond in groups can have both positive and negative manifestations. Throughout most of the history of humankind, people have bonded to create culture, to establish patterns of cooperation, and to ensure their survival. Yet some groups, when they have become large and powerful, have set out to prove that their superiority gives them the right over the material possessions and even the lives of others.

In these instances, we observe a mechanism set in motion whereby the group that is mistreating another also creates a whole range of beliefs designed to portray the group that is being abused as inferior, unworthy, and somehow deserving of abuse. It is as though we humans cannot live with the knowledge that those we are harming are in some way equal to ourselves, and thus we are forced to rationalize our behavior by portraying them as "other."

Differences in religious beliefs, traditions, language, and physical features have all been used as justification for establishing superiority over another group, which is then assigned a wide variety of other supposed characteristics to justify their status. There is a surprising similarity across cultures in the attributes projected onto a group that is being dominated. For example, these projected attributes include childishness, impulsiveness, laziness, lack of responsibility, exaggerated sexuality, and simplemindedness. Groups as distant geographically, ethnically, and historically as Native Americans and Finnish people have been portrayed with the same characteristics by their oppressors (Skutnabb-Kangas, 2000; Skutnabb-Kangas & Cummins, 1988)

Young children born into the dominant culture are taught at an early and impressionable age to regard members of the subordinate culture as "other," "different," "inferior," and "not fully human." Because children have a natural curiosity, openness, and desire to become close to other humans, these early learning experiences tend to be painful and confusing. Furthermore, they typically become shrouded in silence, as there are few opportunities to talk about such experiences. As a result, the pain and confusion tend to persist and harden into a generalized unwillingness to explore these issues or to question the culture's established prejudices and biases. In turn, this widespread individual conformity allows larger patterns of social injustice to continue.

At the same time, we see oppression not only between members of different cultures, but also among subgroups within a given culture. Within a cultural group, it is common for differences in gender, age, physical ability, and many other areas to become polarized, with one "standard" becoming the "norm," and those who are different from that "standard" being seen as inferior. It often seems that the more competitive and warlike the culture, the more any groups within it that are considered "weaker" or "more vulnerable" are treated in an oppressive manner.

EXPLORATION 1

It is important for all of us as adults to have opportunities to remember and reflect on our early experiences with difference. It is especially helpful when we can share these experiences with others in a supportive and respectful setting. We can also experience a sense of release by writing about these experiences.

This is a good place to begin exploring some of our early conditioning. We invite you to take a few minutes to think about one of your earliest experiences of becoming aware that you were "different" in some way from others. This could be a difference in gender, size, skin color, physical ability, class, ethnicity, sexual orientation, language, origin, religion, or any other dimension.

When was this? What happened? How did you feel?

Now take a few minutes to write down some of your reflections in your journal.

PREJUDICE, BIAS, AND OPPRESSION

One way to define *bias* is "an attitude or belief about the inferiority of the members of another group that supports the unfair treatment of the members of that group as a result of their identity." As we mentioned earlier, prejudices and biases passed on to children effectively prevent them from becoming close to other humans in different circumstances. As a result of this separation, fear, lack of information, and misunderstanding between different groups are perpetuated.

In turn, these attitudes help keep oppression in place by leading individuals to passively collaborate with established social and institutional practices. These established practices, often termed "institutionalized oppression," work to keep one group in a position of greater decision-making and economic power than another. They are reinforced by bias and also perpetuate bias.

The importance of prejudice-reduction or anti-bias work is that it helps human beings learn about one another and get in touch with our shared humanity. The more we realize what we have in common, the greater empathy we develop with another person. Once we feel connected and begin to learn what the world looks like from another perspective, we naturally become motivated to help change the oppressive circumstances that cause pain to the members of that group.

Some of the forms that social oppression takes include:

Racism—One of the more visible forms of oppression, based on the skin color, physical features, and/or ethnic heritage of a person. Racism is used to both justify and perpetuate the subordination of people of a given ethnic background.

Religious Oppression—The oppression of a group of people identified by their religious beliefs. It has often led to tragic results.

Linguistic Oppression or Linguicism—The institutionalized devaluing of a language. It can easily lead to linguistic genocide, the destruction of a culture by the annihilation of its language.

Classism—A set of beliefs and practices that values some human beings more than others based on their economic resources. This system is used to justify and perpetuate the unequal distribution of resources in society, and to allow the most basic human needs to go unmet.

Sexism—The discrimination against, unequal opportunities for, and social and physical oppression of women in most cultures.

Homophobia—The institutionalization of social policies motivated by fear and hatred of gay men and lesbians. Homophobia results in discrimination and attacks against people due to their sexual orientation.

Ageism—Discrimination against elders and against youth.

Ableism and Mental Illness Stigma—Attitudes, actions, and institutionalized practices that subordinate those who have physical challenges or suffer from any form of mental illness and prevent their full access and participation in society.

Although anyone can hold prejudiced views with regard to another, we are reserving the words *bias* and *oppression* to describe situations in which there is an unequal power relationship between two groups. Thus, by definition, we would not use them indiscriminately to include any kind of prejudice.

For example, imagine a society with two classes of people, the stripes and the polka dots. The stripes are the dominant group, wielding greater economic and political power. Therefore, they have greater decision-making power in the government structures, are treated more favorably in the classroom, and represent the canon of beauty. As part of the structure of domination, there is widespread cultural bias about the polka dots, who are widely regarded as overly emotional, childlike, impulsive, and not quite human.

In such a situation, some polka dots might believe the cultural bias about themselves, causing them to dislike other polka dots and look up to stripes. However, other polka dots might react by developing the belief that stripes on the whole are nasty, insensitive, selfish, and arrogant and overall "not quite human."

Yet, given the stripes' greater economic and decision-making power, the prejudice held by some polka dots toward the stripes would not result in a societal pattern of injustice toward the stripes . . . unless somehow the societal and power inequality were to be completely reversed. On the other hand, the existing pattern of oppression continually reinforces the bias the stripes hold against the polka dots. That bias in turn helps perpetuate the systemic oppression of the polka dots.

The reason we have spent time clarifying this distinction between prejudice (what polka dots felt), on the one hand, and bias and oppression (what stripes exercised), on the other, is that each concept is important and has its place. To create a world of peace and justice for all, we need to have a clear understanding of injustice, acknowledge the existing social patterns that support it, and create a language that allows us to speak about these patterns in an intelligible manner.

At the same time, we need to have allies. To achieve this, we need to heal and transform *all* of our prejudices. In this way, we can reach out and connect with the humanity of everyone, including those behind the mask of "the oppressor" and those behind the mask of "the oppressed."

EXPLORATION 2

All of us experience multiple identities in our lives as a result of our gender, our religion, our economic circumstances, our physical abilities, our family circumstances, and so on. In some of those identities, we experience what it is like to be a member of a dominant or privileged group, whereas in others we experience what it is like to be a member of a subordinate or oppressed group.

The following is a list of possible identities. You can add or delete to this list to better fit your experiences:

taller than average	shorter than average
physically fit	physically unfit
thin	fat
white	person of color
urban	rural
man	woman
heterosexual	homosexual
rich	poor
at least one parent with higher education	parents without higher education
nonabusive parents or caretakers	abusive parents or caretakers
nonpresence of alcoholism in the home	presence of alcoholism in the home

From the list, choose two identities you have personally experienced as a member of a privileged group. Also choose two identities you have experienced as a member of an oppressed group. Then, for each identity think about the stereotypes and prejudices you may have acquired about members of the opposite group.

In what ways did you learn to think about them as "not fully human"?

Use your journal to write down some of the prejudices you learned about others as a part of each identity.

LIBERATION: BEYOND PREJUDICE, BIAS, AND OPPRESSION

One of the fundamental tenets of Transformative Education is that all human beings are born inherently good, with the natural desire to love and be loved. No human being comes out of the womb predisposed toward prejudice, hatred, and the mistreatment of others. Although our essential core can become clouded and obscured by subsequent experiences, the inherent desire to love and be loved remains with us for the rest of our life.

A basic goal of Transformative Education might be described as helping to create a world that works well for everyone, without resorting to the mistreatment or exploitation of any group or class. In order to do so, we believe it is necessary to restore the human capacity to feel close and connected to all other human beings, without exception. Of course, we will always have challenges to work through with individuals in our lives, as this is part of how we grow. Feeling "close and connected" does not mean we do not have any differences. It does mean that we are able to learn and grow from these differences because we respect and honor the basic humanity in one another.

Yet the norm in the world today is very different. For most of us, there are whole classes of people from whom we feel separated or distant, or about whom we are uncomfortable. Although we may mistake this for "the natural state of things," it is more accurate to view this as precisely the result of the various oppressions that exist in the world today.

This discussion of our goals highlights a key premise of our work: Everyone is hurt by oppression, in the sense that everyone, both "oppressor" and "oppressed," is held back from experiencing a full humanity. At the same time, the unequal aspect of the oppressor/oppressed dynamic is also very real. As members of a privileged class, part of our privilege implies being able to remain ignorant about the injustice that members of the subordinate group experience on an everyday basis.

From a global perspective, we are privileged by the mere fact that we are writing and/or reading this book. The majority of the people in the world lack easy access to food and clean water or to shelter for sleeping and protecting themselves and their families. The mere fact of living in an economically developed country is a privilege that gives us access to possibilities not available to the majority of the people in the world. Of course, these privileges should be the norm for all human beings, yet we need to be aware of how far our current reality is from our vision. Still, being able to experience and affirm our human connection with one another, despite differences in economic circumstances, culture, or religious belief, constitutes the seed of a new reality.

EXPLORATION 3

Think about an experience in which you felt close to someone who was different from you in some significant way.

What was the experience?

What meaning does that experience hold for you?

What are your feelings as you recall the experience?

✤ HOW OPPRESSION IS PERPETUATED ✤

Given our premise that all human beings are born with the natural desire to love and be loved, how do we explain the many kinds of suffering we see around us? Although there is no single explanation, we know that various factors contribute to both the perpetuation of individual mistreatment and the perpetuation of larger patterns of social mistreatment. Some of these factors include (1) how extremely vulnerable we are to being hurt as children; (2) how as adults we instinctively avoid anything that reminds us of that early vulnerability; (3) our tendency when we have not healed to pass on the hurt we have experienced to others; and (4) our tendency to internalize the experience of oppression.

OUR VULNERABILITY AS CHILDREN

Part of the reason we are so powerfully influenced by our childhood is that we are all born physically helpless and dependent on others for our survival. If we do not receive the love and understanding we need, our growth can be stunted in a variety of ways. For example, we might internalize a sense of helplessness and dependency, and grow up with a fear of not having enough or not being able to survive. In later life, this can lead to a compulsion to secure much more than is necessary for personal survival, often at the expense of others.

As children, few of us experience full respect and care from our parents, elders, and teachers. However well-meaning the adults around us might have been, they may have been suffering under the weight of their own painful histories. Once we are grown, many of us want to distance ourselves as much as possible from the vulnerable child we carry within ourselves. Out of our own fear and desire for self-protection, we tend to identify with those social identities that accord status, prestige, and power, and to distance ourselves from any reminders of our vulnerability.

If we are in a disadvantaged social position, we may simply give up any hopes for a better life, as hope can make us too vulnerable to our pain. Or we may focus all of our efforts on escaping our individual circumstances and be unwilling to look back once we have done so. If we are in a position of privilege, we may feel hesitant about reaching out and becoming too close to someone of lesser privilege for fear that we may lose our own privilege or be rejected by our social group. Or we may feel guilty and afraid of becoming a target for the anger of someone in a subordinate position.

Regardless of our relative privilege or lack thereof, our childhood experiences may have left us with a lack of confidence in our ability to work with others to make change and create a better world. We may settle instead for trying to reach whatever positions of power are available to us. And we may tend to treat others the way we ourselves were treated as children, or as students, or in any other situation in which we felt powerless.

EXPLORATION 4

Think about an early experience of schooling, in which you remember feeling young and vulnerable.

What happened?

What were your feelings in this situation?

Spend at least five minutes describing the situation on paper, with as many details as you can remember. Next, spend some time thinking and writing about the following question:

What are some of the ways in which you as an adult protect yourself from ever being in a similar situation?

OUR TENDENCY TO PASS ON HURT TO OTHERS

The tendency to pass on our hurts, or to treat others the way we have been treated, is a central part of what keeps oppression in place. People living in difficult conditions may end up venting their frustration by turning on others who are weaker. Men frustrated by poverty and discrimination may take their frustration out on the women in their lives, whereas women oppressed by their husbands or by other men may in turn take their anger and pain out on their children. Of course, this behavior also happens among wealthy families, who can suffer from great emotional dysfunction and pain regardless of their material circumstances. The alternative to passing on our pain is to heal from our wounds. This requires both courage and a supportive environment so that we are able to open up to and feel our pain instead of fleeing from it. Engaging in our own healing process is an essential part of unlearning our biases because it allows us to become more able to listen to others and empathize with their pain. As a result, we become more able to make contact with others at a very human level.

If we have been too wounded ourselves and have not been able to touch our own pain, we will not be able to listen to the pain that others carry. And so we may find it easier to distance ourselves, to not recognize the full humanity of those who are different from us.

In addition to the painful everyday forms of neglect, disrespect, and shame that most children experience, many children suffer from extreme abuse and quite horrible circumstances. Of course, not all of these children grow up to be abusers; many are able to find ways to heal. Yet the vast majority of people who commit terrible crimes were in fact abused as children; they are the unfortunate ones who were not able to heal from those traumas.

Among these seriously wounded people we would include those who, having reached positions of great power in society, fan the flames of hatred and intolerance in others in order to serve their own selfish ends. Although we recognize that these people also were abused, this kind of crime plays a significant role in perpetuating the cycle of oppression in our society.

EXPLORATION 5

Most of us can recall an instance when we have "passed on a hurt," hurting another person in the same way we ourselves were hurt. Although we usually have a great deal of regret as well as other painful feelings associated with these memories, they can also be a source of learning. Take some time now to write in your journal about one such experience in your life and what you feel you have learned from it.

THE INTERNALIZATION OF OPPRESSION

Another mechanism that contributes to keeping oppression in place is the internalization of oppression. When we are subject to mistreatment by others who have power over us (children oppressed by adults, students oppressed by teachers, people oppressed by others with higher economic or political power), we have a tendency as human beings to internalize the experience. That is to say, our self-confidence can be easily damaged, and we often come to believe the message that we are in some way inferior and deserve to be treated poorly. This internalization can be quite obvious and explicit, or it can take very subtle forms.

It could be argued that the unstated purpose of most school systems in the "developed" world is not, in fact, to help students achieve their potential. Instead, their real purpose might be seen as convincing the great majority of their students that they lack intelligence and creativity. As a result, most of the adults who end up with the less desirable jobs society has to offer believe they do not deserve to be treated fairly nor compensated decently for their work. After all, it must be "their own fault" that they were unable to "do better."

One clear symptom of internalized oppression is the disdain for members of our own group. For example, as women we might find other women intolerable and prefer to be in the company of men. Or we might take special pains to point out that we are not at all like "those other" members of our group.

Another form of internalized oppression is a tendency to engage in conflict with other groups who are in a situation similar to ours, instead of becoming allies and working together to change the larger social condition. For example, in many impoverished areas of the United States, different ethnic groups are often in conflict with one another. Even though the different groups may be in a similar situation with regard to poverty and discrimination, the internalized oppression can make building alliances a challenge.

EXPLORATION 6

Think about three different groups you are a part of that are "disadvantaged" or "low status" in comparison to another group. (If you want to, you can refer to the list in exploration 2, or use some of the same groups you have explored in a previous exercise.)

What negative messages have you come to believe about yourself as a member of those groups?

Or, if you see yourself as an exception,

What negative messages have you come to believe about other members of that group?

Write down these messages and think about what it would feel like to share what you have written with your classmates or in another public setting.

What feelings come up for you?

Now, write three positive traits about each of these same groups you belong to.

What would it feel like to read these traits aloud to others?

❖ BREAKING THE CYCLE OF OPPRESSION ❖

NAMING THE OPPRESSION

Naming a social problem is necessary for transformation to occur. As Paulo Freire eloquently expressed it, "to say the right word is to change the World." Identifying a problem, exploring its causes and its possible consequences, is the first step toward creating solutions and bringing about transformation. As well as exploring the broader form taken by a social problem, we need to examine our own personal role in the matter.

EXPLORATION 7

Recall a time when you learned there was a name for something you were experiencing, something that was significant for you. Describe the experience and how it felt to learn there was a name for it.

UNLEARNING BIASES

It is important to recognize that all of us have been taught to be prejudiced and biased against others. It is not our fault that we have been shaped by societies full of prejudice and bias. Since we were very young, the people around us have expressed bias both through their words and their actions, and many of these biases have come to feel like second nature.

Yet, once we develop sufficient awareness of this process, it becomes our responsibility to "untrain" ourselves so that we can develop appreciation and respect for all human beings. As we unlearn our biases, we regain our ability to develop closeness with people from many backgrounds. Our understanding is enriched as we learn to see the world from many different perspectives. And we become better able to work together with others in order to create a world that works well for all.

Some ways to become more aware of our own biases include paying attention to the language we use and the jokes we make. We can also observe our judgments of others to discover whether they are based on an individual's characteristics or on the fact that the person belongs to a particular social group. We can look at who we choose as friends and with whom we prefer to spend time.

In addition, we can listen and learn from the experience of people from circumstances very different from ours. We can read fiction, nonfiction, and autobiographies written by authors who belong to groups with which we are unfamiliar. We can also make a point of reaching out and developing authentic, respectful relationships with people in circumstances different from ours. Although we will inevitably make mistakes based on our ignorance, we can begin by admitting our ignorance and communicating a willingness to learn from our mistakes.

Last but not least, we can learn from other members of our own group who are willing to share their own processes of recognizing and unlearning their biases. This frees the members of the "target" group from the burden of having to "teach" us about the injustices they suffer. If we do not wish to become dehumanized by our privilege, we need to accept our responsibility for dispelling our ignorance about the injustices from which we are shielded.

EXPLORATION 8

Choose a group you belong to that is "subordinate" with respect to another group.

What are some of the injustices you experience as a member of that group, injustices that members of the "advantaged" group might not even realize?

Ask yourself the same question again with respect to another "subordinate" group of which you are a member.
Now think about an "advantaged" group of which you are a member.

What might you do to learn more about the injustices experienced by those who are not members of that "advantaged" group?

BECOMING AWARE OF OUR PRIVILEGES

An important aspect of the process of unlearning oppression is becoming aware of the specific privileges we enjoy as members of privileged groups. Many of the basic things we take for granted are in fact determined by the accident of our birth. These privileges may include access to good educational opportunities, good medical care, being treated respectfully and fairly by social authorities, having positive images of our group represented in the media, not being looked at with suspicion when we enter a store, and so forth.

Yet the central fact of privilege is precisely that we are able to take these things for granted because the privileges we enjoy may seem to us to be "the norm." Because the tendency in our society is always to compare ourselves to those who have more, we may tend to think about privilege as something that belongs to others who have greater advantages than our own. As we take a broader view, we realize that in our present social and cultural arrangements the simple things we take for granted are not shared equally by others.

It is important to clarify that we are *not* saying that any of us should feel guilty because of the advantages we enjoy. Quite the contrary. Although discussions about bias, oppression, and privilege often elicit uncomfortable feelings in all of us, guilt is not only unnecessary but often counterproductive. In fact, "Guilt is unnecessary, change is essential" has become a guiding insight in the world of anti-bias education. Guilt tends to paralyze us and make us ineffectual, or worse, motivate self-righteous attempts to justify our attitudes and conduct.

As human beings, we are not responsible for the circumstances into which we are born, or our resulting ethnic, linguistic, and cultural background or our gender or sexual orientation. Any disadvantage or privilege associated with our birth is neither our fault nor the result of our personal merit. However, we are certainly responsible for how we *respond* to the circumstances of our birth. We can choose to use our advantages as resources toward the work of creating a more just and equitable world in which these advantages are truly the norm that all human beings enjoy.

Even when we realize that we have actively taken part in perpetuating oppression, it is important to distinguish between unhealthy guilt and beneficial regret. Although we may regret our past actions, we do not benefit anyone by punishing ourselves. Instead, beneficial regret can inspire us to take responsibility for our actions by undertaking the task of working toward a positive future. Our willingness to forgive ourselves and to learn from our experiences will strengthen our ability to apply ourselves to the work at hand.

EXPLORATION 9

Now think about two groups you belong to that are "privileged" in comparison to another group. For each group, explore the following question:

What are some of the things you can easily take for granted because of your membership in that group?

It might help to imagine what would happen if someone waved a magic wand and you were suddenly placed within the body of a member of the disadvantaged group.

What would be different? What could you no longer take for granted as you went about your daily life?

BECOMING ALLIES

As we begin to recognize the many ways in which we experience privilege in our lives, we can use that awareness to strengthen our dedication to creating a better world for all. One of the steps we can take is to become an ally of those in more difficult circumstances than ours.

Becoming an ally is an ongoing process, closely related to continually exploring and unlearning our own biases. For if we are not aware of our own biases, attempting to help others can easily become an expression of paternalism. Paternalism, however well-intentioned, only reinforces inequality. It happens when, viewing ourselves as superior, we offer to help someone we view as inferior. Being an ally is very different. To be an ally, we need to connect with another person as an equal human being, while at the same time acknowledging the privilege we have and placing it at the service of our fundamental equality.

A significant element of being an ally is recognizing the mutuality of the interaction. Because of our privilege, we may be able to offer our advocacy, our expertise, or our economic or legal assistance to someone. Yet, if we are truly being an ally, we will find ourselves grateful for what we are learning and receiving in the process: a deepening ability to connect with other human beings.

EXPLORATION 10

Think about one of the disadvantaged groups of which you are a member. Now think about a time when a person from the corresponding advantaged group acted as an ally to you.

Who was the person? What did the person do that was helpful?

As a member of that disadvantaged group, think about what sorts of things are helpful and what sorts of things are *not* helpful.

Are there any general principles you can deduce from your own experience?

EXPLORING OUR ROLES AS BOTH OPPRESSOR AND OPPRESSED

As we have seen, all of us have experienced what it is like to be a member of a group that is treated unfairly. As we uncover and heal our experiences of powerlessness, we bring more strength and confidence to our work for justice and freedom. And, as we obtain deeper insight into our own painful experiences, we develop greater insight into the suffering of others.

For example, if we are members of a dominant culture, we may experience a great degree of privilege in many ways. However, as women we may have internalized a lack of confidence in our abilities to speak out and become a leader. The more we can heal from our own internalized oppression as women, the better allies we can become for members of other marginalized groups. Of course, we also need to remain aware of our privilege with regard to other groups and be willing to continue to learn how to help in ways that are empowering instead of oppressive.

EXPLORATION 11

Consider these questions. If possible, answer them in writing:

What kind of things might make it hard for us to explore the ways in which we have experienced being *both* "oppressor" and "oppressed"?

Why do you think it might be easier to identify with only one or the other?

What might be the consequences of not looking deeply at either side of our experience?

❖ TAKING ACTION WITH OTHERS ❖

We need to remember that the purpose of gaining a deeper awareness about our own conditioning is to take more effective action in the world. The actions we take can range from speaking out as allies when we see biased behavior, to organizing for change in institutions and organizations, to educating others about bias, oppression, and human liberation.

Some organizations have focused specifically on anti-bias education, such as the Museum of Tolerance in Los Angeles. Others, such as the National Coalition Building Institute of Washington, D.C., have focused on helping community members intervene effectively in everyday instances of prejudice and bias. In the United States, Louise Denmar-Sparks has concentrated on working with early childhood educators, as well as developing the field of antibias education within the world of academe. Ricky Sherover-Marcuse, an early pioneer in the field, developed effective workshops on the subject of unlearning racism. Her visionary work has been continued by many others. Today, many anti-bias educators work as consultants to the business world, helping to create a less biased climate within the workplace.

All of us, wherever we find ourselves, can make a difference in the lives of those around us by our example, our courage, and our actions, however small. Yet those of us in the field of education have a special responsibility. As our actions directly affect the lives of many young people, we are in a position to make a significant difference. As educators, we do not have unlimited freedom. We are constrained to a greater or lesser degree by the traditions of the institutions in which we work, by the demands of our job, and by the expectations of the larger community. Nonetheless, given all the external constraints we experience, it remains true that often the greatest constraints are internal. Most of us have a greater degree of freedom than we utilize, and in many cases, more freedom than we are aware of.

Realizing that those who oppose us are motivated mostly by fear will help us remain focused on the goal of being of benefit to everyone. We can avoid becoming disheartened and overwhelmed by temporary obstacles, and instead continue extending the invitation to others to join us in a worthwhile endeavor.

Most important, we need to nurture the supportive relationships we have with others who share this vision, even if at first we are only a few. Because of the challenging nature of this work, it is not something that can be done well alone or in isolation. We need to be continuously renewing ourselves with the very closeness and connectedness that we seek to make possible in the world at large.

EXPLORATION 12

Think about a time you took action about something in which you believe.

How would you have felt if you had not chosen to take action?

What did you learn from the experience?

What might you do differently next time?

SOME RESOURCES FOR FURTHER STUDY AND ACTION

In the United States, there is a growing variety of social justice education and anti-bias curricula (Lee, Menkhart, & Okasawa-Rey, 1997). Some of these curricula are designed to address a particular form of oppression, such as to combat sexism or to address homophobia. Other curricula are designed for a particular age or grade level, or linked closely with a particular subject matter, such as literature or history. *Resistance in Paradise* by Debbie Wei is an excellent example of a curriculum designed to invite reflection on a historical moment. *Rethinking Schools,* a newspaper written by teachers, incorporates articles by teachers and educators committed to a continuous analysis of school practices. Educators for Social Responsibility, Teaching for Change, Teaching Tolerance, California Tomorrow, the Museum of Tolerance, and the Oliver Button Project are some of the organizations that provide resources for reflective education geared to the development of a just society.

In addition to designing and implementing new curricula, as reflective educators we need to examine and evaluate critically the existing curricula in all subject areas for the presence of unconscious bias or oppressive statements. Of course, existing school practices also need to be reexamined and reevaluated. Because children begin to learn biases very early in life and receive countless biased messages from their social surroundings, our goal is for all of our curricula and our classroom practices to be actively anti-biased, and geared toward justice.

In general, it is important that we resist viewing anti-bias or social justice activities as peripheral, add-on activities. Instead, it is helpful to incorporate social justice and anti-bias education throughout our existing curriculum with a commitment to liberation, justice, and equality by:

◆ Adapting existing curriculum activities, or creating new core curriculum activities, so that we can simultaneously teach basic academic content as well as a bias-free and socially just perspective.
◆ Taking every appropriate opportunity to model socially just and anti-biased behavior and to reflect on practices that promote democratic expression, compassion, and supportive attitudes.
◆ Creating an inclusive environment through posters, photos, books, and other publications that promote inclusion and respect for all people.
◆ Learning about transformative and anti-bias teaching practices that we can incorporate into the core of our teaching
◆ Making an effort to overcome our fears and release unhealthy guilt.
◆ Using our experiences as a source for learning and growth and letting go of defensiveness.

The teachers with whom we have worked through the years have constantly rekindled our faith in humanity and our hope in what can happen when caring teachers are willing to let go of fear and open their imagination to a future of possibility. Thank you, dear reader, for being open to considering new perspectives to add to your already rich practice.

C H A P T E R 2

AUTHORS IN THE CLASSROOM

❖ PROVIDING MODELS FOR CREATIVE EXPRESSION ❖

As we know, students learn more from our actions and our examples than from what we say in our lessons. Children naturally tend to imitate adults and adolescents to emulate them. As a result, when teaching reading, significant emphasis has been placed on modeling the reading process for children and adolescents. Teachers are encouraged to share their joy as readers with their students. Although this is an exemplary practice, not enough emphasis has been given to the equally important need for modeling the process of writing and creative expression.

In educational courses or professional inservices, teachers are often encouraged to model the pleasure of reading. They are offered techniques for reading aloud effectively and suggestions on how to create a "reading for pleasure" time in the classroom. Teachers are also frequently encouraged to invite other adults to read in the classroom. Administrators, staff members, community members, and relatives are all suggested as models who can help share the pleasure of reading with children and adolescents, all of which is excellent. Yet the need to provide models of writing and authorship of books has not been equally emphasized. It is true that authors of books for children and young adults are occasionally invited to schools. If done right, this can be a wonderful model for children and leave a lasting impression. But it is something too few children ever have the opportunity to experience.

In addition to lacking an abundance of models for writing, students are also given few opportunities to speak purposefully in front of a group. When they have occasion to do so, it is usually to report on something they have read or been assigned to research. But opportunities to speak in order to explore and expand one's reasoning abilities, to learn to organize logical trends of thought, to develop convincing arguments, and to delight in creating beautiful expressions through language are sadly lacking for most students.

In this, as in many other aspects of education, there are of course great disparities from district to district and school to school. Public speaking and writing one's thoughts are leadership activities. The emphasis on creative activities connected with leadership tends to be reserved for the education of the elite. If we are to help all our youth develop their ability, courage, and strength as leaders of a more just society, further attention needs to be given to the development of voice, both spoken and written.

Of course, we do not mean to diminish in any way the importance of listening and reading. All four aspects of language—listening, reading, speaking, and writing—contribute to the process of intellectual growth, to the development of personality, and to creating and nurturing relationships with others. If approached as critical skills, even the receptive aspects of language—listening and reading—can be undertaken in an active and creative manner.

Public education has a long history of emphasizing passive and receptive practices, which Freire (1970, 1997) clearly describes as the "banking education" model. Even now, as education moves toward more interactive and creative methods, we find that listening and reading continue to be presented as the passive receiving of the words of others. Of course, this is not separate from the larger question of whose voices are heard and by whom, which has been amply addressed by educators concerned with pedagogy for a more just society (Freire, 1970, 1997; Cummins, 2000; Greene, 1995; hooks, 1989; Shor, 1992; and Wink, 1997, among others).

Yet creative listening is not a passive act. Instead, it involves developing an awareness of the presuppositions and the point of view of the speaker, an empathy that allows us to listen from the speaker's perspective. When we listen creatively, we are thoughtful about what we hear, asking the important questions about what is being said and its possible consequences. At the same time, we are engaging in dialogue, whether spoken or merely silent, with the words being said. As in any act of language, we bring to the act of listening our previous knowledge and experience, and we respond with emotions brought about not only by what is being said in the moment, but also by the memories that the words may be awakening.

Creative reading, similarly, involves an active process of dialogue with the text, a process that will be explained more fully in the next chapter. Both creative listening and creative reading are the natural precursors to speaking and writing. Yet, in most traditional educational settings, listening and reading are presented only as receptive skills that provide information about the words of others. Of course, this varies from school to school, reflecting the "savage inequalities" denounced by Jonathan Kozol (1991). There is a tendency for children of less affluent parents to be taught to read and write in a more mechanical way, with more emphasis on skills than on content, more attention given to the ability to reproduce the text than to question it, and much less access to the world of literature.

The disempowering effect of conventional education is clear when we consider that although most teachers feel comfortable with their ability to read aloud to their students, not many feel equally comfortable with their ability to author their own books and share them with their students. However, once they are given the opportunity to experience the process, most teachers discover that creating a book was far easier than they had initially thought, and that they are in fact far more skilled than they had ever imagined.

If we want children to imagine themselves as capable of exploring a variety of professional options and opportunities, it is helpful to expose them to people who are engaged in diverse professions. In the same way, if we want our students to think of themselves as writers, it is important that they see the process unfolding in front of their eyes, and that they are able to see their teachers as authors.

✤ STRENGTHENING TEACHERS' PERSONAL VOICES ✤

In the history of our work in this area, we have often witnessed with pain how many teachers feel uncomfortable about their own abilities to express themselves in writing. Teachers who feel passionately about issues of social justice and equality, or who have thoughtful opinions about educational practices, often find it difficult to write a letter to the editor or an article expressing their views. Valuable teaching ideas remain unheard and unknown because the excellent teachers who devise them do not feel at ease writing a book or article on methodology.

To be able to write what one thinks, feels, imagines, and dreams is extremely liberating and powerful. Often it depends far less on possessing a particular set of skills than on having the confidence and the willingness to try.

As teachers gain a greater sense of their own voice, students benefit in turn. By sharing with students the process of their own writing, teachers offer a valuable model. By acknowledging that ideas are not always easy to formulate, that it can be a struggle to express feelings in a satisfactory manner, or that words are sometimes elusive, teachers free students to take greater risks with their own writing. The more empowered teachers feel, the more able they will be to help their students become empowered.

✤ CLASSROOM-GENERATED BOOKS AS CULTURAL BRIDGES ✤

As students gain greater confidence in their ability to express themselves in writing, and as they are encouraged to write books that reflect their own experiences, valuable bridges are built between the worlds of home and school. Although all students benefit from a stronger home–school interaction, the benefits are even more significant for students who come from a marginalized culture. For unless students feel that the two worlds of home and school understand, respect, and celebrate each other, they will feel torn between the two. A program designed to promote creative self-expression about home and community history and experiences can begin to heal that rift.

Students who experience conflict between the worlds of home and school can easily internalize shame about their parents, their families, and their culture. They may feel compelled to make a painful choice between academic success and loyalty to their community. Although some students are undoubtedly able to find a way to reconcile both even in the most difficult circumstances, our job as educators should be to help students benefit more easily from what schools have to offer, rather than placing in their path obstacles to surmount.

One of the major discrepancies between home and school cultures may be precisely the relationship to literacy. Whereas the school may emphasize "book culture," the home may share and transmit wisdom in a different way. Because schools emphasize the value of books, it is the school's responsibility to ensure that students' families and communities are fully represented in those books, that they are inclusive rather than exclusionary. It is the school's responsibility to ensure that the world of books and literacy is not presented as a wedge between parents and their children, but instead fosters their interaction. Writing and publishing books in the classroom can be a helpful tool for honoring the communities to which the children belong, for portraying the life experiences of children's families, and for recognizing the accumulated wisdom of parents and relatives.

The books authored by teachers not only encourage students' own writing, but also play a significant role in helping to create a bridge between students and their parents or relatives. Teachers begin by writing a personal book about themselves, their families, their aspirations, or their life experiences. When they subsequently invite their students to share this book with their families, they are opening the door to a closer relationship with parents.

Many parents from economically or culturally marginalized groups may feel intimidated by the school. They may have lacked the opportunity to attend school themselves, or their own school experiences may have been painful. They may look on the teacher with respect, but they may also feel a great distance. By choosing to create books about themselves, their families, or their life experiences, teachers open up a different route of communication with parents. There are certain human experiences we can all relate to. We all have names, we all have relatives and friends, we all have life experiences. In everyone's life there is someone who has served as a model, an inspiration, someone who can be remembered with kindness and appreciation. At this very human level, there are no false distinctions between the teacher and the parents.

These books written by teachers can serve as a catalyst to help parents or caretakers feel more comfortable sharing information about their own histories and life experiences. When their stories subsequently become the subject matter for books written in the classroom by students, a circle of connection has been created.

✤ AWAKENING THE AUTHOR WITHIN ✤

Teachers attending Author in the Classroom courses or workshops have frequently expressed their surprise at the ease with which they wrote their first book within the classroom or workshop setting. The structures we use as templates for the creation of personal books have evolved throughout the course of our work with thousands of teachers. The results we present here include many creative ideas teachers have shared with us. Each time we have presented one of these themes, it has been enriched by the experiences from previous presentations. We encourage teachers, as we encourage you, to trust the words that have been growing within you in silence. Whenever a teacher has dared to put these words on paper, we have celebrated with joy the birth of a new author.

Each of the units in Part II offers several works that illustrate different literary and aesthetic examples of authorship. We have requested these authors' permission to reproduce their work here so that you can be inspired by their example, as they were inspired by the example of other teachers.

Awakening the author within sometimes means tapping into painful hidden truths. When this is the case, our advice is to begin by keeping the text private, first sharing it with an intimate circle before deciding whether you are comfortable with publishing and distributing it. Many teachers have told us about the healing powers of writing, rereading, and sharing these texts with intimate others.

Some teachers have chosen to make two versions of books that deal with painful personal experiences. One version becomes the published, public version that often uses metaphors and images to convey the message. The other, the more descriptive and revealing version, remains a private diary or a therapeutic journal.

Before publishing a text, teachers need to consider the audience and the sensitivity of the subject. This, of course, is equally important when publishing the words of students and parents. It is necessary to acknowledge the authenticity of every experience, the importance of feelings, and the significance of a story. But sometimes it is important to not rush into publishing a text that could cause any kind of shame or embarrassment. Sometimes it may be best to acknowledge the value of the writing but suggest that it be saved. Publishing makes a text public, and thus it is necessary to use judgment about what ought to be published, when, and how.

❖ TYPES OF BOOKS WRITTEN BY TEACHERS ❖

The books teachers have created with the Authors in the Classroom program are as unique and diverse as the teachers themselves. Many of the books have been of an autobiographical nature and have taken a variety of forms, from sharing a childhood anecdote to presenting a life history.

These books have had a special significance when shared with students' parents or relatives. By choosing to write about their lives, teachers have conveyed their willingness to share on a personal level, thus bridging any distance created by their status as professionals. In addition, these types of books provide an excellent model for children's own writing.

But writing autobiographically is only one of many possible avenues. Teachers have also chosen to write about important people in their lives, about the history of their communities, or about their classroom, their students, or their school. There is no limit to the subjects about which one can write. The teacher-authors with whom we work continually expand our sense of possibilities.

In their willingness to share the wealth they have discovered, numerous teachers have graciously given us copies of the books they have made. We would like to make them all available to the readers of this book because we know that these examples are a constant source of inspiration for other teachers. Although that has not been feasible, we have selected as broad a sample as possible to include in this volume. In each of the units in Part II, you will find many of these books described or reproduced. We want to express our gratitude to the teachers who have made them available so that all of us can continue to be inspired by their creativity, their daring, and their authenticity.

We are in the process of creating a web page, www.authorsintheclassroom.com, where teachers can share the work they are doing as authors and as promoters of authorship among their students and parents. We are, of course, always happy to hear from you.

An example of a book created by a teacher as a gift to her students appears on pages 35–38. Jeni Hammond, a bilingual teacher at Sunnyslope School in Arizona, wrote this extraordinary book to encourage her students to discover their inner richness and strength so that they can face prejudice, discrimination, and other difficult situations with the courage that comes from self-awareness and an open heart. The book is written in two languages and illustrated with powerful black-and-white photographs of her students.

Jeni Hammond followed our suggestion to obtain permission from the students' parents to use the students' photos and to self-publish the book. The book was presented at the National Association for Bilingual Education Conference in Phoenix, Arizona, in spring 2001. Jenny received a standing ovation and was able to sell and sign every copy of her book. This book is now available through Del Sol Books. With her permission, we are reproducing here some pages of the book as a first introduction to the world of teacher-authored books.

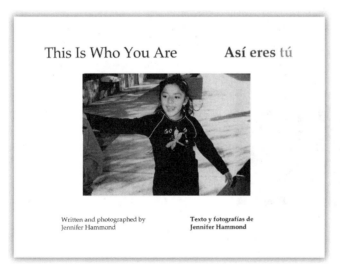

This Is Who You Are   Así eres tú

Written and photographed by
Jennifer Hammond

Texto y fotografías de
Jennifer Hammond

This Is Who You Are by Jeni Hammond

Reprinted by permission of Jennifer Vargas (formerly Hammond), 9501 N. Central Ave., Phoenix, AZ, 85020.

So when they doubt you
and tell you
there is no hope for you...

Cuando alguien dude de ti
y te diga
que no hay esperanza...

Remember the strength
that is in you and be
who you know you should be.

Recuerda toda la fuerza
que hay en tu alma y atrévete
a ser quien sabes que debes ser.

2

When they try to shame
where you come from and
trivialize the very core of
your being...

Cuando traten de humillar
el sitio de donde vienes
y trivializar lo más profundo
de tu ser...

Remember the pride
that is in you and show them
the power of your culture and
the strength of your spirit.

Recuerda el orgullo que hay en ti
y muestra al mundo
el poder de tu cultura
y la fuerza de tu espíritu.

3

When they tell you that you
are too loud and that you
only stick out...

Cuando te digan que bajes
la voz
y que no sobresalgas

Remember the courage
that is in you and say
what needs to be said.

Recuerda la fuerza que hay en ti
y di lo que es preciso decir.

4

When they tell you
to give up, because
you just don't measure up...

Cuando te digan que te rindas
porque no das la talla...

Remember the fighter
that is in you and do what
they said you could never do.

Recuerda la fuerza que hay en ti
y haz lo que dicen que tu nunca
podrias hacer.

5

When they try to demean
and belittle your character...

Cuando traten de menospreciar y
empequeñecer tu carácter...

Remember the self-respect
that is in you and maintain
who you are
and what you believe in.

Recuerda tu autoestima
y mantén quién eres
y en lo que crees.

7

When cowards surround
you and try to kick you
when you are down...

Cuando te rodeen cobardes
y traten de golpearte cuando estes
en el suelo...

Remember the dignity that
is in you, pick yourself
back up, and hold your head up high.

Recuerda la dignidad
que hay en ti,
levántate y mantén la cabeza
bien alta.

8

When they break your heart
and you question who you
are and if you matter...

Cuando rompan tu corazón
y cuestionen quién eres
y si importas...

Remember the love
that is in you and
keep believing in yourself.

Recuerda el amor que hay en ti
y sigue creyendo en ti mismo.

9

As a starting point in the process of awakening voice, we have identified a number of themes and structures that have proven effective and listed them according to the unit in Part II where each theme is developed:

Unit—Topic	*Structure*
1. Affirming Self	I Am book
2. Recognizing Human Qualities	Acrostic
3. Strengthening Self-Identity	Story of My Name
4. Building Communities	ABC/counting books
5. The Power of Transformation	Contrasting books
6. Understanding the Past/Creating the Future	Childhood memories
7. Discovering Our Capacities and Strength	I Can book
8. Learning to Know	Book of goals
9. Developing Relationships	A Person in My Life
10. From Yesterday to Tomorrow	Where I Come from . . . book

✤ BENEFITS OF AUTHORING BOOKS ✤

The benefits of the Authors in the Classroom process are multiple and significant for each of the groups involved:

Teachers

◆ Develop their own voice and strength as writers
◆ Gain a better sense of themselves as artists and intellectuals by becoming models of authorship, a highly regarded artistic and intellectual activity
◆ Establish stronger relationships with their students and their students' families

Students

- Strengthen their literacy skills
- Increase their interest in books and writing
- Develop a greater understanding of the writing process and confidence in themselves as authors
- Strengthen their sense of identity and self-esteem

Parents or Caretakers

- Experience new opportunities to relate to the school
- Strengthen their role as educators of their children by having their words and experiences receive greater respect from the school
- Develop their own capacity for reflection, creativity, and self-expression
- Enrich their relationship with their children

❖ BENEFITS OF SELF-PUBLISHED BOOKS ❖

The self-publication of books in the classroom or school brings about multiple benefits. Self-published books can:

- Foster reading, vocabulary building, and literacy in general
- Create a meaningful print-rich environment in the classroom and the home
- Build bridges between home and school by sharing life experiences and personal reflections
- Provide an opportunity for children and their parents to create meaningful, lasting memories together
- Facilitate understanding of others by bridging cultural differences
- Invite self-reflection
- Bring out the artist or the creator within each of us
- Build self-esteem by validating life experiences and cultural history
- Empower us, as main characters of our own stories, to look at our lives as protagonists rather than as secondary characters in someone else's story
- Become valued treasures, to be kept as reminders of important moments in our lives or to be given as gifts
- Motivate us to:
  - Remember
  - Reflect
  - Dream
  - Be authors, artists, creators
  - Become whomever we may want to be

❖ WHAT ABOUT STANDARDIZED TESTING? ❖

The overwhelming reliance that public authorities and administrators place on the results of standardized testing sometimes obscures the fact that students who perform well on the tests are not those who have been taught to the test, but the ones who are strong readers, have a wide vocabulary, and know how to think independently (Mayer, 1988; Knepper, 2001).

As students advance through the grades, standardized reading tests increasingly assess range of vocabulary knowledge. Whereas high-frequency vocabulary is found in everyday conversation, low-frequency vocabulary is found primarily, or even exclusively, in books. All of the research data show that extensive reading is the best predictor of reading comprehension performance.

The pedagogical approach proposed in this book is designed to connect students' personal lives and identities with literacy. This promotes students' engagement with reading and writing much more effectively than an exclusive focus on isolated or disembodied skills. As students discover the value of literacy for interpreting and recreating the world, books take on a greater meaning.

As students become active and frequent readers, performance on standardized reading tests increases; this particularly benefits students in the later grades of elementary school when many students instructed in a drill-and-skill approach typically experience the "grade 4 slump." Students who become lifelong readers and writers become lifelong learners. This is a better predictor of academic success than any test results.

C H A P T E R **3**

THE ROLE OF DIALOGUE IN THE CLASSROOM

✤ BENEFITS OF DIALOGUE ✤

Dialogue is one of the most overlooked and undervalued educational tools we have at our disposal. Dialogue can serve a variety of useful purposes in the classroom, all of which are worth exploring in greater depth.

To begin with, dialogue allows us as teachers to build on what students bring with them to the classroom. In the process of conversation, we invite students to share their personal experiences, feelings, and concerns. This facilitates the process of making connections between what students already know and what we are introducing in a lesson, thus generating greater interest and creating a more powerful learning experience.

In addition, dialogue gives students access to higher-order thinking skills and allows more students to participate in thinking about and exploring a topic. Students with low reading and writing skills are often fed a steady diet of low-level skill practice that provides little interest and stimulation. When students are invited to contribute to the dialogue and are received in a welcoming manner by the teacher, they have the opportunity to experience themselves as creative, thinking beings who have something worthwhile to contribute, regardless of their present repertoire of reading or writing skills.

As a precursor to writing, dialogue is the basic entry into self-expression. By inviting students to contribute ideas through brainstorming, to share various possible responses, and to explore a range of variations on a theme, the creative juices are allowed to flow. Students will then be able to turn to the process of writing much more freely, without finding themselves at a loss for ideas.

Dialogue turns the act of reading from a passive, receptive intake of information to a creative process of active engagement through questioning the text. For this purpose, we have developed the framework of Creative Dialogue as a typology of various kinds of questions we can use as we proceed in our group exploration of a text.

❖ PRINCIPLES OF CREATIVE DIALOGUE ❖

Creative Dialogue is a formal elaboration of the natural process that efficient, critically minded adults follow when they read or listen to information (Ada, 1991, 2003; Ada & Campoy 1998a, 1999a). All readers or listeners approach new information with already existing knowledge and experiences and perhaps some anticipation of what the text may contain. On encountering the text or the new information, a dialogue begins.

We describe this process as having four phases, although these phases do not occur separately. When first encountering the text, the reader or listener becomes aware of its content. We call this first phase the *descriptive phase.* It includes discovering theme, characters, setting, and plot, as well as the intent of the author.

Yet the reader's or listener's reaction to the text does not end with the intellectual assimilation of its content. Instead, that content provokes a personal response. This response, which may be wonder or recognition, surprise or confirmation, joy or pain, will depend not only on the content of the text but also on the reader's previous knowledge of the topic and his or her personal experiences. We have labeled this second phase the *personal interpretive phase.*

Aware of the information and having compared and contrasted it with his or her own previous knowledge and experience, the effective reader engages in a process of critical reflection. We have begun to call this third phase the *critical/multicultural/anti-bias phase* to call attention to the fact that to be critical also demands becoming aware of the subtle biases or the ethnocentric views that often permeate a text. An empowered reader or listener will not only ponder the intentions of the writer/speaker, the consequences of the ideas presented, and who would benefit or suffer from those consequences, but also how people of different cultures might relate to the text and what hidden biases it sustains.

The purpose of Creative Dialogue is fulfilled in the fourth and final *creative/ transformative phase.* This time the purpose is not to relate to previous knowledge and experiences nor to explore the feelings evoked, but rather to apply insight and power gained during the reflective process to actions that will shape the future.

We do not often think about the connection between reading, thinking, and action, but it is always present. For example, whenever we read we begin to make decisions—first, whether it is worth our while to continue reading. We may also decide that we want to be sure to remember the name of the author, to search for more works by that author, or to recommend this book to others. Furthermore, we begin making internal decisions—how we will relate to a certain topic, how much more we want to learn about or reflect on it, how we will interact with others or modify our behavior based on these new reflections. This is the ultimate power inherent in dialogue with a text or with one another: It can help us become stronger and better human beings.

Of course, the reader's response to a text, or a dialogue with others in the classroom, will not always proceed in a linear fashion. Nonetheless, we have found it helpful to describe these four phases and to design questions that invite students to think along each of these four lines. Too often the discussions following a reading are reduced to the descriptive phase and designed solely to ascertain that students have understood the information presented. Sometimes an effort is made to include some critical reflection. But in most cases, students' personal responses are not given sufficient validity, and students are seldom encouraged to distill the insights gained from the process and apply them to action that shapes the future.

Each unit of this book presents a text related to the major theme of the unit along with Creative Literacy questions you can use to initiate a dialogue about books or literary pieces related to the major theme of the unit. In this third and final chapter of Part I, we offer some general suggestions for facilitating dialogue in the classroom.

❖ THE ISSUE OF TIME ❖

The current emphasis in education on skill-oriented instruction has had many detrimental effects. Teachers report that they have lost "the joy of teaching." Many have also become extremely concerned with the lack of time for "real teaching" when the drill-and-skill obsession takes up much of the time available.

The difference between educational experiences that are mechanical and those that are transforming is that mechanical activities need to be repeated again and again. Because student interest is minimal, what students retain is also minimal. Thus the need for constant repetition.

When students experience the power of a dialogic process with the text, the way they relate to reading is transformed. Although it make take a few times for this process to become fully internalized, once students acquire it, they do not forget it. The time devoted to the transformative experience is not wasted, nor will it have to be repeated over and over again. Instead, it creates a strong and stable foundation for the future and frees time for meaningful learning experiences.

❖ FACILITATING REFLECTIVE DIALOGUE IN THE CLASSROOM ❖

RATIONALE

One of the biggest (and potentially most rewarding) challenges we all face as educators is how to move from the old model of teaching, in which the teacher does most of the talking, to a more facilitative and participatory style of learning. We should note that this is part of a larger cultural shift: In management terms, it is often described as the move from "sage on the stage" to "guide on the side." Yet this shift may be particularly challenging for educators because we have a tendency to teach in the ways we ourselves were taught. As a result, although most of us may no longer hold the conscious belief that "children and young people should be seen and not heard," it is still the case that in most classrooms teachers do 90 percent or more of the "legitimate" talking.

If we wish to change this situation, we need both the motivation and the means. The motivation can arise from seeing clearly the pedagogical value of conversation: Students benefit from learning how to listen to one another with respect, instead of listening only to the person with the greatest coercive power in a given situation. Dialogue is an exemplary way to learn democracy in action.

Motivation also arises from considering the intellectual value of dialogue as an opportunity to examine and question one's own thinking by listening to other points of view. And motivation is strengthened when we consider the community-building aspect of dialogue: As we create a space for students to bring more of their own experience to the classroom, we help create the greater sense of belonging and care that are essential for an optimal learning environment.

Many books have been written on the benefits of conversation for academic learning, social and ethical learning, and community building. Presented below are a few practical means, or the "how to," of facilitating conversation. At the same time it is helpful to begin by acknowledging the challenges involved.

CHALLENGES OF DIALOGUE

Although it may seem obvious, the fact that students have not been taught to listen to one another or to engage in a respectful group conversation can easily be overlooked. Teachers may attempt to hold a dialogue in the classroom, only to give up in frustration at the first sign of difficulty. Of course, it is easier for everyone involved to revert to the familiar form of teacher talking and students listening, or of the teacher asking the questions and students offering the "right" answers.

Yet with a little patience and conscious intention, other forms of interaction can be learned by all involved. Some of the hallmarks of true dialogue are that students are actively involved in questioning, and a real, in-depth exploration of ideas takes place, in which both teachers and students are engaged in a process of discovery. This sustained process of inquiry requires of everyone involved a sense of discipline, albeit a different discipline than the traditional dutiful listening and offering up of the "correct" answer on request.

It is therefore helpful for teachers to understand that the class is learning a new form of interaction, and to allot time for them to learn this process, instead of expecting immediate results. In addition, it is helpful to involve students in the learning process through group reflection and problem solving, discussing together any challenges that arise and proposing alternative solutions.

SUGGESTIONS FOR FACILITATING DIALOGUE

1. *Norm setting.* It is usually helpful for the teacher to introduce the process of dialogue, making the norms and expectations explicit. ("We are going to be exploring the thoughts each of us has about a topic. There are no 'right answers' in this process. We want to focus on listening to everyone with respect so that everyone can feel comfortable sharing their ideas. Of course, it is fine to disagree, but it's important that we do so in a respectful manner.") It is even more helpful when students themselves are involved in creating the group norms. ("How might we create an atmosphere in which people feel safe sharing their ideas or exploring new ideas they are not quite sure about? What norms can we agree on?")

2. *Awakening participants' interest.* As teachers, we are often tempted to overrely on our authority to compel students to participate in a given activity or assignment. In the process, we lose the opportunity to tap into students' curiosity and interest, all of which are much more powerful motivators than a sense of duty.

Admittedly, it takes greater effort to offer a meaningful reason why students might be interested in a given topic, yet that effort can produce significant results. When students see a connection between their own needs and interests and the topic at hand, the enormous potential of human beings' natural love of learning becomes available.

A necessary step, then, toward meaningful dialogue is finding something of common interest. You can begin by choosing a question or a topic that you think might interest your students, suggesting it to them, and then listening for their response. Or you might begin by choosing a question or topic that truly interests *you,* communicating your interest to your students, and then listening to what they have to say. In either case, listening is an essential part of the process.

3. *Listening to students.* One of the best ways to awaken human beings' desire to participate in dialogue is by communicating that we are truly willing to listen to what they have to say. Although this wonderful principle works just as well for six-years-olds as it does for sixty-years-olds, it can take some effort on our part to put it into practice.

When we are really listening, or "listening to understand" (Covey, 1997), our first priority is not to judge or to evaluate, but simply to understand. It is of course a truism that if we want students to learn to listen, we ourselves need to model what listening looks like.

4. *Communicating that we are listening.* When we are interested in what someone is saying, we sometimes ask them to expand on or clarify what they have said. And when someone has said something we don't understand, we often find it helpful to paraphrase what we have heard and offer it back to them, as a way to check whether we have indeed understood. These are both useful approaches for letting students know we are listening to them. They are also useful approaches to model for students so that they can begin using them in their responses to one another.

One note of caution here: Paraphrasing someone else's words can become tiresome if done to excess. Also, if the teacher takes it upon himself or herself to paraphrase what each student says, he or she can unwittingly end up once again doing most of the talking. So this approach is best used only as needed, keeping in mind that in this case, "less is more."

5. *Asking real questions.* A key way to help ourselves listen more deeply to students is to choose questions that truly interest us instead of asking about things to which we believe we already know the answer. If we are not genuinely open to receiving different points of view, our listening can become superficial.

In addition to the initial questions we use to start dialogue, some follow-up questions arise spontaneously as we engage more deeply in the process. We might become curious about something that has been said or about the connection between two or more different statements that have been made. A genuine question that arises from what students have said, a question that is not from the teacher's guide but from our own minds and hearts, is a wonderful gift to offer our students, especially when it is accompanied by the willingness and patience to listen to and explore the different answers that might emerge.

6. *Inviting different points of view.* A key step we can take toward promoting dialogue is to invite several different responses to the same question. This communicates very clearly to students that we are not looking for "one right answer" and that we are more interested in their responses than in marching through a list of prepared questions.

We can approach this step in two different ways. The easier way is to invite different points of view on questions that have to do with simple matters of taste, such as "What was your favorite part of the story, and why?" The more difficult way, the way we all have a tendency to shy away from, is to welcome disagreement on matters of greater substance. For example, if a group of children has decided that the Big Bad Wolf was obviously a bad guy because he was so mean to Little Red Riding Hood, one might conceivably ask if anyone sees things differently and would like to explain why; or if several adolescents have agreed that men who don't defend their rights, even to the point of violence, are sissies, it would be possible to ask if someone wants to express the point of view of nonviolence as a form of obtaining justice.

Sometimes we might feel that it is important to resolve a difference of opinion. But the greater lesson may well be that we can learn to respect and get along with those who think differently from us, and that we can all continue to learn as we dialogue with one another.

7. *Acknowledging relationships between different ideas.* We live in a competitive culture in which the focus is skewed toward individual performance; too little acknowledgment is paid to all of the help each one of us receives from others. To emphasize the collective aspect of dialogue, it is important that we recognize how our ideas are inspired and influenced by the ideas of others. This includes the ways in which we build on the ideas of others as well as how we define our ideas in contrast to or in disagreement with those of others.

Again, this is an area in which teacher modeling plays a crucial role. A teacher can say something such as: "Oscar, it sounds like your idea is similar to what Emilia was discussing yesterday." Or, "Tyrone, it sounds like your idea is different from Pedro's. What do the rest of you think?" Or, "What Mai-Ling said earlier made me think about another question. . . ."

8. *Making room for all voices, including the shy ones.* Several techniques have been found to help equalize opportunities for participation in the classroom. One is to simply increase the response time between asking a question and calling on a student. In addition to giving all students more time to prepare a thoughtful response, it gives slower students more opportunities to participate and communicates that speed is not the only criterion of value.

Once we have called on students, we can also increase the time we are willing to wait for them to collect themselves to speak. Our own patience and acceptance can serve as models for students of how we would like them to treat one another.

Another technique is to give students a few minutes first to share their thinking with a partner. This is an approach that dramatically increases the number of students able to participate. In addition, students who may be shy about speaking in front of the whole class will be much less so about speaking with just one other person. After students have shared their thoughts with a partner, some volunteers can be invited to share their thoughts with the whole class.

Once the dialogue has been underway for a while, you might want to pause and invite those students who have not spoken up to offer a thought if they wish to do so. Often students who are shyer and hesitate to dive in to the conversation welcome the opportunity to contribute when an opening is created. Of course, we do not want to put students on the spot, because then the talk becomes a forced performance instead of a true dialogue. Therefore, it is important that students know they always have the right to remain silent.

In discussions with a smaller group of students, every student will have a greater opportunity to participate. On the other hand, we lose the richness of various points of view if the group is too small. Somewhere between eight and fifteen students is probably ideal for a small, teacher-facilitated dialogue group. However, we are not implying that it is not possible to hold a dialogue with a larger group.

9. *Being willing to teach, model, practice, and problem-solve.* Learning how to have a rich, stimulating dialogue is not something that happens overnight, either for teachers or for our students. It is important that we take the time and effort to help students learn the skills we want them to master. For example, we can take some time early in the year to practice what it means to "turn to your partner and share your idea with him or her," and then return to the larger group when it is time to do so. This is a worthwhile investment for the remainder of the year because it becomes a common routine that students can move into and out of with ease.

One of the wonderful things about dialogue is that it can be used as a tool for group reflection and problem solving. That is to say, we can shift the topic of dialogue from whatever subject we are exploring to any difficulties we are encountering in the use of dialogue itself. We can do so simply by initiating a conversation about "what is happening between us in our conversations."

As the teacher, it is important to be clear about what is not working for you and why. It is also important to listen closely to students' responses and to invite them to participate in creating a solution that will work for everyone. (For excellent classroom examples of a collaborative approach to problem solving, see Strachota [1996]).

Through participating in teacher-led discussions, whether with the whole class or with a smaller group, students are learning by our modeling and example the kind of interactions that give rise to a fruitful dialogue. Over time they become increasingly able to use these skills independently and to apply them in other settings, such as in cooperative groups of four.

10. *Inviting authentic action.* All of us can become frustrated and dispirited when we feel that talk is "just talk" that seems to lead nowhere. Whether in a quality circle in an organization, a site-based management council at our school, or a creative dialogue in our classroom, it is essential for participants to feel that they are not just spinning their wheels. Wholehearted participation requires that human beings know their ideas and concerns are being taken seriously and that they are truly making a difference in terms of the decisions that affect the conditions of the environment in which they find themselves.

In our classrooms, this means creating opportunities for students to engage in authentic decision making and problem solving about issues that affect them. This by no means diminishes the teacher's leadership role nor its attendant responsibilities.

Instead, it allows us to use our leadership to nurture and support the growing leadership of others.

Of course, there are many ways in which dialogue can lead to action, and some of those ways are personal and individual rather than shared and collective. But if we are to help students learn to make powerful choices in their lives, we need to provide opportunities for them to participate and have a real influence in the collaborative creation of a shared classroom community.

In order to do so, we need to be alert to ideas and suggestions from students that we can collectively implement, and to welcome those ideas and invite the consensus of the group as a whole. Of course, creating a positive learning environment in the classroom is our final responsibility, and it is important that we do not abdicate our own role in offering guidance to our students. Yet the more we can give students real input and responsibility in decisions about group activities, curriculum projects, and classroom procedures, the more they will surprise us by rising to the challenge.

A TRANSFORMATIVE PROCESS

AFFIRMING SELF

Setting forth on the path to becoming an author marks an important point in one's life. As writers we write mostly about our own experiences, our way of seeing and understanding our environment. Writing becomes a means of restoring memories and of discovering the importance and effect that events, people, and places have had on our lives. Writing uncovers silent truths we have carried inside with either pleasure or pain. Writing becomes a tool for learning, beginning with learning about ourselves.

In order to understand, care for, nurture, and support others, we need to understand and care for ourselves. Frequently, a lack of respect and appreciation toward others is the result of a damaged self-respect and an inability to appreciate what is good and positive in ourselves.

This unit offers teachers, children, and parents an opportunity to acknowledge and celebrate their individuality. The intention is not to nurture false self-pride, nor to promote a feeling of superiority, but instead to encourage a sense of comfort and ease with oneself, and a greater awareness of our potential. The purpose of this process is to develop the ability to recognize the uniqueness of self and others, as well as the richness that comes from diversity.

Objectives

- To initiate a process of self-discovery and respect for the uniqueness of everyone in the group.
- To explore the power of words as a form of self-expression and a way to share insights, feelings, and emotions.
- To use writing as a way to express individuality with true respect for ourselves and others.

Teachers	Students	Parents
Teachers are invited to:	Students are invited to:	Parents are invited to:
■ Create their own individual **"I Am"** poem, following the suggestions offered here.	■ Listen to and discuss the book or poem authored by the teacher.	■ Participate in authoring books about themselves and their families.
■ Share the poem with their students, as well as their own experiences in creating the poem. (Some teachers of younger students may prefer to reserve their poems for adults and choose instead to create a book on the same topic in a language and style closer to their students' age.)	■ Participate in a collaborative creation of a group poem.	■ Learn about the objectives of the unit and speak with their children about the need to understand and respect others.
■ Lead an activity to create a collective *I Am* book containing the teacher's poem, a collective poem created by all the students, and individual poems by each of the students. In addition, teachers can help students use their poems to create their own individual books.	■ Create and illustrate their own individual poems, which may be turned into individual books.	
■ Celebrate the production of this collective *I Am* book, publicizing and/or disseminating it.	■ Listen to and discuss the literary selection for this unit and engage in dialogue about their self-worth and respect for others.	
■ Read and discuss with students the literature selection for the unit and facilitate dialogue to promote self-validation and respect for others.		
■ Engage parents or caretakers in the creation of their own *I Am* books, following various procedures to be explained later.		

❖ UNVEILING THE AUTHOR WITHIN ❖

We learn to write by reading. Units 2 through 9 of Part II all begin by suggesting that you gather and share books with your students on the chosen theme for that unit. You will then be invited to explore one of the books using the Creative Literacy process as a preparation for the writing activity. This first unit is somewhat different. Though we also begin by reading, you need not gather books beforehand. Instead, we invite you to read the following poem:

By Myself
Eloise Greenfield

When I am by myself
And I close my eyes
I'm a twin

51

I'm a dimple in a chin
I'm a room full of toys
I'm a squeaky noise
I'm a gospel song
I'm a gong.
I'm a leaf turning red
I'm a loaf of brown bread
I'm a whatever I want to be and anything I care to be.
And when I open my eyes
What I want to be
Is Me.

Now take some time to write your own responses to this poem. What thoughts or feelings arise for you?

In this poem, Eloise Greenfield, one of the foremost contemporary African American poets, has shared with us a great deal about herself through a series of metaphors. Her joyfulness is expressed through two unexpected images. First she tells us she is "a dimple in a chin." Because dimples often appear as a result of a smile, we can understand her description of herself as joyful. She then deepens the sense of joyfulness by adding that she is "a room full of toys." Greenfield also uses contrasting sounds to refer to diverse aspects of her personality. The "squeaky noise," which might represent how most of us sound when tired or frustrated, is contrasted with the vibrant "gospel song" full of hope. And the resounding "I'm a gong" leaves us in no doubt about her willingness to project her voice and the message she stands for.

Just as sounds help describe some aspects of Greenfield's personality, colors hint at her willingness to grow into radiance. "A leaf turning red" has achieved the fullness of possibility. Color also suggests the cultural wealth she draws from her heritage—"a loaf of brown bread"—and her willingness to be sustenance to others.

But though Eloise Greenfield gives us several glimpses into various aspects of herself through her images, the main purpose of the poem is to declare that, out of limitless possibilities, her ultimate choice is to be herself. It is this affirmation and honoring of oneself that we would like to emphasize in this unit. Precisely because all of us are in a process of continual growth, it is key that we accept gladly, gratefully, and joyfully who we are right now.

Now read these two poems (reprinted by permission), written in response to Eloise Greenfield's poem:

By Myself
F. Isabel Campoy,
inspired by Eloise Greenfield

When I am by myself
and I close my eyes
I have short hair and I'm shortsighted,
I'm a bird perched on the telephone wire,
I'm laughter at mid-day.

Uniqueness
F. Isabel Campoy,
inspired by Eloise Greenfield

I am a woman,
creator of life.
I am Latina, passionate, familiar.
I am an emigrant,
conscious of my two horizons.

I'm a long, long train—
on Mondays, the engine
on Fridays, the caboose.
Choo-choo train, choo-choo train.

I'm the fragrance of freshly mown grass.
I'm the Moon in love with the Earth.
I'm two, I'm one.
I'm Latina, mestiza in history and culture.

Within me, the guitar dreams,
With me, the whole world dances.
In one hand I hold my friend's;
on the other, life, as the best of chances.

And when I open my eyes
I run to find a mirror
to tell me, face to face,
how much I love myself.

I am bilingual,
capable of negotiating contradictions.
I am the granddaughter of peasants.
I am the daughter of tenacity and love.
I am mestiza of cultures,
of races, of ways to see life.
I am a voice without fear.
I am here, building new roads.

TEACHERS AS AUTHORS

BOOK 1   Creating a Book Based on a Poem: *I Am*

Now we invite you to follow Eloise Greenfield and close your eyes. Think about your-self. What are the deepest feelings that define you, the hopes, the dreams, the com-mitments that support your life?

Think of an image to describe yourself. If you were a sound, what sound would that be? If your were a color, what color would that be? In the spirit of Eloise Green-field, do not limit yourself to naming a color. You can place that color in context to make it more vivid, like her "leaf turning red." If you were a flower, which one would you be? Which bird? Which animal? Which element of nature? How can you best ex-press who you are?

After you have written several lines, read them to yourself, preferably aloud. Have you captured the essence of yourself to your satisfaction? Are there any signifi-cant elements you need to add? How do you feel about the musicality of your poem? What lines might you want to rearrange? What lines might you want to shorten by pruning unnecessary words? Where would you want to make you poem more visual, or more specific? What details might you add?

Which images feel right, and which ones might you like to modify? Where are you "playing it safe," and where might you take more of a risk in your writing? How might you best honor your own uniqueness?

When you are fully satisfied with your poem, think about with whom you would like to share it. Also think about what format you would like to use to pre-sent it.

Following is a poem by a teacher from San Francisco, María Coronado.

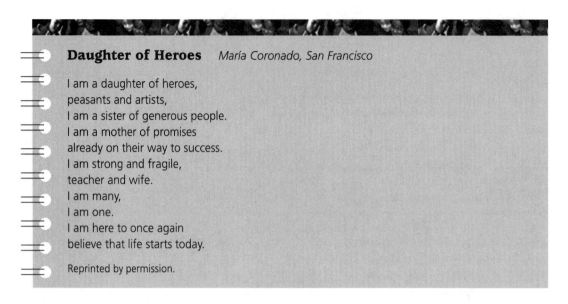

Daughter of Heroes   *María Coronado, San Francisco*

I am a daughter of heroes,
peasants and artists,
I am a sister of generous people.
I am a mother of promises
already on their way to success.
I am strong and fragile,
teacher and wife.
I am many,
I am one.
I am here to once again
believe that life starts today.

Reprinted by permission.

A poem can be transformed into a book. Here is an example by Jennifer Benedict, a creative bilingual teacher in San Francisco. Jennifer used paper of different textures, including fancy wrapping paper, Japanese rice paper, foil, and tissue paper, pasted onto cardboard pieces to create a delicate but striking accordion book.

To achieve a longer or more elaborate book, you may want to follow the conventions of traditional book formats. Although books can have many shapes and innovative designs, usually they include the following elements:

I Am by Jennifer Benedict

Reprinted by permission of Jennifer Benedict, 39 Glen Oaks Dr., Prescott, AZ, 86304.

◆ *A cover.*
Frequently made of heavier paper or cardboard, the cover can be protected by laminating it or covering it with a clear plastic sheet. An attractive cover will invite readers to pick up and read the book. The title of the book, the author, and the publishing house are usually included on the cover. With self-published books, you can invent the name of your own pub-

lishing house. As time goes on, you might even develop different collections with their own names and logos.

◆ *A title page.*

The first page of the book usually repeats the information found on the cover and usually includes the city, or cities, where the publisher is located. If you work and live in different cities, or if you have close friends, relatives, or colleagues in another city, or if more than one city is important in your life, you may want to have more than one location listed for the publisher.

◆ *Copyright.*

This very important page can be on the back of the title page or follow it. Here you should give your full name, a postal address, and any other information (phone, fax, e-mail) that allows readers to contact you in case they want to purchase, reproduce, or even publish your book. (It is frustrating to see a wonderful book and not be able to get hold of the author to request permission!) You should also add the date of publication, preceded by the copyright symbol: ©. In most computers, you get this symbol by typing an open parenthesis, the letter *c,* and a closing parenthesis.

On this page, you should include your intentions with regard to the book. If you would like to have people request permission to reproduce it, say so. You can also grant permission to reproduce it but request that a copy be sent to you. You can find simple wording by looking at the copyright page of a recently published book, including this one.

◆ *Dedication.*

Dedicating your book to someone is a way to give that person a meaningful gift. The page following the dedication can be blank if you prefer to begin on a right-hand page or odd page.

◆ *Table of contents.*

Sometimes books benefit from a table of contents. If you are including one, it comes next.

◆ *Text and illustrations*
  • *Number of pages.*
    For a printed book, the total number of pages is usually a multiple of 8 (16, 32, 48, 64, 96, 128, . . .) because of paper sizes and the design of printing presses and folding machines. Self-published books printed on computer or duplicated on a copying machine do not have these restrictions.
  • *Book design.*
    You may want to think of your book in terms of facing pages or spreads. The page on the left-hand side has an even number. The page on the right-hand side, typically a more visible and therefore a leading page, has an odd number. In designing the book, you may want to consider the relationship between text and illustrations, matching shorter text with larger illustrations and vice versa.
    Of course, there is no limit to the size, shape, or design of your book. Bear in mind that if you want to make multiple copies, some shapes will be more difficult to work with. But do not let this limit you. Sometimes it may be important

to make a one-of-a-kind book for the sake of the experience or the relevance of the content.

- *Illustrations.*

    The teachers whose work you will find described or quoted in this book have used a wide variety of means to illustrate their writing. Sometimes they have used photographs, which provide immediacy and sense of authenticity. On occasion they have made their own illustrations using water colors, markers, or even crayons. Sometimes they have asked their students to provide the illustrations.

    Although computers can give self-published books the feel of a finished professional product, we would caution you about the use of computer clip art. Although it is conceivable that someone might create artistic collages or something exceptionally daring with clip art, in general it trivializes a book by robbing it of authenticity. On the other hand, it is possible to use reproductions of good art to illustrate books provided you are not planning to make multiple copies and sell them. This approach has been used effectively by some of the teachers with whom we have worked. Other possibilities include making collages of photos taken from magazine illustrations and the use of ripped colored paper.

As many authors do, sometimes we use a blank map to outline our books. On page 57 we offer a book map, which can serve as a frame for turning a text into a self-published book.

BOOK 2   Creating a Narrative Book: *I Am*

Now we invite you to create a book about yourself to share with your students. Some teachers have used the poems they have written in response to Eloise Greenfield's to create their book. Others, particularly if they work with younger students, have decided to keep their poem to share with other adults and have created a new text for a book on this topic to share with their students.

We all define ourselves in a multiplicity of ways. We can define ourselves by our relationships, being concurrently brother, son, father, grandson, and uncle, or daughter, granddaughter, niece, mother, cousin, aunt. . . . We can also define ourselves by what we are drawn to—we are lovers of plants, birds, nature, cars, music, art—or by the things we know how to do—we are cooks, artists, builders, listeners. . . .

Some teachers have chosen to define themselves through their relationships with family members, friends, and students. Illustrating their texts with photographs adds realism and authenticity to their books and offers an excellent opportunity for the parents of their students to get to know the teachers better. The beauty of this format is simplicity. This approach is an easy model for students and parents to follow. At the same time, it is very personal; no two books would ever be alike.

The book on pages 58 and 59 was written in Spanish by Lisa Solomon, a first-grade bilingual teacher. She typed her book on a computer using large print, and illustrated each page with large photographs of the people mentioned. Her book has inspired many other teachers to produce similar books. We also offer here an English rendition of her text (pp. 60–61).

	Cover Title Author Illustration	Blank	Title Page Title Written by . . . Illustrated by . . . Publishing house City **(1)**
Copyright © year Full name and postal address **(2)**	**Dedication** Dedication to someone you love or respect or want to honor **(3)**	**Table of Contents or Beginning of Book** Treat these two facing pages as a spread. Decide proportion of art and text. **(4)**	**(5)**
(6)	**(7)**	**(8)**	**(9)**
(10)	**(11)**	**(12)**	**(13)**
(14)	**(15)**	**About the Author** Your photo **(16)**	**Blank** **(17)**

Example of Book Map

The fact that Lisa Solomon's family is not made up of mother and father, and that she chose instead to write about the grandparents who raised her, can be liberating for many students. Many of the students in our classrooms are being raised by grandparents or other caretakers. Seeing families as composed of a diversity of people, especially if one of those families is the teacher's, can convey the important message that a family is those who share a home and the responsibility of caring for one another.

Mi nombre es Lisa Solomon. Yo soy maestra pero también soy mamá, tía, hermana, nieta, y amiga. Quiero presentarles a diferentes personas en mi familia.

I Am: A Photo Essay
by Lisa Solomon

Reprinted by permission of Lisa Gonzales Solomon, 2938 Fallbrook St., Santa Ana, CA, 92706.

Yo soy mamá. Estos son mis hijos. Mi hijo se llama Tyler. Mi hija se llama Victoria. **Los quiero mucho.**

Yo soy nieta. Yo viví con mis abuelos desde cuando tenía cuatro años. Mi abuelita se llama Andrea y mi abuelito se llama Roberto. **Los quiero mucho.**

Yo soy esposa. Este es mi esposo. El se llama Jeffrey.
Lo quiero mucho.

Yo soy amiga. Estas son mis amigas. Se llaman Ruth y Maria. **Las quiero mucho.**

Yo soy maestra. Estos son mis alumnos. **Los quiero mucho.**

In addition to the simplicity of this book, several other elements contribute to its value:

- The recognition of the multiple roles we play
- The teacher's sharing of her or his personal world through words and photos
- The inclusion of the teacher's students and their photos in the book
- The open ending, which invites the reader to respond to the book either through personal reflection or, even better, by creating her or his own book

I Am

A Photo Story *by Lisa Solomon, Santa Ana, California 1998*

My name is Lisa Solomon. I am a teacher, but I am also a mother, an aunt, a sister, a granddaughter, and a friend. I would like to introduce the various people in my family.

❖ ❖ ❖

I am a mother. These are my children. My son's name is Tyler. My daughter's name is Victoria. I love them very much.

❖ ❖ ❖

I am a sister. This man is my brother. His name is Bobby. I love him very much.

❖ ❖ ❖

I am a granddaughter. I lived with my grandparents since I was four years old. My grandmother's name is Andrea. My grandfather's name is Roberto. I love them very much.

❖ ❖ ❖

I am a wife. This is my husband. His name is Jeffrey. I love him very much.

❖ ❖ ❖

I am a friend. These are my friends. Their names are Ruth and Mary. I love them very much.

❖ ❖ ❖

I am an aunt. I have two nephews and a niece. My nephews' names are Bobby and Cris. My niece's name is Aimee. I love them very much.

❖ ❖ ❖

I am a teacher. These are my students. I love them very much.

❖ ❖ ❖

I am
A mother
A granddaughter
A wife

An aunt
A sister
A friend
and a teacher.
What are you?
Whom do you love very much?

Reprinted by permission of Lisa Gonzales Solomon, 2938 Fallbrook St., Santa Ana, CA, 92706.

Other teachers have chosen to write about the many hats they wear and the many roles they fill: In the morning, cooking breakfast, they are a chef; then they become a chauffeur, taking their children to school; then they become a teacher with a classroom of students; then a nurse, bandaging a student's knee; then a counselor, listening to a child's problems, and so forth.

Sharing the Teacher's Book with Students

Introducing the Book to the Students

Before sharing your book with your students, it helps to set the stage by telling them about it. A simple statement that this is a book you wrote and that it consists of your own thoughts and feelings about who you are can be sufficient. Or you might want to share with them Eloise Greenfield's poem as an introduction. In either case, if you help students develop a sense of anticipation, they will be much more attentive as you read.

Teachers report that students of all ages from elementary school to high school are fascinated by the books written by their teachers. The authenticity of the texts gives them a special relevance. Teachers further report that their students' relationship to books in general is strengthened once the idea sinks in that each author is a real, everyday person.

Talking about the Book

After you share your book with your students, you may want to invite their feedback or thoughts. Do they have any questions about the content? Do they want to know something about the process of creating the book? Once they have had an opportunity to ask their own questions, take some time to share with them how it felt to write your book. How did you choose what to include? What parts were easy? Which ones were hard? How many changes did you make? How did you decide when you were finished?

STUDENTS AS PROTAGONISTS AND AUTHORS

BOOK 3   **Students' Collective Writing:** *We Are*

Once you have shared your individual "I Am" poem and/or book, you can invite the students to create a class poem. Each student will contribute a line to the collective writing. To help students complete this activity successfully, begin by inviting them to exercise their creativity and get their ideas flowing. Ask them to complete the following sentence aloud: "I am . . . " If students seem reluctant to go beyond "I am a boy,"

"I am a girl," "I am a student," you may want to use some of the prompts on pages 64–65 to expand their sense of possibility.

Next, introduce the writing activity. Explain that in writing the class poem, there will be a rule, just as in any game: No one is to repeat what someone else has said. So if someone has said, "I am a soccer player" and someone else wanted to say the same thing, the second student would need to modify the sentence in some way.

You may want to suggest that everyone use adjectives as qualifiers; for example: "I am a happy boy, an intelligent child, a thoughtful person. . . ." Then ask each student to contribute a line to the poem by completing the statement "I am . . . " while you record their contributions.

Help your students identify their gifts in order to complete this one line. Students in a high school English class wrote:

I am a vessel, ready to set sail.
I am voiceless, yet full of meaning.
I am sitting on the horizon, waiting.
I am not anybody's image, but my own.

Once the poem has been completed, read it aloud to students in an expressive manner. Then invite the whole class to savor reading it aloud several times. Take time to enjoy and appreciate your collective accomplishment.

Here is an example of a class poem created by very young students that follows this format:

I Am   *By Room 7, Alvarado School, San Francisco, CA 1998*

I am a baseball champion.
I am an artist.
I am a ballerina.
I am a soccer player.
I am the artist that likes to draw.
I am a little TV, because I like to watch TV.
I am excellent at painting, that makes me an artist.
I am a ballerina, that twirls, spins and leaps.
I am a baseball fan excited about the World Series.
I am a really good basketball player who does dunks and stuff.
I am an artist at playing.
I am a racecar to drive.
I am an expert at coloring.
I am the nightlight by your bed.
I am in kindergarten.

Reprinted by permission of teacher Laurie Baker-Flynn, 3872 22nd St., San Francisco, CA, 94114.

BOOK 4   Students' Individual Writing: *I Am*

Once the collective poem has been completed, students can be invited to create their own individual poems about themselves. Encourage them to copy the line they contributed to the class poem and to add a few more lines to create a full poem.

Here are two examples of individual **"I Am"** poems written by students of different ages, a first grader and a seventh grader:

I Am
Jasmine Fuller, First Grade

I am the owner of two dogs; one is named
Rosie and the other is named Buddy.
I am a kid and I am six.
I am funny; I make people laugh.
I am a wonderer; I wonder what's for homework.
I am a friend.
I am a person, caring for people.
I am a cousin, who is nice to her cousin.

Who I Am
John Price, Seventh Grade

I am a crystal that twinkles like a star in the soft evening light.
I am a rose that dreams of rain to come.
I am an explorer who researches other countries.
I am a tree that gives sweet fruit.
I am so beautiful; I look like the moon.
I am a game that only clever people can play.
I am a sun that brings sunshine to the whole world.
I am a lover, who truly loves my family.
I am a light, which not even the lack of electricity can shut down.
I am a zoo; I house many types of animals.
I am a cat, whose green eyes can peer into the darkest night.

Our enthusiasm for books created by teachers, students, and families has extended to the people around us. Many an unsuspecting passenger who happened to sit next to Isabel on a plane has landed having authored a book during the flight. Although we have generally resisted the temptation to present books produced by our friends and relatives, we were pleased when six-year-old Camille Zubizarreta created several books with her mother. We have included two pages from her book *I Am* on page 64.

If you sense hesitation or reluctance on the students' part, or you see the need to help awaken their imaginations, you may want to offer them one or more of the following suggestions:

◆ *Explore sensory experiences.* Invite students to create images of who they are based on sight, smell, taste, touch, and sound. Start by asking them to brainstorm a variety of things they can see, smell, touch, and hear, and create a list of their ideas for each of these items.

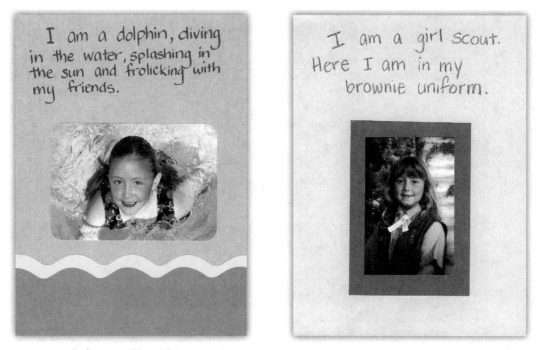

I Am Camila by Camille Zubizarreta
Reprinted by permission of the mother of Camille Zubizarreta, 1148 Pomeroy Ave., Santa Clara, CA, 95051.

◆ *Describe youself as an animal (or plant, tree, flower, place, toy).* Invite students to select an animal they particularly admire and to create images that describe themselves in comparison with that animal. If a child says, "I am a bird," to promote further expression the teacher-editor can ask: "What kind of bird? What is the bird like? What is the bird doing? Why is it important for you to be that bird?" The same can be done with plants, trees, flowers, toys, and so on.

◆ *Identify yourself in your family and in relationships with others.* Talk with students about how all of us have many roles in relation with others. Invite them to list all the things they are: daughter, son, sister, brother, granddaughter, grandson, stepdaughter, stepson, niece, nephew, cousin, friend, student, neighbor, and so on. Ask students to find a way to include these roles in a poem.

◆ *Identify actions important in your life.* Invite students to think about activities that are important in their lives. Let them describe themselves as: "a reader, a listener, a soccer player, an author, a runner, a singer . . . " You can also invite them to modify their statements; for example: "a fast walker, a joyful reader, an extraordinary baseball player, an impressive student, a great person . . . "

◆ *Use sentences frames.* You can ask the students to complete sentences such as these:
  • With a color: "I am . . . like. . . ."
  • With a sound: "I am . . . like . . . "

- With an animal: "I am . . . because . . . "
- With a landscape: "I am . . . because . . . "
- With a toy or game: "I am . . . "

◆ *Create images by comparison.* You may also want to invite students to finish lines similar to:
   - "I am wonderful like . . . "
   - "I am bright like . . . "
   - "I am gentle like . . . "
   - "I am kind like . . . "
   - "I am supportive like . . . "

Sharing Their Work with Other Students

Once the individual poems have been completed, it is important to create an opportunity for students to share them with others. There are various ways of doing this. One option is to have students form smaller groups in which to share their poems. This can allow students to develop greater ease in sharing their work with others.

Another possibility is to give all students who wish to do so the opportunity to share their poems aloud with the whole class. Of course, this does not need to be done all at once, and it is probably best if it is spread out over a few sessions. Also, it is important to make this an enjoyable experience. For example, students may want to have a friend come up and stand next to them as they read their poems. Or students who are not comfortable reading their poem to the class may choose to have someone else read their poem aloud for them. Although the ultimate goal is for everyone to feel able and willing to stand up and share their words, it is important to proceed gradually, ensuring that the experience is not overwhelming for anyone.

Also, remember that at times writing can be a way to express things we are not yet ready to share with anyone. If students express a reluctance to share their writing, it is important to honor their feelings. You can let them know they are welcome to keep their original writing private, and invite them to write another piece to share with others, if they wish.

PARENTS OR CARETAKERS AS TEACHERS AND AUTHORS

Home Conversations: Learning from Parents' Experiences

When students and parents share even a few minutes of meaningful conversation on a regular basis, students' academic achievement improves regardless of the parents' or caretakers' socioeconomic status or their level of schooling (Hewison & Tizard, 1980). Encouraging meaningful conversation at home is also a way teachers can show respect for students' home cultures. This will not only benefit individual students, but also contribute to a better classroom climate.

Conversation Starters

Because the theme of the unit is "I Am," begin by sending home copies of the book you have written about yourself, as well as the collective and individual books the students have written in class. Next, talk with students about the kinds of questions they would like to ask their parents or caretakers to learn more about who they are. Following are some examples of the kinds of questions students can pose at home. Although we have included some examples here, the questions will be more powerful if they are the result of students' brainstorming. Depending on students' ages, they can choose one or more of these questions to take home at a time.

Students can ask their parents or caretakers things about everyday life:

- Tell me about the place in which you were born.
- Who is one of your best friends? Why?
- What is your favorite activity to do alone?
- What activities do you enjoy sharing with other people?
- If you could travel to any place in the world, where would you like to go?

Students can also ask questions to help them understand their parents' outlook on life:

- What is the most important thing you like to see in a friend?
- What things in life make you happiest?
- What things in life make you saddest?
- What is one thing you feel proud of having done?
- What would you like to change in the world?

Classroom Follow-Up

It is important to acknowledge and build on the information students receive from their parents or caretakers. One way to do so is to give students some time to talk in the classroom about their conversation with their parents. You may want to have students share with the whole class, in small groups, or with a partner. If students share in small groups or with a partner, a few of them can be invited afterward to share with the class as a whole.

Another way of validating students' home conversations is to record them in the classroom and later create a collective book titled *Thoughts from Our Parents and Relatives*. This process is described more fully in the next section.

Books That Feature the Voices of Parents

There are a variety of ways in which parents and caretakers can be invited to become authors in the classroom. They can:

- Visit the classroom during or after school hours and write their own books with the teacher
- Participate in an afternoon or evening program to write books collectively
- Write their books independently at home
- Give their children oral and/or written feedback so that students can write books about their parents' thoughts and experiences

Although the first two options may not always be feasible, parents can become authors by sharing their stories and thoughts at home with their children, orally or in writing.

Later, their words can be transformed into books by the students, either at home or in the classroom.

In whatever way you choose to proceed, it is important to treat parents' words with respect. It is also helpful, as far as possible, to find ways in which parents can share their wisdom with one another. This will help contribute to a larger feeling of community among parents.

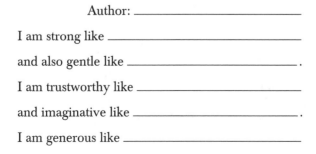

BOOK 5   Parents' Collective Writing: *We Are*

When you invite parents to become authors and to share their voices with your class, you are opening a door that parents never thought existed. Many will welcome this opportunity. Others will doubt they can do it. To promote success:

- Keep the process simple.
- Be natural and positive in your expectations.
- Be patient and constant. Once some parents contribute, others will be more in-clined to do so.
- Share each contribution with the class and celebrate it.

To begin with, send home a copy of your book and invite parents or caretakers to cre-ate a book following yours. This will be easy to accomplish if the book you send home has a clear, simple structure. If you want to offer parents some additional structure, you can send home an invitation to complete a blank poem that you provide. You can use the model outlined below or a similar one.

If parents will be completing their books at home, or giving their children feed-back so that students can create books in class based on their parents' thoughts, start by having a conversation with students in the classroom. Ask them how they can best help their parents complete their book. What might be a good time to approach their parents? What kind of help might their parents need or welcome? If the students will be taking notes from the conversation with their parents to complete the book later, what things might be useful to remember? What steps might they want to take? Stu-dents need to perceive their parents or caretakers as adults who have lived and expe-rienced many things and who have valuable things to share.

I AM

Author: _____

I am strong like _____

and also gentle like _____ .

I am trustworthy like _____

and imaginative like _____ .

I am generous like _____

and courageous like _____ .

I am like _____

when _____

I am _____ .

Once the parents' books are completed, it is important to share these finished products with other families. Parents will welcome the opportunity to hear one another's stories or poems. When you send home the copies of parents' books you have created, they can see their own words in print and read about one another's stories. In this way, you help create a climate of respect and solidarity among parents in which students can thrive.

Following is an example of a book created to share parents' voices. After sharing her own *I Am* book and the classroom *We Are* book, Alma Ricarte, a teacher in Los Angeles, invited each of the families of her second-grade students to send in some statements to share as well as some photos. She typed the parents' words and then re-produced them on bordered paper, which is an inexpensive way to create colorful books. This is a sample of a page translated from the original Spanish:

Our Family

Mother, father, children.
The family.
We are large trees,
with branches, leaves and deep roots,
searching with our roots to plant ourselves firmly in the earth.
The earth where new seeds will grow,
new trees,
shy and tender,
but nourished with the fertilizer, of teaching and education.
Some day, new branches, new leaves, new flowers will bloom,
and deep roots to strengthen the world.

With all our love,
these simple thoughts for our
beloved daughters María
Guadalupe and Verónica Río

Reprinted by permission of Alma Ricarte, 125 1/2 E. Adams Blvd., Los Angeles, CA, 90011.

Hannah Brooks, a mother from Santa Clara, California, created an individual *I Am* book. Hannah uses the metaphor of "a wearer of many hats" to introduce her family and the many aspects of her personality.

I Am by Hannah Brooks

Reprinted by permission of Hannah Brooks, 1148 Pomeroy Ave., Santa Clara, CA, 95051.

BOOK 6   **Parents' Individual Writing:** *Our Children* **or** *Our Family*

Kimberly Persiani, a teacher in the San Francisco Bay area, invited the parents of her fourth-grade students to write about their children. Every family in the class participated by sending a page about their child. Parents talked about the things their children like to do, the things they like to share together, and the characteristics that make their children unique.

Because all of Ms. Persiani's students are English language learners, the parents wrote their contributions in their home language: Chinese, Spanish, or Tagalog. Ms. Persiani enlisted three mothers to translate the texts into English. The texts were then printed bilingually in the original language and in English. The students in turn drew their self-portraits to accompany their parents' words. The great effort and care they put into their self-portraits and the remarkable likenesses they were able to achieve attest to the pride they felt in having the people in their lives, parents and teachers, working collectively to create a book about them.

Starr DiCiurcio, an ESL teacher from Schenectady, New York, decided to write a book about herself as a mother as an example to share with her students' parents. In her book, she describes the process of adopting her son and daughter and shares how they became *Our Forever Family.* Again we see how the willingness to share one's personal history with students' families is a powerful way to generate trust and build community.

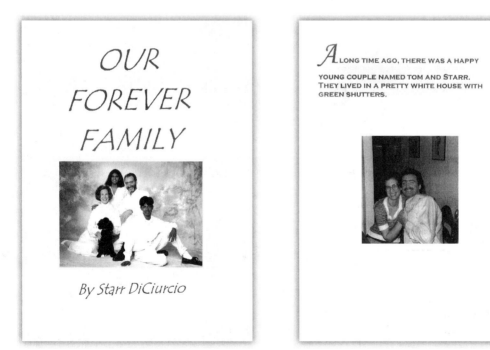

OUR FOREVER FAMILY

By Starr DiCiurcio

A LONG TIME AGO, THERE WAS A HAPPY

YOUNG COUPLE NAMED TOM AND STARR. THEY LIVED IN A PRETTY WHITE HOUSE WITH GREEN SHUTTERS.

Our Forever Family **by Starr DiCiurcio**
Reprinted by permission of Starr R. DiCiurcio, 2255 Berkley Ave., Schenectady, NY, 12309.

ADDITIONAL EXAMPLES OF BOOKS AUTHORED
BY TEACHERS, STUDENTS, AND FAMILIES

Lupita Hightower, a first-grade teacher, created the bilingual book *I Am/Yo soy.* Lupita chose to include a variety of people who constitute the different relationships in her life. Inspired by Alma Flor Ada's book *Strange Visitors,* she used a counting book format based on the days of the week:

I Am—*Yo soy*   *Written and Illustrated by Lupita Hightower, October 1999*

On Monday,	Los lunes,
I am the wife of 1 husband.	soy la esposa de 1 marido.
On Tuesday,	Los martes,
I am the mother of 2 daughters	soy la madre de 2 hijas.
On Wednesday,	Los miércoles,
I am the godmother of 3 goddaughters.	soy la madrina de 3 ahijadas.
On Thursday,	Los jueves,
I am the older sister of 4 brothers.	soy la hermana mayor de 4 hermanos.
On Friday,	Los viernes,
I am one of 5 children.	soy una de los 5 hijos.
On Saturday,	Los sábados,
I am friends with 6 girls.	soy amiga de 6 muchachas.
On Sunday,	Los domingos,
I am part of a family of 7.	soy parte de una familia de 7.
But everyday,	Pero todos los días,
I am the teacher who loves	soy la maestra que quiere
Her students a lot.	mucho a sus estudiantes.

Reprinted by permission of Guadalupe (Lupita) Hightower, 5381 W. Kerry Ln., Glendale, AZ, 85308.

Many teachers have followed in the footsteps of Lisa Solomon and Lupita Hightower. In Brooklyn, New York, María H. Quiñones Antonato added an interesting twist to her book. She wrote it as a brief summary of her life, beginning with her birth in Puerto Rico. On each laminated page, she pasted a small 2" × 1" flap. Upon lifting each flap, the reader discovers a list of categories. Beginning with one word, *daughter,* the list grows along with life events: the birth of another sibling, "daughter/sister;" beginning school, "daughter/sister/student." Sometimes one event, such as a wedding, will add several categories: "wife, daughter-in-law, sister-in-law." The ending invites students to reflect on the process of becoming: "As you can see, I began as a daughter. I have become a sister, student, wife, daughter-in-law, sister-in-law, teacher, godmother, mother. Who knows how many other things I shall become."

Pattern books with simple text, can be given unique formats to descrive an aspect of self. In the beautifully illustrated ***Sometimes/A veces*** (p. 72), Cattryn Somers, a teacher from Sunnyslope School in Phoenix, Arizona, chose to focus on the richness of her personality by talking about the many things she enjoys. By sharing with

I love to feel the sun.

Me encanta sentir el sol.

Sometimes I like to be inside.

A veces me gusta estar adentro.

I love to listen to the rain.

Me encanta oír la lluvia.

Sometimes/A veces by Cattryn Somers

Reprinted by permission of Cattryn I. Somers, 3653 E. Stanford Dr., Paradise Valley, AZ, 85253.

her students that sometimes she likes some things, while at other times she prefers other things, she is giving them the freedom to explore the diversity of life and a multiplicity of possibilities.

Marilyn Maiden Palowitch has grounded her poem in her experience of being a woman. She explores her heritage, aided by the nurturing metaphor of her grandmother's nut bread.

Grandma's Nutbread   *by Marilyn Maiden Palowitch, San Francisco, 2001*

I am many women.

I am a woman of one woman of five women,
   My mother, her sisters, their mother, her mother,
   abandoned by men, by death, by war, by alcohol.
I am their lone house on the hill.
I am their pot-bellied stove.
I am their rain-soaked hillside springing wildflowers.
I am their daughter.

I am a woman of four men,
   my father and brothers.
   keepers, providers, lovers, givers, takers.
What have I learned from them?

I am a daughter of women.
I am their chatter.
I am the humming Singer,
   ever-listening to their stories
   as they sewed their perfect garments.
I am the careening trolley
   that carried them to their jobs in the city.
I am the hard pavement
   they walked in their heels.
I am their new home in the suburbs.
I am the lost letters from their lost brother.
I am their student.
I am their daughter.

I am a wife to a man, a teacher, a learner,
   a musician, a reader, a lover.
I am listening for him. He is watching for me.
We are inventors.
We are authors.
What I have learned with him!

I am a mother of two sons,
   my boys, my little men.
I am their teacher.
I teach about Us,
   their mother, their sister. Their daughters?
I am giver of many women to these boys I love,
   so that they may love a woman.

I am a mother of a daughter.
   We are Grandma's Nutbread.
I am the yeast in the dough she kneads.
She pours the nuts we grind,
   releasing the oily perfume.
I am the dough, spread thin,
   filled with her nutty sweetness.
She is the glaze.
I am the heat of new bread, she is the aroma,
   wafting over a continent,
   to Our house on a hill, that stands no more,
   swirling across an ocean,
   to Our town that is no more,
   yet it will always be.
She is Our daughter.
She is many women.

I am one woman.

Reprinted by permission of Marilyn Maiden Palowitch, 6923 Corte Madrio, Pleasanton, CA, 94566.

Parents and Family Members as Authors

Parents and caretakers invited to participate in this process have made valuable contributions. We would like to share an experience developed by a participant, Nina Montepagani, from Troy, New York, in one of our courses.

Proving that there are no limits to the possibilities of authorship, Nina invited the parents of her ESL students to work with their children to create a class book. She sent a letter home asking family members to identify an object that has a special meaning for the family. To facilitate the writing, she included some questions: "What is the object? What country is it from? What size, color, and shape is it? How did you get the object? Did you buy it? Did someone give it to you? How old is it?" Spaces in which to answer followed each question. The last question was: "Why is this object important to you and your family?" Finally she asked the families to draw a picture of the object on a separate piece of paper.

Nina presented us with a copy of this amazing book, ***Something Special*** (p. 75), to share with other teachers. On the note accompanying the book, she states: "100% of the parents responded. That was a first for me!"

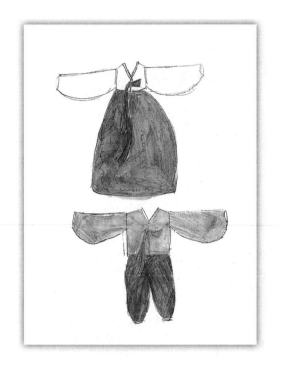

I'd like to introduce traditional cloth called **Ham Bok** in **Korea**. There are many different size, shape and color. It is very smooth. The color is very bright and wonderful. Also, it is very comfortable.

Sometimes parents buy it for children. When I was married parents gives it to me. All of my family have **Ham Bok**. I had five. We often wore it when it was a ceremony.

This is the beauty of our tradition. We have pleasure when we wear **Ham Bok**.

My teapot is from **Saudia Arabia**.
It is silver.
My grandmother give it to me.
It is new.

In our culture we usually drink tea together after meals. Also sometimes we meet with our relatives to drink tea and share talking about our life. Usually, we meet together afternoon.

Also, it is the way to show hospitality for other.

Something Special by **Nina Montepagani**
Reprinted by permission of Nina Montepagani, Enlarged City School District of Troy, Core Curriculum and Instruction, 1950 Burdett Ave., Troy, NY, 12180.

Because the drawings sent in by the families were so extraordinary, Nina decided to bind the book by placing each page in a protective plastic cover. Each left-hand page is a drawing, whereas the right-hand page carries the text, which Nina typed into the computer, along with a flag to represent the country of origin. The entries are from families from all over the world.

A Korean family describes the national dress, or *Ham Bok*, and states: "This is the beauty of our tradition. We have pleasure when we wear Ham Bok." Another Korean family describes a porcelain dish received as a wedding present. For another family, the computer is the special object that allows the mother to communicate by means of the Internet with her relatives who stayed in Korea.

A Pakistani family has drawn a reproduction of a famous mosque; a Chinese family has drawn a cuckoo clock. A family from Saudi Arabia writes about their teapot and the importance of sharing tea: "We meet with our relatives to drink tea and share, talking about our life. . . . Also, it is the way to show hospitality. . . ." A family from Algeria draws and writes about a gold necklace with a medallion representing the hand of Fatima, a piece of jewelry the mother received on her first birthday from her grandparents. "[I]t keeps us in touch with our roots, cultural and religious, . . . to carry on this tradition to the next generation, it will be an honor to give it to my kids." The families included came from Turkey and Puerto Rico, from Mexico and Nepal, from Yemen and Colombia, from Vietnam and Japan. They all had something unique to share.

Not only did the students learn about one another's families and cultures, but they also understood that people from all over the world share the love of family, home, and tradition, even if these are expressed in diverse forms. The parents gained greater understanding of the richness of this multicultural society of which they are now a part. New knowledge was created in this classroom as students learned how to research and learn from one another.

A Book by Teacher, Students, and Parents

Bringing together under one cover the writings of teacher, students, and parents is a powerful way to convey the message that a community of authors has been formed, and that all voices are important and of equal value. Many of the teachers who have chosen to create these books have used three-ring binders as an effective way to incorporate the poems collected.

Ms. Peguero, a kindergarten teacher at E.P. 48M, District 6, New York, collected the poems written by her students' parents to create the book ***Somos, Eres, Soy/We Are, You Are, I Am.*** Here is a translation of one of the parents' poems:

I Am Loneliness and Existence

When I close my eyes
Rain falls
I am loneliness at night.

A swallow fills my soul
Clouding all light and life.
I am a star in a dark night
I am tears in the rain, falling.
I am earth without a plowman.
I am solitude and sadness, like water from a spring.
Within me, lives a tornado,
Breaking down dreams into fears
In one hand I have a handkerchief
In the other rest, as a goal for peace.
When I open my eyes, I run to the mirror
To tell me face to face
All I have to live for,
My children, waiting for me.
When I look to the sky
I wish I could travel there
But my eyes are on this earth
—the world doesn't end here—I say.

RECOGNIZING HUMAN QUALITIES

It is generally acknowledged among educators that children tend to live up to (or down to) our expectations. Teachers' high expectations of students' result in higher academic achievement, a well-known phenomenon that has been termed the "Pygmalion effect." Yet we still have far to go in applying this knowledge to our educational practice in effective and meaningful ways.

In our society, the recognition of positive qualities in ourselves and others tends to be less frequent than critical or negative comments. Parents may praise their children while talking to relatives or friends, yet seldom offer that praise directly to the children. Instead, parents frequently criticize the way their children look, dress, and keep their room, and even criticize their character, perhaps with the hope that these criticisms will help improve children's behavior. Likewise, children seldom define their parents by their positive qualities, and this is too often the case with siblings, relatives, and spouses. Of course, the amount and kind of appreciation offered varies from family to family as well as from culture to culture.

As educators we are responsible for encouraging the best in our students by recognizing and celebrating their good qualities. We also need to help our students see the best in others, instead of reacting negatively to characteristics such as national origin, language, features, skin color, religion,

Objectives

- To analyze books that contribute to the understanding of the richness of human beings.
- To continue the process of self-discovery and generating respect for everyone in the group.
- To expand our perception of positive qualities in ourselves and others.
- To discover and express the richness of personality and the power of language.
- To develop a vocabulary of appreciation and practice ways to contribute to a positive sense of self in ourselves and others.

Teachers	Students	Parents
Teachers are invited to: ■ Identify books that show the richness of the human spirit and make them available to their students. ■ Involve the students in the analysis of one or more of these books. ■ Generate an alphabetical list of the qualities they most admire in human beings. ■ Create an acrostic of their first name and last name, choosing positive adjectives that begin with each letter of their name. Or create a variation of this acrostic by writing a positive sentence of appreciation for each letter of their name. ■ Create an acrostic about their students and share it with them, displaying it prominently in the classroom. ■ Alternatively, create a book in which each page is an acrostic about an individual student.	Students are invited to: ■ Engage in the Creative Literacy Dialogue. ■ Collaborate in the ongoing creation of an ample list of positive adjectives. Depending on the students' ages, this list can be posted on the classroom wall or kept individually in a folder or notebook by each student. ■ Create an acrostic of their own name using words from the list. ■ Participate in creating a collective book. Each student will have a page in the book with his or her acrostic. The book can be illustrated with photos or self-portraits. ■ Participate in additional activities using acrostics to celebrate all the students in the class. ■ Create one or more acrostics to give as gifts to their parents or caretakers and/or other members of their families.	Parents or caretakers are invited to: ■ Participate with their children in the creation of a family book of acrostics consisting of one page for each family member. ■ Help create a **Book about Our Families** to which each family will contribute a page. This book will be circulated among all families. Whenever possible, it will be duplicated so that each family can own its own copy. ■ Express their appreciation for their children on a regular basis. ■ Appreciate the human qualities of all people.

clothes, or gender. When students are members of a group that is subject to prejudice and bias, it is especially important that we encourage their ability to appreciate their own parents and other members of their group. Internalized oppression can lead members of oppressed or marginalized groups to develop low self-esteem, feel shame about their family, and dislike others who are like themselves.

We need to clarify, however, that when we encourage appreciation, we are not speaking about false praise, nor a mechanical "pat on the head," much less about comparing one student with another. Instead, we are speaking about authentic and genuine responses. All human beings have talents. All of us have positive qualities. Regardless of our failures, all of us are working hard to do the best we can each day. It takes conscious effort to go through each day without taking our frustrations out on others or giving up on difficult or taxing tasks. It is not always easy to make the effort to treat others with patience and kindness while meeting our many commitments, being on time, and fulfilling our responsibilities.

Yet we tend to give ourselves and others little credit for all we do and in turn receive little appreciation for our efforts. Sincere words of recognition can be a valuable encouragement for all of us. As we find ways to appreciate one another, we also become less fearful of differences and better able to appreciate the qualities that we share as human beings.

I Am a Student of Life
F. Isabel Campoy

I am a student of life,
no more, no less than you.
I am a believer in learning,
in caring and justice.
I am a seeker of happiness,
a creator of peace.
I want the best for my children,
no more, no less than you.

Reprinted by permission.

✤ THE CREATIVE LITERACY PROCESS ✤

Well-chosen books can provide helpful opportunities for students to explore the subject of human relationships and the need for appreciation and respect. Begin this unit by inviting students to read books that show the multiple qualities of the human spirit. You will find a list of suggested titles at the end of the chapter.

Next, choose a text for engaging in Creative Literacy Dialogue with your students. An important aspect of being an author is learning to hold conversations with the books one reads. This is a learned skill that we can model for students. Students learn to engage in dialogue by being invited to take part in an open-ended conversation centered on a shared text.

We have included two selections in this unit to serve this purpose. The poem by Alma Flor Ada, "Song about All the Young People in the World," celebrates the basic human qualities that unite us regardless of our differences: the desire to play, to laugh, to dream, to learn and grow, to understand the world around us, to be happy. *The Gold Coin,* also by Alma Flor Ada, is a story of transformation. Juan, trying to steal doña Josefa's gold, follows her through the countryside. Their travel through the fields is also a journey from greed to generosity. Alternatively, you may prefer to select another book of your choice.

It can be helpful to introduce the reading by eliciting students' previous knowledge about the topic and inviting them to make predictions about the book. Once you have finished reading the book, use the corresponding questions to initiate the conversation. (If you have chosen your own book, you will need to spend some time designing thoughtful questions beforehand. The four stages of the Creative Literacy process are described in detail in Chapter 3 on p. 42. Additional tips on facilitating dialogue are included in Chapter 3, pp. 44–48.)

Song for All Young People of the World/
Canción de todos los jóvenes del mundo

When here is nighttime	Cuando aquí es de noche
dawn breaks where you are.	para ti amanece.
We live very far away,	Vivimos muy lejos
doesn't it seem so to you?	¿no te lo parece?
When here is summertime,	Cuando aquí es verano
you are wearing a coat.	allí usan abrigos.
If we are so far apart	Si estamos tan lejos,
can we possibly be friends?	¿seremos amigos?
I don't speak your language	Yo no hablo tu idioma,
and you don't speak mine.	tú no hablas el mío.
But I laugh	Pero yo me río
for the same reasons as you.	cuando tú te ríes
You study. I study.	Estudias, estudio.
I learn and you learn.	Aprendo y aprendes.
You dream and I dream.	Sueñas y yo sueño.
I know you understand me.	Sé que me comprendes.
We live very far away,	Vivimos muy lejos,
we are not close by.	no estamos cercanos,
But I tell you	pero yo te digo
we are brothers and sisters.	que somos hermanos.

If you want to show your students photographs of children from around the world that illustrate each line of this poem, you can use the regular size or the big book edition of *Canción de todos los niños del mundo,* published by Houghton Mifflin (ISBN 395-78863-5). There is also a cassette on which the author reads the poem in Spanish, and Suni Paz sings it to music she composed. The cassette is produced by Del Sol Books. (Both can be obtained from Del Sol, 29257 Bassett Rd., Westlake, Ohio, 44145, delsolbooks@hotmail.com)

✜ QUESTIONS TO INITIATE THE DIALOGUE ✜

 DESCRIPTIVE PHASE To develop an understanding of the content of the book.

1. When it is day where you live, what is happening in other parts of the world? Can you name a place where it is nighttime?
2. When it is summer where you live, what is happening in other parts of the world? Can you name a place on Earth where it is summer at the same time that it is winter where you live?
3. What kinds of things do all the young people in the poem share in common?
4. In what ways are they different?

If you have a copy of the book, you can ask:

5. Looking at the book, can you find two pictures that show children doing things that are similar?
6. Can you find two pictures in which the children are doing the same thing, such as learning, but in very different surroundings?

 PERSONAL INTERPRETIVE PHASE To encourage the expression of feelings and emotions elicited by the text and to relate the book content to the reader's experiences.

1. All over the world young people enjoy learning. What do you like to learn?
2. All over the world young people like to play. What do you like to play?
3. What are some of the dreams you hold in your heart?
4. In what ways are you different from other young people?
5. What do you share in common with all young people of the world?

 CRITICAL/MULTICULTURAL/ANTI-BIAS PHASE To promote higher-thinking skills. To encourage reflection about the themes of equality, inclusion, respect, and justice leading to peace.

1. Sometimes people think that their language is better than the language of others. What can happen when people think this way?
2. Sometimes people believe that their way of dressing [eating, living, thinking] is the only good way. What can happen when people think that?
3. All the children in this book are beautiful, each in their own way. What happens when we appreciate different kinds of beauty?
4. All children and young people have the right to be treated well. Yet this does not always happen. Why do you think that is?

CREATIVE TRANSFORMATIVE PHASE **To encourage creative, constructive action toward greater understanding and respect. To encourage taking responsibility for bringing about positive changes in our own reality.**

1. How do we want to be treated by others?
2. What does this tell us about how we need to treat others?
3. When other people are different from us in some way, what can we do to let them know we want to get to know them better and become friends?

The Gold Coin
by Alma Flor Ada

If you have the opportunity, share the complete book with your students and enjoy the illustrations by Neil Waldman (New York: Atheneum). If you don't own the book or are not able to obtain it in the public library, here is a synopsis of the story.

This original folktale tells the story of Juan, who has been a thief roaming the countryside for so long that he does not have a single friend. After Juan sees doña Josefa, an elderly healer, holding a gold coin and saying she must be the richest person on earth, he ransacks her cabin. Not finding her treasure, he sets off in pursuit of doña Josefa. Wherever he arrives he finds that she has just left, having healed a sick person and offered the person a gold coin. This makes Juan even more determined to catch up with her. However, to continue his journey, he has to work in the fields so that someone in turn will row him across a river, give him a ride on a wagon, or accompany him on horseback. So for the very first time in a long while he is out in the open air, working and sharing with others. When Juan finally catches up with doña Josefa in front of her home, a major storm is approaching. In response to Juan's demands, the old woman hands him the gold coin that everyone else has refused, asking her to save it for someone with a greater need. At that moment a young girl arrives requesting that doña Josefa help her mother, who is about to have a baby. The healer is very worried that the storm will destroy her ransacked cabin. Overhearing her concern, Juan regrets his action and promises he'll fix the cabin. Then he offers the gold coin back to doña Josefa, suggesting the newborn baby should be the one to have it.

Some of the themes suggested by this book are:

◆ Generosity
◆ Solidarity, working together
◆ The healing qualities of nature
◆ True values and inner wealth

Some of the ideas suggested by the book are:

◆ The most valuable things in life cannot be purchased with money.
◆ Many times by working together we can find the solution to our needs.
◆ There is much to be discovered in the people around us.
◆ Generosity brings unsuspected fruits.
◆ People can be transformed given the right opportunity.

Some of the ways in which the book may relate to the experiences of students and of many families, particularly immigrants or ethnic minorities, include:

◆ The experience of feeling alone, without support
◆ The experience of feeling alienated from others
◆ The desire for material comfort

✚ QUESTIONS TO INITIATE THE DIALOGUE ✚

 DESCRIPTIVE PHASE **To promote understanding of the message of the book.**

1. How would you describe Juan?
2. Why was Juan without family or friends?
3. Why could doña Josefa say she was "the richest woman on earth" when indeed she did not have any money?
4. What are some of the riches we all share?
5. What do you think this book is trying to tell us?

 PERSONAL INTERPRETIVE PHASE **To promote self-expression of feelings and emotions and to relate the book content to the reader's experiences.**

1. Have you ever felt like Juan (alone, without friends, envious of others)?
2. Who do you know who is helpful to you and others like doña Josefa?
3. How do you feel when you are generous toward others?
4. What are the riches in your life?

 CRITICAL/MULTICULTURAL/ANTI-BIAS PHASE **To promote higher-thinking skills. To encourage reflection about equality, inclusion, respect, and justice leading to peace.**

1. What do we need to learn to be able to participate well in a group?
2. What do we need to know to make good decisions?

3. Why is it important to have family, friends, and the support of others?
4. What do you think causes some people to steal or hurt others?
5. What do you think helps people find a good path?

 CREATIVE TRANSFORMATIVE PHASE **To encourage creative, constructive action leading to understanding and respect for others, and to become more responsible for bringing about positive change in our own reality.**

1. How can we tell our family, friends, and classmates that they are important to us, that they are indeed our treasures?
2. What can we do to become friends with someone we do not know well?
3. How can we make sure that everyone in the class feels appreciated?
4. How can we solve difficulties with our friends?
5. What riches do we have and want to increase?
6. What riches can we share with others?

✤ UNVEILING THE AUTHOR WITHIN ✤

TEACHERS AS AUTHORS

If we want to invite children and parents to appreciate themselves, it can be help-ful to begin by modeling our own self-appreciation, as well as by communicating our appreciation of our students. The books in this unit are designed to invite you as a teacher to recognize and celebrate your own strengths, as well as those of your students.

 BOOK 7   **Teacher's Acrostic: *Myself***

Many adjectives can be used to describe human beings. To create this book, it is help-ful to begin by expanding our sense of possibility, much as an artist might select a broad range of colors for his or her palette.

Before reading any further, please take a moment to write down some of the ad-jectives you might use to describe someone who is close to you. Once you have done so, read the list we have included on page 86. See which of the adjectives you wrote are included in our list. Next, create your own list, using our list of adjectives as a start-ing point, and see what you might add to it.

A	B	C	D	E
accommodating	balanced	capable	decisive	efficient
admirable	beautiful	caring	dedicated	empathetic
adorable	becoming	compassionate	dependable	energetic
affectionate	best	considerate	devoted	enthusiastic
alive	bilingual	conscientious	diligent	excellent
amicable	blessed	courageous		exciting
angelic	brave	creative		exquisite
animated		cultivated		extraordinary
appreciative				
articulate				
artistic				
attractive				
authentic				

F	G	H	I	J
fabulous	generous	happy	idealistic	jolly
fair	gentle	hardworking	imaginative	joyful
fantastic	genuine	helpful	independent	jubilant
fine	good	high-spirited	innovative	just
fun	gracious	honest	intellectual	
		honorable	intelligent	
		humanitarian	interesting	
			inventive	

K	L	M	N	O
keen	lovable	magical	natural	open
kind	loving	magnificent	neat	open-minded
knowledgeable	loyal	majestic	nice	optimistic
		marvelous	noble	orderly
		mature	nurturing	outgoing
		merciful		
		motherly		
		motivating		
		multilingual		
		multitalented		
		musical		

P	Q	R	S	T
patient	questioning	radiant	self-assured	talented
peaceful	quiet	real	sensitive	tenacious
persevering		reasonable	sharing	terrific
perspicacious		reflective	sincere	thankful
positive		reliable	splendid	thoughtful
precious		remarkable	sociable	truthful
productive		resilient	stupendous	trusting
		responsible		trustworthy
		responsive		
		romantic		

U	V	W	X	Y
unique	valiant	wonderful	eXceptional	youthful
universal	vibrant	wondrous		
unselfish	virtuous			Z
	vocal			zealous

List of Adjectives That Describe a Person

Now write your name vertically and add one or more adjectives to each letter to create a simple acrostic such as the one below:

T alented
E nterprising
A ctive
C reative and caring
H ardworking
E ducated
R esponsible
S tewards of the future

Choose words that on some level you know to be true. When you are finished, take a moment to read your acrostic and notice how it feels to appreciate yourself. Notice any feelings of awkwardness or embarrassment. These feelings can indicate the ways in which we have been taught to not appreciate ourselves.

The basic acrostic framework can be elaborated on in a variety of ways, as shown in the following examples. Once you have completed writing and illustrating the text pages, you can finish your book by adding a cover, a title page, a copyright page, and a dedication page. Alberto Rodriguez, from Los Angeles, wrote an acrostic book using his name.

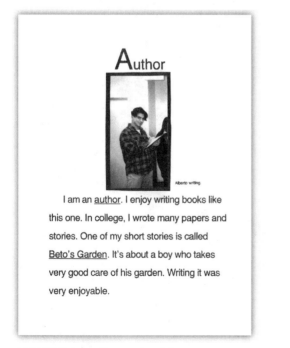

Author

I am an <u>author</u>. I enjoy writing books like this one. In college, I wrote many papers and stories. One of my short stories is called <u>Beto's Garden</u>. It's about a boy who takes very good care of his garden. Writing it was very enjoyable.

Best

Whenever I do something, I try my <u>best</u> to do it right. I like doing things as well as I can. I put a lot of effort into my schoolwork, hobbies, and profession. For example, when I write a paper, I always double check it before I turn it into a professor. This is how I turn in my <u>best</u> work and sometimes I get rewarded for it.

ALBERTO by Alberto Rodriguez
Reprinted by permission.

Alberto chose the following words:

A uthor
L earning
B est
E xplore
R esponsible
T eacher
O K

He then devoted a page to each word, explaining the personal associations that word holds for him as a person who loves to learn, to explore, and to always do his best. He enlivened the book with photographs of himself in various situations, including a photo of his students, to illustrate his role as "Teacher."

Marisol Carrillo, from Brentwood, New York, explores the potential of the acrostic format in order to introduce herself to her students and their families. In addition to acknowledging her personal qualities, she also incorporates information about her family history. Her striking book makes good use of large, bold lettering and contrasting colors. She used heavy paper in pastel colors, onto which she glued the text. Under each cut-out letter of her name, she inserted a tab. When the tab is pushed, a hidden photo is revealed. Here is the text of her book:

M.A.R.I.S.O.L   *By Marisol Carrillo, Illustrated by Marisol Carrillo,*
H.A.M. Publishing, Brentwood, NY

I dedicate this book to the two most
important people in my life.
Thank you,
Mami & Papi

❖ ❖ ❖

M
Marisol, a name given to me by my father. I was born on February 18, 1974, in Bogotá, Colombia, on a Monday morning at 3:00 a.m.
[When the tab is pushed, we see a baby picture of Marisol.]

❖ ❖ ❖

A
Animal lover, defender and friend
[When the tab is pushed, we see a photo of her 4 dogs.]

❖ ❖ ❖

R
Delicate and fragile, but vibrant and strong like my grandmother whose name was Rosa.
[When the tab is pushed, we see a photo of her grandmother framed by a red rose.]

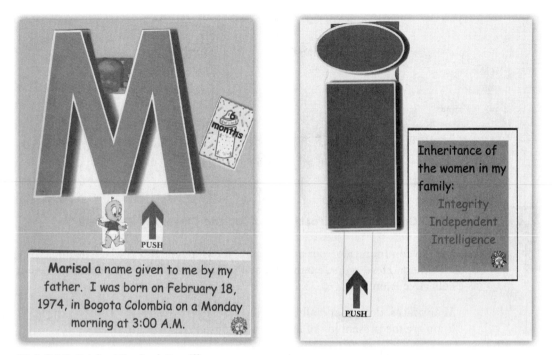

M.A.R.I.S.O.L by Marisol Carrillo
Reprinted by permission of Marisol Carrillo, 354 Washington Ave., Brentwood, NY, 11717.

❖ ❖ ❖

I
Inheritance of the women in my family: Integrity
                                          Independence
                                          Intelligence
[When the tab is pushed, we see a photo of Marisol with her mother and grandmother.]

❖ ❖ ❖

S
"Smile at the world and the world will smile back." Unknown author
[When the tab is pushed, we see a photo of Marisol, smiling, next to a photo of the Earth.]

❖ ❖ ❖

O
Only child of Arleth P. Carrillo and Henry Carrillo, married on March 10, 1973.
[When the tab is pushed, we see a photo of Marisol's parents on their wedding day.]

$$\Diamond \; \Diamond \; \Diamond$$

L
Lefthanded
    Lady
        Laughter
            Love
                Latina

Reprinted by permission of Marisol Carrillo, 354 Washington Ave., Brentwood, NY, 11717.

BOOK 8   **Creating an Acrostic Book for the Class:** *My Students*

One way to communicate your appreciation for your students is to create an acrostic book for them. Here is one example that a group of teachers created in a workshop as a collective exercise:

M any faces, diverse and all beautiful
Y ou are the present joy of life and a promise for a better tomorrow.

S tudents today, friends always,
T alented, you are frequently my teachers.
U nique, each of you a world to be discovered,
D evoted to your work,
E nergetically enthusiastic
N othing is too difficult for you.
T houghtful of your choices in life, I give you
S incere thanks.

Sharing the Teacher's Acrostic Book with Students

You may wish to introduce your book by asking your students how we feel when someone else says good things about us. Why is that? Who in their life says good things about them? To whom do they say good things? Let your students know that you are committed to helping everyone in the class learn how to appreciate themselves and others better. Then share your acrostic with them.

Creating an Acrostic Book in Honor of a Loved One

Some teachers have chosen to model for their students how to create an acrostic book in honor of a parent or family member. Oneida Mateo, a teacher from Central Islip, New York, used the acrostic format to write a book, ***Reflection of Love,*** in honor of her mother. Each of the words she chose to represent her mother inspired a page of text about that quality or trait, which she then illustrated with authentic photographs. A color border and the use of a contrasting color of ink for the text adds to the quality of this brief but moving book.

My mom is *única* (unique). She became a widow at the age of 27. She never remarried because she did not want a stepfather for her children. She raised 5 children without the help of any man.

She was *capaz* (capable) to raise her family without any schooling skills, but has had the honor of seeing her children finish their schooling and become professionals in different fields.

Reflection of Love by **Oneida Mateo**
Reprinted by permission.

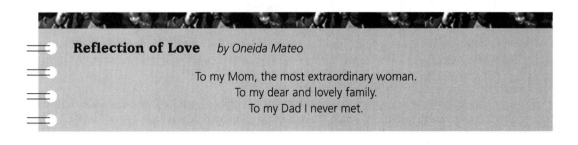

Reflection of Love   *by Oneida Mateo*

To my Mom, the most extraordinary woman.
To my dear and lovely family.
To my Dad I never met.

❖ ❖ ❖

DULCE

D edicada	Dedicated
U nica	Unique
L uchadora	Fighter
C apaz	Capable
E nergética	Energetic

❖ ❖ ❖

My mom has always been an incomparable person. She was always very *dedicada* (dedicated) to her parents, brothers and sisters. When she had children of her own, she was very dedicated to them as well. When she had grandchildren, they also had the opportunity to enjoy her love and dedication.

❖ ❖ ❖

My mom is *unica* (unique). She became a widow at the age of 27. She never remarried because she did not want a stepfather for her children. She raised 5 children without the help of any man.

❖ ❖ ❖

My mom has been always a *luchadora* (fighter). She always did both the possible and the impossible in order to raise her 5 children. We never lacked for anything.

❖ ❖ ❖

She was *capaz* (capable) of raising her family without having had any schooling. Yet she has had the honor of seeing her children finish school and become professionals in different fields.

❖ ❖ ❖

I'm going to remember my mom as the most *energética* (energetic) woman. She was never too tired to do chores and to take care of her children, grandchildren, brothers, sisters, nieces and nephews.

❖ ❖ ❖

My mom is all that and more. She has been my inspiration to be a dedicated person, a fighter, to love and care for my family, to reach my goals, and to be energetic. For that and much more, "Mom, you are my hero. I love you and I'm very, very proud of you."

Reprinted by permission.

STUDENTS AS PROTAGONISTS AND AUTHORS

Once students have seen the books you have created, invite them to create their own acrostic books on the theme of appreciating self and others.

BOOK 9   Collective Book: *We Are Friends* or *Our Classroom Community*

Invite students to write their own acrostics. Let them know that, in order to do so, you will first create a collective word bank that everyone in the class will be able to use.

- Create a grid with the letters of the alphabet. You can use chart paper or a blank transparency.
- Invite each student to contribute one positive adjective. Ask them, "What are some of the things we like or admire about others? What are some of the characteristics we would like to develop in ourselves?" Write each of the adjectives they contribute on its appropriate place on the grid.
- Continue as long as the students can come up with new adjectives. (You also can contribute some words to the list as needed.)
- Read the list aloud with your students. Remind them that all of us have the potential to develop these qualities in ourselves, and one way to do so is by noticing and appreciating them in others.

Plan to keep the alphabetic list of adjectives accessible. You may want to post it on the wall of the classroom. Students could also copy the list into a notebook, a computer file, or a set of file cards. In any case, encourage them to continue adding words to the list.

Next, invite students to create a collective book. One way of doing this is to take the name of each student, one at a time, and invite the whole class to suggest positive adjectives to create that student's acrostic. Alternatively, students could work in small groups helping one another create their acrostic page. Afterward, encourage students to illustrate their page with self-portraits or photos. Collect all of the pages and bind them to make a class book. Create a sign-out system so that students can take the book home overnight to share with their families. If at all possible, make copies that each student can keep.

BOOK 10 Individual Book about a Friend: *Allow Me to Introduce . . .*

Invite each student in the class to make an acrostic about another student using phrases or complete sentences for each page. This can be a good opportunity for students who do not know one another very well to get to know one another. They can work together in pairs to create an acrostic for each other based on the other person's interests. In order to do so, they will need to ask each other questions about their likes and dislikes.

Have students begin by brainstorming as a large group the kinds of questions they may want to ask their partner. They may come up with questions similar to the following ones, or they may come up with different ones. You may want to suggest some questions as well. Of course, the more the students "own" the questions, the more engaged they will be in the subsequent process.

- What are your favorite games [sports, pastimes]?
- What do you like to do after school?

- Who is your best friend outside of school? What do you enjoy doing together?
- Are there any celebrations you share with your family?
- What do you like most in people? Who is a person you admire?
- What are your dreams for the future?

BOOK 11 **An Acrostic about a Parent, Caretaker, or Family Member**

Invite students to create an acrostic about a member of their family such as a parent or caretaker. Depending on their age, students can write for each letter of the person's name a single word, a sentence, or a paragraph. This acrostic can be used to create a card or turned into a book. In any case, encourage students to illustrate their work in order to create a finished product that reflects their appreciation.

PARENTS OR CARETAKERS AS TEACHERS AND AUTHORS

Here we present a variety of suggestions for including parents in this unit on appreciation and inviting their authorship as a way to enrich the classroom learning experience.

Home Conversations: Learning from Parents' Experiences

Let parents know that you are working on developing awareness of the positive qualities of human beings. Ask for their support at home in identifying positive qualities and in offering appreciation to their children. Also, let them know that you will be asking them to help their children create a family book.

- As a homework assignment, have children ask their parents for positive traits they admire in others. Invite students to share their lists in class, and add any new adjectives to the classroom's ongoing list.
- Invite children to write an acrostic about one or both of their parents or caretakers and then take these acrostics home to share with their family. Once parents have seen the acrostics made by their children, it will be easier for them to participate in creating their own.
- Send home copies of the acrostic you wrote about your students. You may also want to create another acrostic about your students' families as a way of expressing your appreciation for them.

Books That Feature Parents' or Caretakers' Voices

In this unit, as in many of the others in this book, we suggest that you invite parents to work with their children to author an individual "family book." In addition, we suggest that you invite parents to contribute to a collective book that will later be shared with all of the families, as a way of helping develop a community of solidarity and support.

***Gabriel* by Camille Zubizarreta**
Reprinted by permission of the mother of Camille Zubizarreta, 1148 Pomeroy Ave., Santa Clara, CA, 95051.

Inviting Family Members to Write Acrostics about One Another

Send home a blank page, like the one that appears here, that parents or caretakers can use to make an acrostic about their child. You can enclose a simple set of directions, such as:

Please write the name of your child vertically, one letter on each blank square. Then use each line to write one of the many wonderful qualities of your child. The idea is to begin each line with the same letter written in the square.

Once you have completed this acrostic, please send it back to school to be shared. It will later be returned to you.

If parents have already seen some acrostic books made by the teacher and by their children, it will be much easier for them to complete the acrostic. You can also invite students to work with their parents on this activity.

When students return these completed acrostics to school, allow time for them to share their acrostics with a partner, a small group, or the whole class.

Acrostics Page

BOOK 12 **Writing a Family Book through Acrostics:** *Our Family*

Invite students to work with their parents to create a family acrostic book. First, have the students make blank books, with a page for each family member. Next, send these books home, along with a simple set of directions such as:

Please help your child create a book of family acrostics. The idea is to have a page for each family member.

Write the name of the person vertically, one letter on each square. (Add additional squares as needed.) Then use each line to write positive qualities about that person. (The idea is to begin the line with the letter that is in the box.)

Encourage your child to illustrate the book.

Once completed, please send the book back to the school to be shared with the class. It will be returned to you later.

Family Acrostics Book

Again, when these books are completed and returned to the school, it is important to give students time to share their family acrostic book in the classroom. If possible, you may want to make a copy of each one before sending the original back home.

Creating a Classroom Book That Includes All Families

Let parents know that you would like to create a collective book that includes all of your students' families so that everyone can get to know one another a little better and appreciate one another more. Send home a blank page like the one that appears here. Enclose simple directions such as:

Please use this page to write an acrostic about the activities your family enjoys, the celebrations that are important to you, and the things you value in your friends and relatives. Feel free to illustrate your page with a photograph or with a drawing made by any member of the family.

Sample Book Page

You may want to send home a sample page about your own family to serve as a model. Because many children do not live with their birth parents and many parents have different last names than their children, you may want to use a generic name such as "Our Family" for the acrostic instead of asking families to use their last name. Once each family has returned their page, you can bind them together to create a class book that children can borrow to take home and share with their parents.

ADDITIONAL EXAMPLES OF BOOKS AUTHORED BY TEACHERS, STUDENTS, AND FAMILY MEMBERS

A participant in one of our presentations in Ontario, California, a teacher by the name of Yma Sumac, gave us an excellent suggestion for using the acrostic with older students. The idea is to invite students to identify people whom they admire. The class can create a bank of names, similar to the bank of adjectives suggested earlier. Then students select appropriate names from the list that correspond with each letter in their own names and write a phrase that defines the struggle, courage, determination, or creativity of each of those individuals.

Students will have more options if you suggest that they use either the first or last name of the people on the list to create a match. These are some examples of names that students have used to create their personal acrostics.

> **Joan Báez**—a voice to sing for justice
> **César Chávez**—seeker of justice through peace and unity
> **Angela Davis**—outspoken woman for equality
> **Albert Einstein**—hero of the mind
> **Mahatma Gandhi**—transformation through peace
> **Martin Luther King, Jr.**—champion of human rights
> **Abraham Lincoln**—seeker of unity
> **José Martí**—education and truth will set us free
> **Mother Theresa**—embracing generosity

Another possibility is for students to write adjectives and then match them with an individual:

> *Artistic,* like Frida Kahlo
> *Courageous,* like Angela Davis
> *Compassionate,* like Mother Theresa
> *Forgiving,* like José Martí
> *Outrageous,* like Pablo Picasso
> *Talented,* like Plácido Domingo

3

STRENGTHENING
SELF-IDENTITY

A person's name is one of the strongest marks of identity. Most cultures have ceremonies connected with the bestowing of a name. Whereas in some cultures a name is given for a lifetime, in other cultures the name of a child changes when the individual reaches adulthood so that the adult name can better reflect the character of the individual. Some cultures add honorific titles to the names of all adults to express respect for their standing as adults; in others, honorific markers are acquired by only a few. All in all, names are a significant cultural element.

There is a story behind every name. Someone chose the name, usually selecting it from among various options. The namers usually had reasons for the choice or a process to make the decision. Most names have both a general meaning and a specific meaning within the family. Whether one has a unique name or a name that is shared with others, there is a story to be told about the experience of bearing one's name.

People have different relationships to their names. Some may like their name; others may not. Some may have changed their name several times during their life, whereas others may have always used the original name they were given. Regardless of our relationship with our name, we all have a way we prefer to be referred to by

Objectives

- To read and analyze books that present the topic of names and engage in dialogue about their message.
- To continue the process of discovering self and others by learning and sharing the stories of our names.
- To affirm that we all have valuable stories to tell, and that exploring our own family history will produce valuable information.
- To invite teachers, students, and parents to experience the power of authorship through writing the story of their names.
- To support collaborative relationships between teachers and parents or caretakers through the sharing of the teacher's own **Story of My Name** book.
- To strengthen home relationships by encouraging parents to share family stories about the names of various family members.
- To help build supportive community among parents by providing opportunities to learn more about the various families in the community.

P R O C E S S

Teachers	Students	Parents
Teachers are invited to:	Students are invited to:	Parents are invited to:
■ Identify existing books on the theme of names and share these books with their students.	■ Engage in the Creative Literacy process.	■ Reflect on their own names, how they were chosen, and their feelings about their names.
■ Create their personal book on **The Story of My Name.**	■ Brainstorm a list of questions regarding what they would like to know about their names.	■ Create, or help their children create, books about the parents' names or the names of other family members.
■ Share the book they have authored with their students, along with insights about their process of writing the book.	■ Interview family members to research information about their names and how their names were chosen.	
■ Share their book with parents, either by circulating a single copy or, whenever possible, making additional copies to give to each family.	■ Create books about the story of their names and share their books with classmates.	
	■ Decide what they would like to know about the names of their parents, caretakers, and/or other relatives.	
	■ Research and write a book about the name of a family member.	
	■ Research the life of a famous person who shares the same name as the student (or as one of the student's family members).	

the people with whom we interact. Often we have different ways of being addressed depending on the circumstances.

When we acknowledge a person's preference about what he or she likes to be called, we are honoring that person's individuality. Likewise, learning to pronounce someone's name correctly is a simple way to show our respect. When we invite a person to share the story of his or her name, we are acknowledging our commonality—we all have names, we all have life stories—as well as showing our willingness to learn more about that person's uniqueness and personal history, how he or she has become the person we know today.

✦ THE CREATIVE LITERACY PROCESS ✦

Invite students to read books in which a character's relationship with his or her own name is featured prominently. You will find a list of suggested titles at the end of this book. Make these books (or others on the same theme) available to students.

Choose a text for engaging in Creative Dialogue with your students. We have included here a synopsis of *My Name is María Isabel* by Alma Flor Ada to serve this purpose. Alternatively, you may prefer to select another book of your choice.

It can be helpful to introduce the reading by eliciting students' previous knowledge about the topic and inviting them to make predictions about the book. Once you have finished reading the story to them, use the corresponding questions to initiate the conversation. (If you have chosen another book for the Creative Dialogue, you will need to design your own questions. See Chapter 3, p. 42.) Additional tips on facilitating dialogue are included in Chapter 3, pp. 44–48.)

My Name Is María Isabel
by Alma Flor Ada

For the protagonist of the book, María Isabel Salazar López, the hardest part of being the new girl in school is that the teacher does not call her by her real name. Because there are already two Marías in the class, and because the teacher doesn't realize that López is María Isabel's second last name, her mother's last name, she decides to call her Mary Lopez.

But María Isabel Salazar López does not recognize herself when the teacher calls for María López. She fails to answers the teacher, again and again, and this creates a terrible situation for her in the class. Worst of all, María Isabel, who has a lovely voice and loves to sing, gets excluded from participating in the Christmas pageant.

María Isabel has been named after her father's mother, María, and after Chabela, her beloved Puerto Rican grandmother, who wants María Isabel to study to have a better future. María Isabel has been finding company in books. She has been reading *Charlotte's Web* and is moved by the plight of the little pig who did not want to be eaten. She hopes Charlotte will find a way to save Wilbur's life, and she hopes she can find a way to retain her name.

Can María Isabel find a way to help her teacher understand that if she loses her name, she will lose a very important part of herself? What would you do?

If you have the book available to share with your students, the following questions may be useful to initiate the dialogue. If you do not have the book available, you can share this synopsis with them and follow a dialogue along the line of the questions.

✤ QUESTIONS TO INITIATE THE DIALOGUE ✤

 DESCRIPTIVE PHASE **To promote understanding of the message of the book.**

1. Why did the teacher want to change María Isabel's name?
2. What happened when the teacher called on María Isabel using the new name she had given her?
3. What made it hard for María Isabel to let the teacher know what the problem was?
4. How did she feel as she was reading *Charlotte's Web?* Why did the book mean so much to her?

PERSONAL INTERPRETIVE PHASE **To encourage the expression of feelings and emotions and to relate the book content to the reader's personal experiences.**

1. Do you know anybody whose name has been changed?
2. Has your name changed? In what ways?
3. How do you feel when someone gives you a nickname or calls you by a made-up name they invented for you?
4. How do you feel about your name?

CRITICAL/MULTICULTURAL/ANTI-BIAS PHASE **To promote higher-thinking skills. To encourage reflection on the themes of equality, inclusion, respect, and justice leading to peace.**

1. Sometimes when immigrants arrive at a new country, their names are changed to sound more like the language of the new country. What would be difficult about that for the people whose names are changed? What is your opinion about this practice?
2. Sometimes people choose to change their own names in order to fit in better. Many times they later discover that it was not necessary to change their name to be accepted. Do you believe that people should have to give up their names? Or should they be welcome with their own names? Should some names be more acceptable than others? What are your thoughts about this?

CREATIVE TRANSFORMATIVE PHASE **To encourage creative, constructive action leading to greater understanding and respect for others; to encourage taking responsibility for bringing about positive change in our own reality.**

1. How can we express our respect for other people's names, traditions, and cultures?
2. What more would you like to know about the history of the names in your family?

✦ UNVEILING THE AUTHOR WITHIN ✦

TEACHERS AS AUTHORS

The process of writing **The Story of My Name** has resulted in wonderful books created by teachers, parents, and children. Of course, once the books are finished they are often not titled the **The Story of My Name** but instead receive a more descriptive title. Some of the types of books created through this process include:

1. *Books based on acrostics.* Expanding on the previous unit, some teachers have chosen the acrostic as a structure to guide their writing. There have been many variations

My Closet

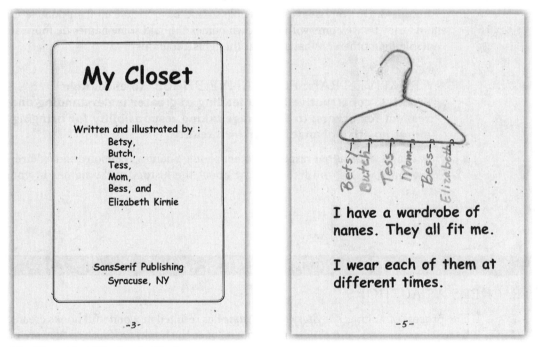

My Closet

Written and illustrated by :
Betsy,
Butch,
Tess,
Mom,
Bess, and
Elizabeth Kirnie

SansSerif Publishing
Syracuse, NY

-3-

I have a wardrobe of names. They all fit me.

I wear each of them at different times.

-5-

My Closet **by Elizabeth Kirnie**

Reprinted by permission of Elizabeth Kirnie, 1128 Westcott St., Syracuse, NY, 13210.

"Butch" is my father's
sweater, wrapped
about me as he carries
me sleeping to my
room.

—7—

"Tess" is the warm,
fuzzy slippers my
sister and I wear when
we stay awake late,
giggling quietly.

—8—

"Elizabeth" is a long,
warm overcoat, given to
me on the day of my
birth. It fits over
everything I wear.

—11—

on this theme, from a simple format of devoting one page to each letter to much more elaborate constructions.

2. *Books centered on a feature of one's name, such as initial letters or syllables.* The linguistic elements of one's name can trigger the imagination and become an organizing structure for a book. For example, *Mi letra G* (*My Letter G*) by Gladys Guzmán introduces a variety of people, animals, and objects that are dear to the author, all of whose names begin with the letter *G.*

3. *How one's name was changed.* Having one's name changed is a rather frequent occurrence. Often someone is given a name at birth, but relatives later decide to call that person by a different name. Or the family moves to another country and the name gets changed, or teachers at school modify the child's name. Several of the books teachers have written about their names have to do with a name change.

4. *The person for whom I was named.* For some teachers, the invitation to write a book about their name has offered an opportunity to recognize and celebrate the person for whom they were named.

5. *A changed appreciation of one's name.* Often as children we do not like our name until a special circumstance helps us appreciate it. This is the theme of the autobiographical book *Un nombre a secas* (*Only One Name*) by Lidia Goberna.

6. *A hidden name.* Sometimes, for cultural reasons or other circumstances, children have additional names that are unknown to others. This is the theme of *Un nombre escondido* (*A Hidden Name*) by Vivian Valentino, from Miami.

7. *Overcoming teasing.* Children often experience teasing as a result of their name. How she learned to overcome the teasing is the central theme of *Así soy yo* (*This Is Me*) by Amparo Espinosa.

8. *Relationship between name and identity.* The author of the book *¿Elsa? ¿Celín?* believes that she has two different personalities reflected by the two very different names she has been called throughout her life.

9. *Relationship to others.* Elizabeth Kirnie, the author of the book *My Closet* (see pages 104 and 105), explores the various nicknames one can have and the connections those names create with special people. She builds her highly creative book around an intriguing metaphor: Her many nicknames are different kinds of clothes, all hanging in her closet. Her full name is an overcoat, which covers any other piece of clothing she may choose to wear. The author uses very brief text enhanced with striking collages composed of fabric, ribbon, fur, buttons, and costume jewelry, as well as wire hangers. The cover of the book features a set of closet doors that open to reveal her collection of names inside.

10. *Family histories.* The teacher who wrote *Why I'm Named Yolanda* told the story of her father, who was in a prison camp in Italy during World War II. His only solace during that time was watching an Italian child named Yolanda. Later, he chose that name for his own daughter. In *El origen de mi nombre* [*The Origin of My Name*],

Hace muchos años que vivía en la isla de Puerto Rico, un joven muy trabajador. Se llamaba Pedro Antonio Brignoni y era el mayor de 8 niños. Con la bendición de sus padres, Pedro y Montserrat, Pedro Junior decidió viajar a Nueva York para conseguir dinero para mandar a su familia.

5

Junior no viajaba sólo a Nueva York así que su hermano, Miguel, lo acompañó. Los dos trabajaban muy duro en su nuevo barrio. En poco tiempo ganaron bastante dinero para ayudar a su familia en Mayaguez.

6

¡Que alegres se pusieron Pedro Junior y Miguel! Iban a ver a su familia de nuevo. Iban a estar juntos como las familias deben de ser.

9

Volando muy alto en el aire, el piloto se fijó que descompuso un motor. Pasa lo que pasa se estrelló el avión en el Océano Atlántico.

12

El origen de mi nombre by Evangelina Cronin

Evangelina Cronin, a Puerto Rican teacher living in California, tells the story of how her father decided to name all of his children after his brothers and sisters, who died in a plane crash while traveling from Puerto Rico to join him in New York City.

11. *Predictable structures.* There is no limit to the creativity with which a writer can approach a given topic. But when a writer is struggling to find the right voice or appropriate format for a particular book, the use of predictable structures can be helpful. Juan Carlos Rodríguez from Miami, Florida, used the predictable structure of the days of the week to create an original book about his name. In ***Un nombre de cariño es . . .*** (***An Affectionate Nickname Is . . .***), the young protagonist encounters different native birds each day of the week. Each of these birds calls him by a special name. At the end of the week, having received seven different nicknames, he discovers that they are all forms of endearment.

12. *A simple name for an interesting person.* In the course of our work with teachers, there have been a few instances in which individuals felt that the story of their name was too commonplace to offer much material for writing. Nonetheless, this did not deter them from writing about themselves as the person bearing that name, thus proving that whenever we are willing to write a story, there is a story waiting to be told.

13. *Variations of a name during a lifetime.* ***A Daughter Named Laurie*** by Laurie Baker-Flynn, a teacher in San Francisco, focuses on the many variations a name can experi-

***A Daughter Named Laurie* by Laurie Baker-Flynn**
Reprinted by permission of Laurie Baker-Flynn, 3872 22nd St., San Francisco, CA, 94114.

ence throughout a lifetime. The book is particularly poignant because the author illustrated it with photos of herself from her christening day to the present. The refrain appears on the odd-numbered pages, building anticipation for the photos encountered on the even pages. Here is the text:

A Daughter Named Laurie *by Laurie Baker-Flynn, Bakersam Publishing, San Francisco, 1999*

This story is dedicated to
my sister, Carleen

❖ ❖ ❖

My mom always wanted a daughter named Laurie, but when they took me to be baptized, the priest said . . .

❖ ❖ ❖

"A saint's name is what she needs, so you'll have to name her Laureen Dolores Baker."

❖ ❖ ❖

My mom always wanted a daughter named Laurie, but whenever I did something I shouldn't, what I heard was . . .

❖ ❖ ❖

"Young Lady, what are you doing now?"

❖ ❖ ❖

My mom always wanted a daughter named Laurie, but when I started first grade, Sister Francis taught me to write . . .

❖ ❖ ❖

L a u r e e n

❖ ❖ ❖

My mom always wanted a daughter named Laurie, but each year brought a new teacher and a new name.

❖ ❖ ❖

Laura
   Lorene
      Loura
         Lori
           Lorray

❖ ❖ ❖

My mom always wanted a daughter named Laurie, but when I finished college I wanted a more theatrical name so

❖ ❖ ❖

Everyone started calling me "LB."

❖ ❖ ❖

My mom always wanted a daughter named Laurie, but when I got married and started teaching . . .

❖ ❖ ❖

I became known as Ms. Baker-Flynn.

❖ ❖ ❖

My mom always wanted a daughter named Laurie, but once my own daughter was born . . .

❖ ❖ ❖

I was always called "Sara's Mom."

❖ ❖ ❖

My mom always wanted a daughter named Laurie, but then Dylan was born . . .

❖ ❖ ❖

and I was now one of the "Flying Baker-Flynns."

❖ ❖ ❖

My mom always wanted a daughter named Laurie, and if that's what you call me, I'll have an end to my story.

Reprinted by permission of Laurie Baker-Flynn, 3872 22nd St., San Francisco, CA, 94114.

BOOK 13 **Creating the Teacher's Book: *The Story of My Name***

To begin writing your own book about your name, you may want to experiment with one or more of the following processes:

- ◆ Share with someone, a friend or colleague, the story of your name.
- ◆ Jot down all you know about your name and all you can think about your name. Look at the number of letters in your name, the words that rhyme with your name, the nicknames or different versions that exist of your name, and so on.
- ◆ Use a journal to respond to the following questions:
  - • Who chose your name?
  - • When was it chosen?
  - • Were any other names considered?

- What considerations were used to choose the name?
- Are there other members in your family with the same name?
- Do you know anyone else with that same name? Do you share your name with any famous person? Is your name unique?
- What are your feelings concerning sharing (or not sharing) a name with someone?
- Have you always been called the same? What other names have you been called? By whom? When?
- What are your feelings concerning your name? Have they changed over time? In what ways?

◆ Consider using a predictable structure to support your story, such as an ABC book or a counting book. Other formats include following the days of the week, the months of the year, or the seasons. Alternatively, find a metaphor that you can use to frame your story.

Sharing the Book with Students

Read your book about your name to your students. Share with them the elements of your writing process. Why did you choose to write the story the way you did? What other forms did you consider? How did you choose the title? What process did you use to illustrate your book? Invite your students to ask any questions they might have.

STUDENTS AS PROTAGONISTS AND AUTHORS

Once students have seen the book you have created, invite them to create their own book about their name. You may want to set the tone by beginning with the following conversation.

Class Dialogue

Use the theme of names as an opportunity to emphasize respect for diversity. Explain that although names are important in all cultures, they are treated differently in each one. For example, some cultures give children the name of a deceased ancestor, whereas others never use the name of a deceased relative. Some cultures give children a name that is intended to last their whole life, whereas other cultures give their youngsters new names at their coming-of-age ceremonies. Some cultures have a tradition of consulting with people outside the family to help choose a name, whereas others go by the saint's day on the calendar. In still others, the sound and popularity of the name are the primary concern. All of these different cultural traditions are valuable, and there is no one right way to name people.

Next, ask students to share what they know about how names are given in their own cultural tradition. Who are they named for? Does anyone in the family share their name? What do they know about how their name was chosen?

In closing, emphasize how, underneath the diversity, there are some universal values across cultures: All of us consider names important, and all of us understand that treating names respectfully is a way to show respect for others.

BOOK 14 Creating an Individual Book: *The Story of My Name*

Help students brainstorm a list of questions about what they would like to know about their name and the way it was chosen. Encourage them to take their questions home and discuss them with their parents or caretakers. It will be helpful if you have already shared with families the book you have made about your own name. This will encourage greater participation from parents, and give them a better idea of what their children are working toward.

Once students have a sense of their story, invite them to write or dictate the story of their name. When they have completed their books, create a display and invite other classes and/or parents to come see the stories. You can also have some of your students visit other classes to talk about the stories of their name.

Students can create at least one additional book about the name of a parent or family member. Invite them to repeat or adapt the process they used to write about their own name in order to write this next book.

PARENTS OR CARETAKERS AS TEACHERS AND AUTHORS

Here we present a variety of suggestions for including parents in the unit on names and inviting their authorship as a way to enrich the classroom learning experience.

Home Conversations: Learning from Parents' Experiences

If you have not already done so, share the book about your name with the parents. If you have the means to make copies for each family, as the author you may want to write a brief personal dedication in each book. Encourage your students to ask their parents to talk about the parents' own names. The students can take home questions generated in class for that purpose. Suggest to students that they extend the conversation about names to include the names of their siblings, their grandparents, and other members of the family.

BOOK 15 Parents' Individual Book: *The Story of My Name*

Encourage parents or caretakers to create their own book about the story of their name. Alternatively, they can share their story with their child, so that he or she can create a book in class about the parents' names. Suggest that students begin by sharing with their family the process they have used in class to create their own books, the various types of books that were made, and the different stories they have learned about the names of their classmates. This can help encourage parents to tell their own stories and/or create their own books.

Make sure parents understand that they have different ways of participating in this process. Parents who are not comfortable writing may be more at ease sharing their stories orally with their children. What is important in all cases is that the stories of the names of students' parents and family members are shared and celebrated in the classroom.

HER CHILDREN CALLED HER "MOMMY" AND LATER, JUST "MOM."

FRIENDS FOUND LOTS OF NAMES FOR STARR – LIKE STARRSHINE, STELLA, AND STARRITA. THEY LIKED TO TEASE HER WITH SONGS AND JOKES ABOUT STARS. BUT PEOPLE NEVER FORGOT HER NAME.

MRS. D. WENT TO A COLLEGE FOR WOMEN AND THE GIRLS LIKED TO CALL EACH OTHER BY THEIR LAST NAMES SO THEN SHE WAS "REGAN."

Who?, Who?, Who Is Mrs. D? **by Starr DiCiurcio**
Reprinted by permission of Starr R. DiCiurcio, 2255 Berkley Ave., Schenectady, NY, 12309.

Starr DiCiurcio, a teacher in Syracuse, New York, obtained a positive response from parents when she shared her own book *Who?, Who?, Who Is Mrs. D?* with them as a way to encourage their own writing.

ADDITIONAL EXAMPLES OF BOOKS AUTHORED BY TEACHERS, STUDENTS, AND FAMILIES

As mentioned previously, the topic of the story of an individual's name has yielded a diversity of approaches. Here we would like to share some examples of this diversity.

Pride in One's Name

Pride in one's name is movingly portrayed in the following book by Colleen De Foyd.

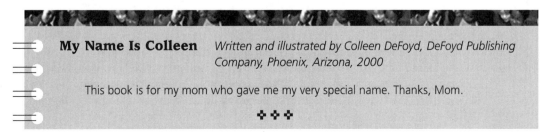

My Name Is Colleen *Written and illustrated by Colleen DeFoyd, DeFoyd Publishing Company, Phoenix, Arizona, 2000*

This book is for my mom who gave me my very special name. Thanks, Mom.

❖ ❖ ❖

My name is Colleen. I always remind people that Irish girls are called "colleens." Lucky for me. It could have meant "ugly wart at the end of the chin."

❖ ❖ ❖

My name is Colleen. Just Colleen. No middle name. That makes me a NMI (no middle initial) person. I asked my mom why she didn't give me a middle name. She said my name was strong and beautiful by itself.
    I said, "You couldn't think of one, could you?"
    She said, "Right."
    But now I think she was right. I think it's a strong name to stand alone.

❖ ❖ ❖

My name is Colleen. I like my name and I would never change it. My grandpa named my mother Mercedes and she's never forgiven him. She always hoped that she would marry a man with an ordinary name like "Smith." She married Jack Croughan. No one can spell it or pronounce it correctly.
[The art in this page shows the mother on her wedding day thinking: Maybe he would consider changing his name to Smith *after* the wedding . . .]

❖ ❖ ❖

My name is Colleen. I'm not named after anyone and I like that. My name tells my story and no one else's. I only have to live up to my standards. I try to keep them high.

❖ ❖ ❖

My name is Colleen, but my brother Jeff calls me "Konie." My brother David calls me "Colleen-chu." My sister, Valerie, calls me "Galouppe." My parents call me "Coll." My husband calls me "Kong." My son calls me "Mom" and that's my favorite.

❖ ❖ ❖

Now, the stories that explain these rather odd nicknames wouldn't make sense to other people. But each one reminds me of a special person, and each one holds a special memory for this colleen.

Reprinted by permission.

Mixed-Up Names

Occasionally there is an unusual circumstance around a name, as in the case of twins. While telling us about her name, Sara Clippinger includes a delightful story concerning her escapades as one of a pair of twins. Her book is enriched with wonderful photographs of the twins, who are difficult to tell apart save for a single distinguishing feature.

The Twins *by Sara Clippinger*

Being identical,
we were called
the twins . . .

Here come the twins . . .
There go the twins . . .
LOOK . . . twins!

❖ ❖ ❖

Although I was Sara
and my twin was Ann

as a young child,
I thought my name was Sara Ann

❖ ❖ ❖

Ann played the piano
with delight.

Sara played but
with fright.

❖ ❖ ❖

Recital time came about . . .

Sara said, "I just can't go out!"

❖ ❖ ❖

We dressed
exactly the same

So we decided
to play a game.

❖ ❖ ❖

Yes! On recital day,
Ann played the piano for two.

Surely, they wouldn't guess
who was who!

❖ ❖ ❖

We asked our other sister
"Who played better?"

She said: "I bet you *both*
get fan letters!"

❖ ❖ ❖

Only our brother
gave a wink that he knew.

So we asked him,
"What gave you the clue?"

❖ ❖ ❖

He said, "Ann forgot to change
the part in her hair.

But, don't worry, the others aren't aware!
Sara . . . Ann . . . You two are quite a pair . . . "

Reprinted by permission of Sara Clippinger, 21545 Erwin St., #106, Woodland Hills, CA, 91367.

To add to our satisfaction as readers, Sara concludes her book by saying: "This is not the end . . . ," letting us know that we can look forward to more stories about these delightful twins.

The Journey of Acceptance

With something as personal and unchanging as a name, it is not surprising that not everyone cares for the name they have been given. In doing this work, we have often encountered people who began by not liking their name until a special circumstance arose that changed their feelings. (Of course, others chose to change their names instead!)

Sometimes, reaffirming one's name may be a way of honoring those who chose it for us. Susan Cromer, from Schenectady, New York, illustrated her book with lilies of different sizes.

Tell Them Your Name Is Susan   *By Susan Cromer*

With thanks to my mom
who never called me Sue
and to my Hungarian grandparents
who got to call me Zuska
. . . just because . . .

❖ ❖ ❖

My name is Susan

❖ ❖ ❖

. . . not Sue
   or Suzy
      or Suzanne.

❖ ❖ ❖

My mom and dad named me Susan because
they thought it was a beautiful name.

❖ ❖ ❖

Susan means "lily."

❖ ❖ ❖

"Be proud of your name," said my mom.
"Do not let them call you Sue.
Tell them your name is Susan."

❖ ❖ ❖

"Her name is Susan," she proudly said to everyone.

❖ ❖ ❖

I, of course, wanted to be Kathy, or Debbie, or Linda. It didn't matter to me if people wanted to call me Sue.

❖ ❖ ❖

My teacher called me Sue. "Her name is Susan," said my mom. But it really didn't matter to me.

❖ ❖ ❖

My first boyfriend called me Suzy. "Her name is Susan," said my mom. But it really didn't matter to me.

❖ ❖ ❖

Our friend from France called me Suzanne. "Please, call her Susan," said my mom. But I really didn't care.

❖ ❖ ❖

And so it went. . . . Suze, Susannah, Suki, and Suey. Always my mom reminded them, "Susan, please."

❖ ❖ ❖

My mom is gone now.

❖ ❖ ❖

One day my new boss called me Sue.
Her voice whispered in my ear.
"Tell him your name is . . . "

❖ ❖ ❖

"Susan," I said.

Reprinted by permission of Susan Cromer, Paige Elementary School, 104 Elliot Ave., Schenectady, NY, 12304.

Being Teased Because of One's Name

Being teased is a hardship children often encounter. Aware of this problem, Lorena Valdez, a sensitive teacher from Texas, created *Mariposa* (*Butterfly*) a lovely book designed to help children think about this issue. Mariposa was "a beautiful child, with a huge smile, brown eyes, long straight hair and fabulous freckles." Yet other children often teased her about her freckles. One day, someone suggested she use lemon juice to erase her freckles. When Mariposa attempted to do so, all she did was irritate her skin. Another child suggested she scrub her freckles away. When Mariposa tried to do so, her face turned an angry red. Other children told her she should find a cream to make her freckles fade, and she tried many. Until one day, her grandmother explained that Mariposa's freckles were the kisses of angels who had arrived to welcome a beautiful baby.

The students from Room 7 in Alvarado School, San Francisco, used information about their names to create a collective guessing book, ***Who Am I?*** Each child brought a baby picture from home. With information provided by parents and grand-parents about the meaning of their names and the reasons they had been chosen, and with the help of their teacher, each child created a riddle to accompany his or her baby picture. The answers to each riddle are found on the last page of the book. Here are some examples:

My name means "princess." It is a name my father picked out for me. My cousin gave me my middle name, Stephanie. Who am I?

My name means "hard working." I was named after a Kate Wolf song called "Emma Rose," (Rosalind is my middle name), only Emma isn't my first name because they liked **** better. Who am I?

My name means "administrator" or "person in charge." I was named after my great grand-mother Sadie and after a famous movie actor (my parents like to watch movies). They both agreed on this name because they liked it. If my name had been left up only to my dad, I would have been called "Cosmo"! Who am I?

My name means "Poet." I was named after a singer from the group Jocdi De'vanta Swing. More than a thousand kids share my first name. Who am I?

After reading the book *My Name Is María Isabel,* the students in Mrs. Lacock's grade 5/6 class at Davis Hill Elementary in Hillsboro, Oregon, wrote a collective book titled ***Why My Name Is Important.*** This book explains why their names are special to them, just as María Isabel's name was important to her.

Mrs. Lacock gave each student a page with an attractive border. Next she invited them to explain why their names were special to them. After the students finished writing their pages, each page was photocopied onto colored paper to create the final book. The students made a beautiful cover by gluing colored tissue paper onto white drawing paper. Here are some of the things the students wrote:

My name is special because I am named after my dad. His name is Gustavo too. It is also special because my parents gave it to me.

Gustavo

❖ ❖ ❖

My names are special because they are all from different countries. Sam comes from Hebrew. My middle name is from America. Also my last name is from France. It means the world to me because I know I am different.

Sam

❖ ❖ ❖

My name is Jessica Dawn. This name is special because when I was born I was an Elizabeth Marcie. After my dad went on a walk with me in his arms, he came back to my mom's room. He put me in my mom's arms and said: "Here is your daughter, Jessica Dawn." I think this is special because my dad's love for me changed my name. I love my dad and I think his name is special also.

Jessica Dawn

✧ ✧ ✧

My name means everything to me. Because it is my identity. It is also my way to my own life. My name is Verónica Denise.

Verónica Denise

✧ ✧ ✧

When my father was a young boy, one of his baby brothers died. His name was Fabián. Later, when I was born, I was named Fabián. This is why my name is special and important.

Fabián

U N I T 4

BUILDING COMMUNITIES

Humans beings are social beings. We need one another for survival. In the process of living together, we have created elaborate social systems and technologies to meet our needs. We have also created a collective history, which allows to us to pass on greater information and knowledge to new generations than previous ones enjoyed. Through the use of language—a shared social product—we learn to analyze our social realities; we transmit our history, in order to preserve it; and we participate in projects to shape the future.

Yet as populations have increased and towns and cities have grown, the sense of community we have enjoyed in the past has greatly diminished. Although we are much more dependent on other human beings than earlier generations that lived closer to the land, we may never see the people who provide for our survival. We no longer know the shoemaker who makes our shoes, nor the tailor who sews our clothes, nor the pharmacist who mixes our medicines, nor the farmer who plants the food we eat. As a matter of fact, we may live surrounded by articles produced on the other side of the globe, by people who will always remain anonymous to us.

This transformation in the way we live occurred so suddenly in the last half of the twentieth century that there has not been

Objectives

- To identify, read, and discuss books that use the alphabet or a counting structure to present their content.
- To continue the process of self-discovery, exploring one's physical and social surroundings.
- To develop an extended classroom community that encourages respect, understanding, and appreciation for uniqueness, as well as a sense of solidarity in the common human adventure.
- To foster community building among students' families by providing opportunities for them to learn about one other.
- To explore the idea of community using the alphabet or counting book format as a tool for creating and structuring a book.

PROCESS

Teachers	Students	Parents
Teachers are invited to:	Students are invited to:	Parents are invited to:
■ Bring to class several models of ABC books and counting books to share with the students. ■ Engage students in the Creative Literacy process. ■ Create an ABC book about an aspect of their life or their community. ■ Read the book to their students and share with them their process of authoring the book. ■ Encourage students to brainstorm a number of topics concerning community that will then become the basis for collective and individual ABC books.	■ Engage in the Creative Literacy process to dialogue about the content of an alphabet book. ■ Brainstorm various aspects of their social and historical reality that can become the topic of their individual and collective ABC books. ■ Research their topic and create their book.	■ Consider their own life and community experiences as topics worthy of a book. ■ Share stories about their life experiences with their children in order to provide information on the topic selected for the ABC books. ■ Collaborate on the development of a family ABC.

sufficient time to reflect deeply about these changes. Nonetheless, the results are felt in many destructive ways.

All this has considerable implications for schools because schools may be called on for help as one of the last remaining avenues through which to create a solid sense of community. Much educational discourse refers to "students' communities" as if it were generally the case that when students go home, there is a close-knit community supporting their families. The truth is that in too many cases the reality is quite different.

But schools can strengthen their own sense of community and strengthen the communities of their students as well. As a learning environment, an effective classroom is a community of learners in which students learn with and from one another, receiving benefits from the talents of the whole group. As a social environment, the classroom can also become a community in which students care for, respect, and support one another. In turn, that sense of community can extend outward to students' families when we help provide opportunities for them to get to know, respect, and appreciate one another.

The process of authorship and sharing books written by teachers, students, and families can be a vehicle for building community. One way to do this is to dedicate some of the books we write in our program to an exploration of the physical and historical communities to which students and their families belong. The ABC format we are suggesting for this unit lends itself extraordinarily well to the topic of community.

Although one may be tempted to believe that ABC books are only for beginning readers, the truth is otherwise. The ABC format is a well-loved structure that allows writers to organize varied content for readers of all ages.

✦ THE CREATIVE LITERACY PROCESS ✦

Alphabet and counting books are not only for the young. Authors have used these structures to create books for readers of all ages, including adults. Invite students to find, read, and look at as many alphabet and counting books as possible. You will find a list of selected titles at the end of this book.

Next, choose an alphabet or a counting book for engaging in the Creative Literacy process with your students. One possibility is *Gathering the Sun* by Alma Flor Ada. Although we have not been able to include the text here for copyright reasons, it is an easily available book. We have included the questions for the dialogue. Of course, you may prefer to select another book of your choice.

It can be helpful to introduce the reading by eliciting students' previous knowledge about the topic and inviting them to make predictions about the book. Once you have finished reading the book, use the corresponding questions to initiate the conversation. (If you have chosen a different book, you will need to spend some time designing thoughtful questions beforehand. See p. 42. For additional tips on facilitating dialogue, see Chapter 3, pp. 44–48.)

Gathering the Sun
by Alma Flor Ada

This poetic ABC book, appropriate for readers of all ages, offers one poem in English and one in Spanish for each letter of the alphabet. The poems are illustrated by Simón Silva, a well-known Hispanic painter.

The book is a celebration of migrant farmworkers. These laborers, mostly of Mexican origin, work in the agricultural fields of the United States, migrating from place to place to follow the crops. Their wages and living conditions are often extremely poor, yet their work provides nourishment for all of us.

This ABC book explores various aspects of farmworkers' lives—their work, their families, their dreams and hopes. It was selected for this unit as an example of how the ABC format can be used to present a social reality. Simón Silva's bold and powerful paintings depict an intimate knowledge of farmworkers' lives.

Gathering the Sun was awarded the Once Upon a World Award of the Simon Weisenthal Center of the Museum of Tolerance as a book that recognizes the dignity of a community of human beings. May it serve as an inspiration for many more such books.

✤ QUESTIONS TO INITIATE THE DIALOGUE ✤

 DESCRIPTIVE PHASE **To develop an understanding of the message of the book.**

1. What have you learned about the life of the Mexican farmworkers in the United States that you did not know before?
2. What is your favorite poem in the book? Why?

 PERSONAL INTERPRETIVE PHASE **To encourage the expression of feelings and emotions in response to the book and to relate the book content to the reader's experiences.**

1. What do you know about the life of your parents and your grandparents when they were children? What would you like to know?
2. What are some of the things you feel proud about with regard to your own family, community, and culture?

 CRITICAL/MULTICULTURAL/ANTI-BIAS PHASE **To promote higher-thinking skills. To encourage reflection on the themes of equality, inclusion, respect, justice, and peace.**

1. Millions of people depend on farmworkers for the food they eat. Yet farmworkers' lives and working conditions are very difficult. How do you feel about this?
2. Many children of migrant farmworkers have grown up without ever having had a home of their own, and having had to change schools several times a year. Why would this be hard on you? What are your thoughts about this?
3. Part of the reason why migrant farmworkers are mistreated is that they belong to a different origin and culture than the people in power. Can you think of other cases in which the people's differences have been used to oppress them?

 CREATIVE TRANSFORMATIVE PHASE **To lead to creative, constructive action that encourages understanding and respect for others and to become more responsible about for bringing positive change in our own reality.**

1. What are some of the things in our life we can be grateful for having?
2. What things do we have in common with farmworkers? With all other human beings?
3. What can we do to help others who are not being treated fairly?

❖ UNVEILING THE AUTHOR WITHIN ❖

TEACHERS AS AUTHORS

Exploring Possibilities

The theme of this unit is family and community, and we invite you to use an ABC structure as one way to explore this theme. You may want to begin by looking at a variety of ABC books before attempting to write your own, exploring some of the many possibilities.

Some ABC books use alliteration. For each letter of the alphabet, sentences are written using words that begin with that letter. Whether the page contains words, rhyming couplets, a complete poem, or a paragraph, alphabet books are valuable tools for expression because they lend themselves well to a multitude of topics. Students seldom have the opportunity to read books that relate to their immediate reality. Using the ABC format, teachers can easily generate such books.

Although we are highlighting here the theme of community, ABC books need not be limited to that theme. Some of the topics that teachers have chosen for their ABC books include:

- ◆ My school or my classroom
- ◆ My students
- ◆ My community, neighborhood, or city
- ◆ Family, friends, and people in my life
- ◆ Authors whom I admire
- ◆ My favorite works of art
- ◆ Quotes that have inspired me

Additional examples of ABC books created by teachers are found in the last section of this unit.

 BOOK 16 Creating and Sharing the Teacher's ABC Book

Begin by choosing a topic for your book. You may derive some inspiration from looking at several examples of ABC books.

Knowing that many of her students from the Dominican Republic do not often see themselves and their homeland depicted in the books they encounter, Yadira Cruz of New York decided to write an ***ABC of the Dominican Republic.*** She used each letter to describe one of the important geographical features of the Dominican Republic.

While pursuing graduate studies in education, Bess Ilano-Tenorio created an ***ABC Filipino Style*** as a way to celebrate her own culture. Some of the elements she includes are related to food and festivities, whereas in others she highlights significant relationships in Filipino culture: "Ninang/Ninong are Filipino godparents. A Ninang can be an auntie or a friend of the family. A Ninong can be an uncle or a friend of the family. They are there for you at your baptism, confirmation and wedding." The author also incorporates values important to the culture: "*Pakikisama*. This is the word used in Filipino for getting along with other people. It is important to try to work in groups and be helpful in your family."

Another Filipino teacher chose a different approach. Erlinda A. Antonio of the Filipino Education Center in San Francisco decided to create *The ABCs of San Francisco* (see page 126) for her fourth- and fifth-grade students, who are all newcomers to the city. Selecting examples of well-known landmarks for her book, she made a point of including additional information for each landmark. The results include: "B is the Bay Bridge, where traffic goes inbound on the top deck, and outbound on the bottom" and "Y is the Yerba Buena Gardens, where everyone yearns to skate on roller blades." At times she personalizes her entries: "D is Diana, my dear friend, who lives on a dangerously steep hill," or she makes a delightfully unexpected choice: "W are the white clouds of fog that travel through the city." The ink-and-watercolor illustrations combine with the text to create a striking book.

Once you have decided on the topic and the format for each page, you can proceed to create and illustrate your book. After your book is finished, read it aloud to your students and share with them some aspects of your creative process.

STUDENTS AS PROTAGONISTS AND AUTHORS

BOOK 17 Students' Collective Writing: *Our Classroom ABC*

After you have read your ABC book with your students, invite them to create a collective ABC book for the classroom. Consider one teacher's example. To create the book *I Spy—A Classroom ABC,* Laurie Baker-Flynn, a teacher from San Francisco, asked her first-grade students to identify and group objects in the classroom according to the initial letter of each object's name.

Then she asked each student to stand next to the group of objects whose name began with the initial letter of the child's name. She then photographed the students together with the objects. As a result, all of the children are represented in the book. Of course, sometimes several children are on a given page, whereas other pages depict only objects because no student's name began with that letter.

This process was carried out over the course of several days. Some of the letters required quite a bit of creativity on the part of both students and teacher, but the results were worthwhile. At the back of the book, the teacher chose to include a key to each page listing the names of the children and of all the objects shown on that page.

If you are working with older students, you may want to create a similar book, exploring other ways of representing the classroom community. For example, instead of focusing on classroom objects, the book might include classroom rules and behaviors, classroom activities, subjects or topics studied, and so forth.

Of course, the students' collective ABC book need not be limited to experiences taking place within the classroom walls. A field trip to visit the redwoods in the Muir

is the Golden Gate Bridge
may not be gold
but oh, so glorious !

is Alcatraz
the Rock sitting very composed
in the middle of the bay.

are the VICTORIAN Houses
that climb the streets

are the TWIN PEAKS
where one drives to get
the panoramic view
of the Bay Area.

The ABCs of San Francisco by Erlinda Antonio

Reprinted by permission of Erlinda A. Antonio, 474 Holyoke St., San Francisco, CA, 94134.

Into Muir Woods: An ABC **by Paula F. Mah**

Reprinted by permission.

Woods north of San Francisco was the inspiration for a book written by the fourth- and fifth-grade students in Paula F. Mah's class at Sutro Elementary School. With their teacher's help, students wrote cinquains and created ink-and-watercolor drawings to explore the community of nature. We include here some excerpts from *Into Muir Woods: An ABC.*

Acorn
Round, spiky
Growing, falling, sitting.
Waiting to be eaten.
Acorn

Chipmunks
Fast, furry
Climbing, running, playing
With lightning fast reflexes
Chipmunks

Hawks
Feathery, mighty
Soaring, flying, hunting
Beauty in the sky
Hawks

Insects
Small, colorful
Flying, crawling, eating
Peacefully in Muir Woods
Insects

Ladybug
Orange, spotty
Flying, munching, watching
Afraid to be caught
Ladybug

Reprinted by permission.

BOOK 18 Student's Individual Writing: *ABC of My Community*

In preparation for students' writing, bring to class a number of ABC books, or invite students to bring ABC books from the public and school libraries. Explore with them the various forms these books can take. Then invite students to create their own ABC books on the subject of community. Begin by having a conversation with students about the idea of community and the significance of belonging to a community.

Help students see that although some people belong to only one community in which they work, play, and worship, it is also possible to belong to several communities at different times and for different purposes. Explain that as students, they are members of a school and a classroom community, in addition to belonging to their home community. Then invite them to create a list of the various communities to which they belong.

Once the students have decided which community they will select as the focus for their book, encourage them to observe, ask questions, and reflect on what they want to include in their ABC book. Invite parent participation by having students brainstorm the kinds of questions they might ask at home to gather more information about their home communities. Send home the questions developed by students as dialogue prompts, and remember to give time in class for students to share what they have learned.

Once students have created drafts of their texts, encourage them to come up with original designs for the cover of their books. Suggest the use of colored paper, cloth, and innovative materials for binding.

After students have written an ABC book about a community to which they belong, they may want to explore another topic. Invite students to consider the following possibilities:

◆ An ABC of my favorite toys or games
◆ My travel ABC (most important trips, excursions, visits to relatives, etc.)
◆ An ABC of my favorite books (this can focus on book titles, authors, characters, settings, or a combination)
◆ An ABC of my country of origin (or the country of origin of my parents, relatives, or ancestors)
◆ An ABC of things I like to collect (or would like to collect, or wish I had collected)

PARENTS OR CARETAKERS AS TEACHERS AND AUTHORS

Home Conversations: Learning from Family Experiences

Let parents know of your intention to support the development of an extended classroom community by creating more opportunities for the families of your students to meet and get to know one another.

 BOOK 19 **Parents' ABC Books**

Send home copies of your ABC book, the classroom ABC book, and/or students' individual ABC books as a way of inviting parents to write their own books. Some possible topics that parents might write about include:

Our family's ABC book
An ABC book about the place I was born
A community ABC book
An ABC book about our family's various skills and talents

Another possibility is to create classroom ABC books in which each page has been written by a different family. These books can be on different themes. For example, each family could write a page about their own family, and the pages could be organized by the first letter of their last name. Alternatively, students and families could choose a letter of the alphabet and use that letter to write a page that highlights one of the many features of the local community in which the school is located.

In an ESL classroom with many immigrant students, you may want to have each family create a page about their place of origin (country, region, or city). Ask each family to write the place name prominently on the top of the page. Once you have all the pages, you can organize them alphabetically to create an ABC book.

Once you have completed a classroom book based on families' writing, make sure that parents have the opportunity to see the finished product. If possible, make various copies of the book so that each family can have one for their home library. Or you may want to send the book home with each child for a limited period. Parents will greatly appreciate the opportunity to come to school and meet other parents, especially once they have had the opportunity to learn a bit more about one another through the collective book.

As we mention throughout this book, it can be helpful when encouraging parents to write to begin by sharing personal examples of your own writing. Because many teachers are also parents, a book on the subject of parenting is one way to forge a common bond with the parents of your students.

Deborah Ramírez Lango created an ABC book for her young son, Michael Tomás Lango, that richly conveys the experience of awaiting his arrival.

On Becoming Your Mom: The ABCs of Bringing You into My Life

Created for Michael Tomás Lango; Written by Deborah Ramírez Lango; Illustrated by Peter and Michael Lango

Anxiously awaited your amazing arrival
Before bedtime you began to beckon.
Carrying you closely within me would come to a closure.
Daringly you dazzled us with a delightful delivery.
Endless excitement enveloped me as you entered.
Feeling fantastic that you were finally here.
Gathering to gaze; gorgeous you were and gorgeous you remain.
Happiness had never been so hopeful.
Imagining your identity was no longer an illusion.
Jauntily you became our jewel.
Keeping you within, knowing you were not for keeps.
Looking at you; learning how life is truly lovely.
Mindful to make moments fond memories.
Naturally you nestled closely.
Overwhelmed with observers not opposed to their objective.
Proud to be your mom, promising to be purposeful.
Quickly stillness filled you as you napped quietly in my arms.
Realizing royalty looking at your rosy cheeks.
Soft and supple skin left me spellbound.
Tomorrows will be tantalizing, today is truly not a tease.
Unbelievable this may be, it is the ultimate life experience.
Vanity was not part of this venue, vulnerability will also vanish.
Worthiness never felt so wholesome.
eXtremely excited to be your mom.
Yesterday you were not here, I will no longer yearn.
Zeal, zip zoom through as we begin to live life as mother and son.

Reprinted by permission.

A Is for Arianne Rose: An Alphabet Album for My Daughter is another book written by a parent about her own child, an inspiring tribute to an exceptional daughter. Sally Gelardin used large color photographs to create this outstanding book, which conveys the intimacy and understanding between mother and daughter. The reader is left with the feeling that Sally understands what is important in her daughter's life, from significant family events to the small things that bring her joy.

ADDITIONAL EXAMPLES OF BOOKS AUTHORED BY TEACHERS, STUDENTS, AND FAMILIES

The ABC format presents us with unlimited possibilities. Likewise, counting books offer the advantage of a preestablished structure that can be used to explore a wide variety of topics.

Community and Cultural Pride

Inspired by Gateways to the Sun, a series that utilizes Hispanic masterpieces to illustrate books for young readers, Jeni Hammond decided to illustrate her ABC book with excellent reproductions of Latino and Latino American art. *ABC of the Man of My Life* is a book written by a teacher for a more adult audience, in which she uses each letter of the alphabet to describe the qualities of this extraordinary man:

A—ADORE	He adores me.
C—CHICANO	He is Chicano and proud of it.
H—HONESTY	It won't work without it.
L—LOVE	Lets me be me and loves me for it.
V—VALUES	Values what is important to me

The book's dedication states:

To you,
wherever you may be.
Please, come find me.

Reprinted by permission of Jennifer Vargas (formerly Hammond), 9501 N. Central Ave., Phoenix, AZ, 85020.

Through this ABC book, Jeni expresses her own values and the values she expects and appreciates in a relationship. Today Jeni, now Jennifer Vargas, confirms that "he" did indeed find her and that she has just married him.

Margie I. Berta-Ávila shares with Jeni the love of good art and pride in her culture. After seeing Jeni's book, she decided to follow the example of using existing masterpieces to illustrate her book. But taking into account the difficulty involved in

SELF-**D**ETERMINATION:

The right, el derecho, to call ourselves
Chicanos y Chicanas. The right to
determine how we want to live our
lives and what we want to do with it.
The right to speak the language we
choose and pray to whom and what
we want.

JUSTICIA:

It is what we are looking for. La
justicia we fight for is not for
ourselves or our life time. It is for the
seventh generation to come that we
will never meet.

The ABCs del movimiento Xicana/Xicano by Margie I. Berta-Ávila

Reprinted by permission of Margie I. Berta-Ávila, 535 Garden Place, Hayward, CA, 94541.
Marg102594@aol.com

obtaining permissions, and hoping to publish her ABC commercially, she decided to use photographs of public art instead. Her book is illustrated with pictures of the murals in the Mission district of San Francisco. The ***ABCs del movimiento Xicana/Xicano (ABCs of the Xicana/Xicano Movement)*** introduces us to the history, values, and aspirations of this significant political and cultural movement.

ABC Books about Self and Family

Myrtis Mixon used the ABC structure to create a book for her granddaughter: ***ABC Adventures with Kate Collins on Her Fourth Birthday*** (p. 133). To make the book more meaningful to Kate, she is the protagonist, and multiple references are made to her world of family, friends, and play. The illustrations combine line drawings, pastel colors, and collage. Photos of Kate, her family members, and friends have been cut out and glued onto the line-drawn characters, adding to the whimsy and realism of this wonderful birthday gift.

Personal and Professional Interests

Charlene Lobo created a powerful ABC book on a musical topic: ***Jazz People A to Z.*** This black-and-white book features one jazz musician for each letter of the alphabet,

Daddy drew an invitation for the party with dancing dalmatians and daring dolls.

Everyone's coming, even Eyore and his elegant elephants enter on the elevator.

ABC Adventures with Kate Collins on Her Fourth Birthday **by Myrtis Mixon**

Reprinted by permission of Myrtis Mixon, 1959 Golden Gate Ave., San Francisco, CA, 94115.

from Louis Armstrong, Chet Baker, and John Coltrane through Ella Fitzgerald and Billie Holiday, to Lester Young and Aziza Mustafa Zadeh.

This passionate and artistic tribute to jazz consists of a spread (two facing pages) for each letter. Each spread includes a photograph of the featured musician, as well as a list of words beginning with that letter that can be used to describe jazz music.

Awesome
    Accelerate   A is for Louis Armstrong
        Admire
Ascendant

❖ ❖ ❖

Electrifying
    Energetic
        Enlightening   E is for Duke Ellington
    Elation
Effervescent

Reprinted by permission of Charlene P. Lobo, charlobo@aol.com.

At the end of the book, the author presents a list of all the artists in the order in which they appear in the book, as well as a brief biography of each.

Sharon Willey, pursuing doctoral studies, used her research to create an alphabet book on *Female Indian Writers*. Each letter introduces a different author, using either first or last name to create the correspondence: **A,** Anita Rau Badami; **B,** Susham Bedi; **C,** Chitra Banerjee Divakaruni; **D,** Anita Desai. . . . In a few cases, she uses creative flexibility to forge the match, as in **E,** Shashi dEshpande. (Used by permission of Sharon Willey, 5881 El Dori Dr., San Jose, CA, 95123.)

As a children's literature project, Bobbi Kyle created an alphabet book that features a variety of characters in children's books. Here is an example from *A World of Letters—Characters in Multicultural Children's Books from A to Z,* a book we hope to see published very soon.

E Emi

Emi is a Japanese American girl, who along with her family is sent away to an internment camp in 1942. The United States and Japan are at war and all Japanese Americans are gathered and sent away. Emi's friend gives her a gold heart bracelet as a going away gift. But she soon learns that home and friends and the things left behind are carried in their hearts, no matter where they are sent.

[Yoshiko Uchida. (1993). *The Bracelet.* New York: Philomel.]

Reprinted by permission of Roberta Kyle, 12 Davies Pl. # 1, Poughkeepsie, NY, 12601.

A Is for ACTOR: A Theatrical ABC was written by Tracy Heffernan, a professional actress who also coordinates BookPALS, Performing Artists for Literacy in Schools. This program of the Screen Actors Guild Foundation brings performing artists to the

A Is for Actor: A Theatrical ABC by Tracy Heffernan
Reprinted by permission of Tracy Heffernan, 518 11th Ave., San Francisco, CA, 94118.

classroom. Sharing the vocabulary and concepts of the stage through an ABC book was a task that Tracy embraced with enthusiasm. The book is written in couplets:

A is for ACTOR
who speaks the words.

❖ ❖ ❖

B is for BALCONY
where the words are heard.

❖ ❖ ❖

G is for GRID,
which holds the lights.

❖ ❖ ❖

H is for "HOUSE"
where the audience delights.

With the collaboration of artist Mary Dilts, Tracy decided to give the book a "turn-of-the-last-century" feel. The characters and the stage were initially created as hand-carved rubber stamps, which were then scanned by computer so they could be used in a variety of ways.

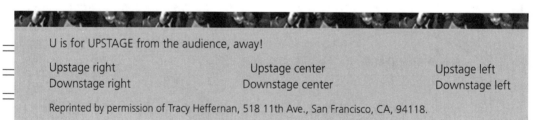

U is for UPSTAGE from the audience, away!

Upstage right	Upstage center	Upstage left
Downstage right	Downstage center	Downstage left

Reprinted by permission of Tracy Heffernan, 518 11th Ave., San Francisco, CA, 94118.

For self-published handcrafted copies, contact: MMI Publications, 518 11th Avenue, San Francisco, California, 94118.

Elizabeth Kirnie wrote ***Through a Child's Eyes: The ABC's of Timeless Wisdom.*** Using the first letter of the author's last name as the organizing element, she presents words by such diverse authors as William Blake and Confucius, Helen Keller and Lao-tzu, illustrating each thought with a beautiful color photograph of children.

Counting Books

Patricia G. Ramos, a second-grade bilingual teacher from El Paso, Texas, created a wonderful counting book ***Contemos con los niños (Let's Count with Children).*** Her goal was to create a book that reflected her students' realities and incorporate them as characters. She illustrated her book with drawings, collage, and photographs.

Let's Count with Children   *By Patricia G. Ramos*

ONE teacher, at the classroom door, greeting her students daily with enthusiasm and love.

TWO languages, Spanish and English, that we speak, read, and write throughout the day.

THREE seasons; multi-colored fall, white cold winter, and warm beautiful spring, pass by the classroom windows.

FOUR groups of students, working cooperatively, on school projects and difficult problems.

FIVE girls, sweet as sugar, dancing and playing during recess.

SIX hours, on the clock, keeping track of the time we enjoy together.

SEVEN boys, smiling and curious, asking questions incessantly.

EIGHT crayons, coming out of their boxes every morning and every afternoon to draw, draw, draw.

NINE months, that fly away, reading and writing interesting stories.

TEN fingers, sometimes clean, often dirty, pointing, cutting, writing, never stopping.

ELEVEN, a simple number, like a pair of sticks, or small arms waving in the air, with questions, with answers, or just moving.

TWELVE students, well-loved by their teacher, who have passed on to third grade, leaving her sad, tired, and happy to see them grow, enjoy themselves, and make good progress.

THE POWER OF TRANSFORMATION

The essence of life is transformation. Nothing that is alive remains the same. Transformation can be a mere physical change brought about by age, but it can also be a profound change born out of learning and experience.

As we can see from the many examples offered by human beings whom we admire, the human spirit has the potential to evolve by embracing generosity, kindness, courage, patience, honesty, and peacefulness as ways of being. Because society is the creation of its members, all social transformation begins within individuals. At the same time, because society is composed of institutions and norms, improving society requires that individuals transform existing institutions and norms.

It is disconcerting that human beings tend to be so hesitant about creating social change, because as a species we seem to feel compelled to test the limits of nature and break free from any limitations imposed by nature. Human beings have devised ways to live in the most inhospitable environments, from deserts to Arctic lands, to the bottom of the ocean to outer space. We have also defied all limitations imposed by our physical bodies. We fly faster than any winged animal, and we observe farther into the outer reaches of space and into the tiniest microscopic realms than any other terrestrial being. We have not

Objectives

- To explore the human potential for transformation as expressed in literary works for children and adolescents.
- To explore through dialogue the human potential for transformation and our individual responsibility to work toward equality, justice, and peace in our communities.
- To catalyze students' reflections by analyzing social conditions and challenging the idea that the way things are is the only way they can be.
- To understand that naming injustice is the first step in the struggle toward eliminating it.
- To use the writing process to develop a greater understanding, expressiveness, sense of confidence, and power.

PROCESS

Teachers	Students	Parents
Teachers are invited to: ■ Identify and share with their students books that explore the human potential for transformation. ■ Create a personal book, ***How It Is and How It Could Be,*** about an individual or social condition that merits improvement. ■ Read their books aloud to their students ■ Share with their students some reflections on the topic of transformation as well as on the process of creating their book. ■ Invite students and parents or caretakers to share reflections at home about transformation.	Students are invited to: ■ Participate in the Creative Literacy process. ■ Engage in classroom discussions about human transformation. ■ Help identify an issue in the classroom that can be improved, and work together to create a collective ***How It Is and How It Could Be*** book. ■ Create an individual book on ***How It Is and How It Could Be.***	Parents or caretakers are invited to: ■ Dialogue with their children on the topic of transformation by sharing life experiences of change. ■ Provide material for their children to write a book (or create a book themselves) on the topic "One Day That Changed My Life."

allowed the "human condition" to restrict what we can do in technological arenas, and every day sees a new frontier being explored, including organ transplants and genetic manipulation.

Yet, when it comes to social evils—war, violence, racism, poverty—human beings make excuses and defend our limitations by saying that these things have always existed and that they are the product of human nature.

It is true that some experiments in social transformation have not succeeded in bringing about an improved society. The French Revolution is a classic example. The revolution set out to create a better society, but instead yielded the Reign of Terror and an empire. A great deal of cruelty took place during this process.

Nonetheless, the ideals of the French Revolution have changed Western history and still have relevance throughout the world today. Among their lasting effects was their influence on the movements for independence in many Latin American nations. The world will never be able to forget the cry of "Liberty, Equality, and Fraternity," which continues to be the hope of many today.

The goal is to learn from our mistakes in earlier attempts to implement our ideals, not to abandon our ideals. In any area, progress has always depended on continued efforts in the face of failure. The history of flying is a case in point. To be able to fly was a dream of the human species for many centuries. The story of Icarus is only one of the many failed examples. Attempts to develop "flying machines" were numerous, and many ended in catastrophe. Nevertheless, those who were intent on finding a way to fly did not cease their efforts, and even today humans continue to explore new frontiers in aeronautics.

It is certainly a double standard to not apply the same principles of persistence and optimism that we apply to physical transformation to the area of social transformation. If we are to commit ourselves to bringing about a just, equitable, and peaceful society, we cannot take the easy way out and simply blame human nature for the current conditions. Instead, we need to continuously and sincerely search for ways to encourage respect and solidarity among human beings. We can certainly begin on a modest scale in our own lives: our families, friends, classrooms, and schools. At the same time, we also need to contemplate the larger picture.

Furthermore, we need to help our youth keep a sense of possibility and hope alive by creating opportunities for them to develop skills in peaceful interaction and responsible conduct. The activities in this unit are designed to provide students with opportunities to reflect on the differences between how things are and how they could be. We want to help students develop a sense that transformation is possible and that, as active protagonists in our own lives, all of us can make choices that affect our own lives as well as the world around us.

❖ THE CREATIVE LITERACY PROCESS ❖

Invite students to read books that show how the protagonist undergoes, or brings about, a meaningful transformation. You will find a list of suggested titles in the appendix on recommended books. Make as many of these books as possible available to the students.

Select a text for engaging in the Creative Literacy Dialogue process with your students. We have included a selection below that can serve this purpose: the text of *The Kingdom of Geometry,* a picture book by Alma Flor Ada. Alternatively, you may prefer to select another book of your choice.

Before you begin sharing the book, elicit students' previous knowledge about the topic and invite them to make predictions about the book. Once you have finished the shared reading, use the corresponding questions to initiate the conversation. (If you have chosen another book, you will need to spend some time designing thoughtful questions beforehand. See p. 42. For additional tips on facilitating dialogue, see pp. 44–48.)

The Kingdom of Geometry
by Alma Flor Ada

The central theme of this modern fable for people of all ages is the destructive effect of discrimination and racism. The story's ending suggests that persistence, courage and solidarity can lead to creative solutions for the problems we encounter, no matter how difficult they may seem. Here is the tale:

The Kingdom of Geometry was a beautiful country. It had green rolling hills, happy brooks, bountiful orchards and a sky covered with songbirds. And the population was joyful and hardworking.

And in the Kingdom of Geometry it all went more or less fine. That is to say, some days were better than others, but on bad days one could always hope that the next day would be better.

The inhabitants of that kingdom were of very different shapes. Some, the triangles, had three sides. Others, the rectangles, diamonds, squares and trapezoids, had four. Sometimes, their sides were all of the same size. And sometimes they were not. But the inhabitants of the kingdom had never been bothered by their differences. On the contrary, they found them interesting and fun.

Until the day a new king was crowned. King Square VII held to some very strange ideas. The ideas came from a few of his counselors, who had said:

"Squares are perfect shapes."

"Their four sides are identical."

"Their four angles are equal, too."

"No matter from what angle you look at them, they are perfect."

King Square VII thought that all sounded very good. That is why he approved when his counselors proposed:

"A Perfectly Square king should have a perfectly square palace, with square courtyards, square doors and square windows."

And he gave orders to renovate the entire palace. The royal architects changed the beautiful gardens into square courtyards. The doors and the windows also became square.

The counselors congratulated the monarch. And King Square VII was filled with satisfaction when they asserted:

"A Perfect Square king deserves a perfect palace."

He smiled when the oldest counselor stated:

"Squares are the only perfect figures."

Then the counselors proposed:

"Only squares should enter a perfectly square palace."

And so the king ordered that anyone who was not a square should be removed from the palace.

They fired the cook, who was a triangle, even though he made the most delicious desserts. And they fired the gardener, who was a rectangle, even though his yellow roses were the most beautiful in all the land. And they fired the musician, who was a trapezoid, in spite of the fact that his melodies enlivened the evenings and delighted young and old alike.

And now it seemed that throughout the kingdom, at least for everyone who was not a square, bad days were followed by worse ones.

The only jobs to be had were for the squares. In the market, the best food went to the squares. The streets were filled with square guards, and anyone who was not a square needed special permission to pass.

When it seemed things could not get any worse, a true catastrophe took place.

King Square the VII, at the suggestion of his counselors, ordered that a strong wall be built, enclosing a square piece of land. Then he ordered:

"All triangles, diamonds, rectangles and trapezoids, that is, everyone who is not a square, will live inside these walls. There they can grow vegetables for the perfect citizens, the squares."

And then he commanded his guards:

"Only squares will be allowed to enter and leave the walled land."

The diamonds and trapezoids tried to protest. The rectangles and triangles requested an audience with the king. But the only answer they received came from the guards:

"Only squares are allowed through these gates."

Happiness had disappeared from the kingdom. No laughter or songs were heard. Many of the squares had neighbors and friends who were diamonds and triangles. Some of them had cousins who were rectangles. But the king's orders were so firm, and the square guards so stern, that no one dared to do or say anything.

And this was the state of things, until the day that Rose, a young square who missed her best friend, a young triangle named Violet, decided that something had to be done.

So, after thinking about it for some time, and taking advantage of being a square, Rose went to the walled section. The guards let her go through. After hugging Violet, she announced proudly:

"I have an idea that will let you and your brothers and sisters escape. Look, if two triangles like you bond together they can form a square. The guards will let you through."

"But . . . " replied Violet "not all of the triangles here can come together to form a square. And we will not leave them behind! Besides, we wouldn't leave the other shapes behind either."

Taken aback by Violet's refusal, Rose left. But the more she reflected upon Violet's words, the more she understood her friend's position. So she decided to find another solution. She thought, and thought, and thought . . .

In a couple of days, she was back inside the wall.

"We won't have to leave anyone behind!" Rose announced happily to Violet. "Let me show you!"

And Rose began to draw on the earth with a stick. She drew a tangram, a combination of a rectangle and four rectangles, all positioned to form a large square. And she drew many variations, showing how rectangles, triangles, diamonds and trapezoids, if properly combined, could all come together to form large squares.

"Let's get started!" said Violet. And she sent her brothers to gather together all of the shapes.

And so the rectangles and triangles, the diamonds and trapezoids, joined together to make large squares.

Since King Square the VII had said that all squares could go in and out of the walled enclosure, the guards had to let them pass.

After walking for many days, the shapes found a valley, surrounded by rolling hills, with happy brooks, abundant trees, and songbirds of all kinds.

They decided they did not need a king after all. Instead, they would work together to accomplish many things, and try to make each day a little better than the previous one. And so they did!

Some of the ideas suggested in this book are:

◆ Sometimes people believe that another group of people is inferior.
◆ These biases can lead to destructive attitudes.
◆ Injustices do not disappear on their own.
◆ There are often creative solutions to problems if one is willing to search for them.

Most of us have experienced prejudice or discrimination in some form or another. We have found that the ideas suggested by this book have broad appeal.

✤ QUESTIONS TO INITIATE THE DIALOGUE ✤

 DESCRIPTIVE PHASE **To develop an understanding of the message of the book.**

1. Why were the king's counselors able to convince the king so easily that a square is a perfect figure?
2. Why did most of the squares do nothing to prevent the king's actions?
3. What do you think this story is trying to tell us?

 PERSONAL INTERPRETIVE PHASE **To encourage the expression of feelings and emotions and to relate the book content to the reader's experiences.**

1. Have you ever seen someone treated unjustly?
2. Have you ever seen people solve a problem by working together or cooperating?
3. Do you have any friends who are different from you (older, younger, speak a different language, have a different culture)? What have you learned from their friendship?

 CRITICAL/MULTICULTURAL/ANTI-BIAS PHASE **To promote higher-thinking skills. To encourage reflections on equality, inclusion, respect, justice, and peace.**

1. What are some of the reasons it can be good to have friends who are different from us?
2. What can be difficult about having friends who are different from us? How can we overcome these difficulties?
3. In the story, the various shapes succeeded in escaping by pretending to be squares. Why might this strategy be dangerous in real life?

4. What might be some of the problems of pretending to be someone else instead of who we truly are?

5. Can you think of other possible solutions the characters in the story could have attempted?

 CREATIVE TRANSFORMATIVE PHASE **To encourage creative, constructive action leading to greater understanding and respect; to encourage taking responsibility for bringing about positive change in our own reality.**

1. How can we learn to feel good about ourselves in spite of any bias or discrimination?

2. How can we make friends with others who are different from us?

3. How can we cooperate with others to make sure that everyone is treated fairly and well?

Published in Spanish as *El reino de la geometría.* By Alma Flor Ada. Illustrated by José Ramón Sánchez. Torrance, CA: Laredo Publishing. 1993.

✤ UNVEILING THE AUTHOR WITHIN ✤

TEACHERS AS AUTHORS

In this unit, we invite you to write a book about transformation to share as a model for students' and parents' writing.

 BOOK 20 **Creating the Teacher's Book:** *How It Is and How It Could Be*

In every life, some things can be improved. To write a book about something we would like to change can be a way to initiate the process of change. Alternatively, we can gain strength and inspiration by acknowledging the changes we have already lived through and the lessons we have learned in the process

Teachers have approached the topic of transformation in a variety of ways. One possibility is to use a good news/bad news structure, as seen in Alma Flor Ada's book *The Kite.* This structure can be used to create a book of contrasting pages in which the even pages depict things that need change (the bad news) and the odd pages explore how these things can be changed (the good news). Another possibility is to alternate spreads, with one set of pages devoted to what needs changing and the next set to the improvements proposed.

If you want to portray an event or transformation that has already taken place, you may want to use the structure "It used to be . . . ; now it is. . . ." An example of a book written in this fashion, *I Used To* by Diane Dolloff, is included later in this unit.

In any case, it is usually best for the form to be determined by the content. Sometimes a simple narrative form can best convey our message.

Valerie Andriola was a teacher in Salinas, California, when she began writing books for her family and her students. One of these books, ***En mi barrio,*** was illustrated with photographs. When this book was published commercially, the author realized the power of her words and camera. Some time later, when a drive-by shooting resulted in the death of one of her students and her student's brother, Valerie felt compelled to document the wake and burial with photos. Afterward, with the family's permission, she created the powerful book ***Your Light, Flower and Song*** (pp. 145–147) to commemorate the grief felt by the family and the entire community. Written as a litany, the book conveys the finality of death. The author adds a note of hope by showing the increased community awareness created by these senseless deaths, and by proposing the continuous remembrance of these broken lives.

STUDENTS AS PROTAGONISTS AND AUTHORS

Once you have shared your own book with your students, invite them to write their own books on the subject of transformation.

Cuando se troncha una flor...La gente enciende muchas velas.

**Las encendemos.
Las encendemos.**

②

When a flower is taken, we light candles.

***Your Light, Flower and Song*
by Valerie Andriola**

Reprinted by permission of Valerie Andriola Púrpura, P.O. Box 1574, Santa Teresa, NM, 88008.

Los amigos pierden a un hermano.

Los amigos pierden.
Los amigos pierden.

Friends lose a brother.

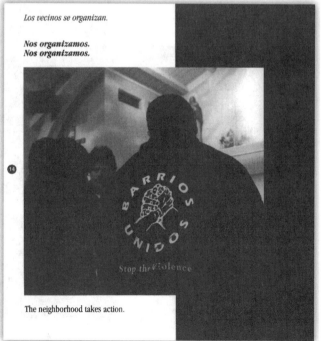

Los vecinos se organizan.

Nos organizamos.
Nos organizamos.

The neighborhood takes action.

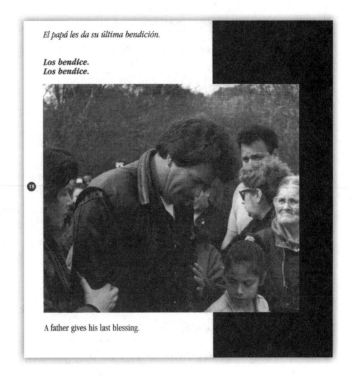

El papá les da su última bendición.

Los bendice.
Los bendice.

A father gives his last blessing.

En el día de tu graduación
soñaremos los mismos sueños.

Te los soñaremos.
Te los soñaremos.

On your graduation day, we'll
dream the same dreams for you.

BOOK 21 Students' Collective Book: *How We Will Make the World a Better Place*

Begin by reflecting with your students on our personal responsibility to help bring more justice, equality, and peace into the world. Next, invite students to create a collective book. Ask each student to offer an idea about how he or she might help make the world a better place.

Explain the guidelines that have been presented before: No one is to repeat what someone else has said. Write students' responses on the board or on chart paper. If students' responses are too brief, encourage them to elaborate. Then give each student a blank page and ask them to copy and illustrate their response onto their page.

You may want to exhibit the pages in a hallway or other visible place before binding them to create a book. Once the book is bound, encourage its circulation. If you have the means to do so, create several copies so that students can offer one to the school library and/or the public library as well as take a copy home.

BOOK 22 Students' Individual Book: *Making a Positive Change in My Life*

Everyone, even young children, is able to make changes in her or his life. The change, of course, will be commensurate with personal circumstances. After the collective book has been completed, encourage your students to think about one aspect of their lives they would like to improve and how they might go about it. Invite them to create a two-page booklet, with one page showing what they would like to improve and the other showing how they intend to do it.

PARENTS OR CARETAKERS AS TEACHERS AND AUTHORS

Home Conversations: Learning from Parents' Experiences

Encourage parents to dialogue with their children about the possibilities of change and specifically about their own efforts to improve their lives. To facilitate the process, students can take home conversation starters (either orally or in writing) such as the following:

◆ Tell me about something in the world that you would like to see changed.
◆ How do you think that we as a family could contribute to that change?
◆ What advice do you have for me (and for other children or youth) about how to help create a better world?

Parents' Books

Parents can express their thoughts on this topic by participating in the creation of a collective book and/or by creating their own books.

BOOK 23 **Collective Book of Transformation:**
   Our Advice for Our Children

Ask each parent to send a sentence (either orally or in writing) that will be used to create a page for a collective book titled ***Making the World a Better Place.*** As a prompt, parents can be asked what advice they would offer their children and other young people.

BOOK 24 **Individual Book of Transformation:** *How Our Family*
   Can Help Make the World a Better Place

Send home a blank book and invite parents to create a family book in which everyone in the family expresses how he or she can contribute to making the world a better place.

BOOK 25 **Individual Book:** *My Dreams for My Children*
   and How I Will Help Them Come True

One way of initiating a more in-depth process of reflection is to create "two-part" books. For example, you could send home an initial question, such as: "What are your dreams for your children?" Once the parents have responded to this question, you can send home a compilation of their responses, along with a follow-up question: "What can you do to help those dreams come true?"

ADDITIONAL EXAMPLES OF BOOKS AUTHORED
BY TEACHERS, STUDENTS, AND FAMILIES

The books written by participants on the topic of transformation vary substantially. Many of them offer students a model of how human beings make decisions and, as a result of time and effort, end up seeing changes in their lives. Other books deal with adjusting to and learning from changes that one may not have chosen, such as a move or the loss of a loved one.

Many students have had to adjust to major changes in their lives, often not of their own choosing. Sometimes the changes have been brought about by a change in location. Insufficient attention has been paid to the profound effects of emigrating from one country to another, a major experience that implies uprooting and loss (Igoa, 1995; Olsen, 1988). Moving from one area of the country to another, though not as dramatic because of the continuity of language and culture, can also be a significant challenge for a child. Even a change of neighborhood and school can lead to a difficult adjustment.

In other cases, students have had to deal with changes in their family structure due to the death of a relative or to a divorce or separation. By presenting them with books that deal with change, teachers can facilitate dialogue about these issues as well as show students that writing can be a helpful way to cope with and process these kinds of challenges.

Diane Dolloff created a magnificently illustrated book to share with her students. Her book explains that though she now lives in San Francisco she originally moved to this city from New York.

I Used To by **Diane Dolloff**

Reprinted by permission of Diane Dolloff, 27 Alvarado St., San Francisco, CA, 94110.

I Used To *Written and illustrated by Diane Dolloff*

I used to live in New York,
where the leaves change colors in the Fall
and it snows in the winter.

❖ ❖ ❖

Now, I live in San Francisco.

❖ ❖ ❖

I used to live with my Mom,
Dad, two older brothers and my baby sister.

❖ ❖ ❖

Now I have to fly on an airplane to visit them.

❖ ❖ ❖

I used to take ballet lessons,
well at least one session.

❖ ❖ ❖

Now I will not wear a tutu for any reason.

❖ ❖ ❖

I used to ride in a school bus to get to school.

❖ ❖ ❖

Now I ride the MUNI to get to school.

❖ ❖ ❖

I used to have two dogs
that I had to share with my siblings.

❖ ❖ ❖

Now I have a very special cat named COCOA.

❖ ❖ ❖

I used to live in this green apartment.

❖ ❖ ❖

Now I live with three wacky women and their pets.

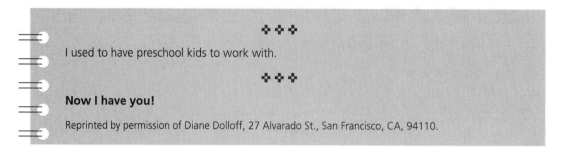

Reprinted by permission of Diane Dolloff, 27 Alvarado St., San Francisco, CA, 94110.

Becoming a Professional

Children and adolescents can benefit from hearing stories about how adults have chosen and grown in their trades or careers, how they have chosen their values, and how they have continued to learn and grow over the years. It is important for children and young people to realize that many adults have not traveled a direct path to becoming who they are today, but instead have gone through several changes or overcome challenging setbacks.

Helping students understand how their teacher has become the person they know today can be a way of providing them with helpful life models. Julie Hodson, from Texas, wrote a book called *I Wasn't Always a Teacher.* In it she describes the various jobs she held after finishing high school: waitress, cashier at a gas station, corn harvester. Each of those jobs was difficult, a point she makes with humor. It is painful to be on your feet all day waiting on people, and often they don't even smile back. Being a cashier was a more restful job, until someone robbed her. Picking corn let her be outdoors, but she couldn't keep up with the machine, and she dreamt all night that ears of corn were falling on her. Then she realized that she could be a teacher. The work is hard but very satisfying.

Another book along these lines was written by Alexandra Román from School P.S. 24 in Brooklyn: *Lo que fui y lo que soy (Who I Was and Who I Am).* The book tells her life story, from arriving at the Sunset Park community in New York from Puerto Rico when she was two months old to her present life as a teacher. The author acknowledges the influence of an excellent teacher, Mr. Hitter, who helped her succeed in school and inspired her to become a teacher.

Sometimes the road to achieving a goal is a long one, and students can benefit from hearing those stories. In *El sueño de una niña (A Girl's Dream),* Kathleen Hughes, currently an educational administrator, shares the story of her long road toward becoming a teacher. Her dream began on her first day of class, and when she finished high school, she began her college studies. But after the birth of her first daughter, she stopped going to school. Kathy and her husband Jim had two daughters, and before the second was one year old, they adopted the first of their nine adoptive children. Caring for a family of eleven did not leave Kathy much time to study!

But as their children grew, Kathy began to read to children at the local library and to take care of preschool children. Her dream, though silent for a long time, was still alive. When her children began to go to college, the author decided to complete her studies and obtain her teaching credentials. It was not easy, with so many family re-

sponsibilities, but Jim and the children helped. On her graduation day, Kathy was surrounded by her children and grandchildren. The book ends with a photo of the author's class and a message to her students about how much she looks forward to learning with them.

Transformation and Identity

Part of the journey of transformation involves learning how to reach out to others. In *Making a Friend*, Matthew P. Hartford and Mizutani Michiyo suggest that the actions that lead to developing a friendship need to be crafted as carefully as each brush stroke of a Japanese character. After beginning the book with one simple stroke and describing one aspect of friendship, for each stroke they add the authors include another effort we need to be willing to make to create and nourish a friendship.

Another example of a transformative book is *This Is Who You Are/Así eres tú,* written by Jeni Hammond to help children discover their inner strength in the face of prejudice, discrimination, and any other major difficulty. The book is presented in Chapter 2.

Making a Friend by Matthew P. Hartford and Mizutani Michiyo

Overcoming Oppression

In response to an invitation to write about the topic "I Wasn't Always a Teacher," Cattryn Somers from Phoenix, Arizona, reflected on social inequalities and the difficulty of creating change. She titled her brief but poignant book *I Wasn't Always a Teacher . . . but I've Always Been a Woman.* The book lends itself well to initiating reflection and dialogue for a social studies unit. We are pleased to be able to reproduce it here in its entirety, thanks to Cattryn Somers's generosity.

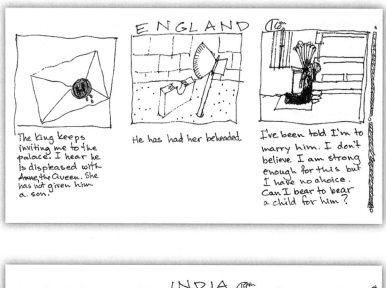

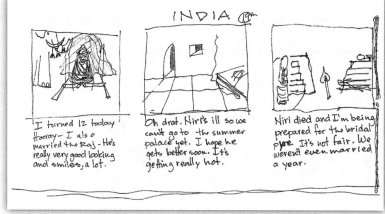

I Wasn't Always a Teacher . . . but I've Always Been a Woman by Cattryn Somers

Reprinted by permission of Cattryn I. Somers, 3653 E. Stanford Dr., Paradise Valley, AZ, 85253.

I Wasn't Always a Teacher . . . but I've Always Been a Woman

By Cattryn Somers

Who's Come a Long Way, Baby?
1. England—16th century
2. India—19th century
3. United States—17th century
4. Africa—21st century
5. The many other tales not told

❖ ❖ ❖

ENGLAND 16TH

The king keeps inviting me to the palace. I hear he is displeased with Anne, the Queen. She has not given him a son.

He has had her beheaded.

I've been told I'm to marry him. I don't believe I'm strong enough for this but I have no choice. Can I bear to bear a child for him?

❖ ❖ ❖

INDIA 19TH

I turned 12 today. Hooray—I also married the Raj. He's really very good looking and smiles, a lot.

Oh, drat. Niri's ill so we can't go to the summer palace yet. I hope he gets better soon. It's getting really hot.

Niri died and I'm being prepared for the bridal pyre. It's not fair. We weren't even married a year.

❖ ❖ ❖

UNITED STATES 17TH

The mixture worked. Martha's daughter will survive with prayer and care.

I sometimes have to hide my smile when the girls ask me to perform a "spell." As if I could. But I see no harm in giving them joy and hope with little trinkets, bits of herbs and silly incantations.

Again, the magistrates speak of witchcraft evil. Even Father John's sermons have become less uplifting. What is happening?

❖ ❖ ❖

AFRICA 21ST

Tomorrow is the ceremony. At last, I'll be a woman. I'm too excited . . . and scared to sleep.

They threw it out to the chickens. I cannot move.

The bleeding hasn't stopped. I feel so weak. Mother cries all the time.

The many other tales
    to tell and tell
        and tell . . .

- elongated necks
- bound feet
- anorexia/bulimia
- shame via the Koran (veiled shame)
- domestic violence
- rape
- baby factories
- discarded or destroyed girl-children
- second-class citizen

and the list goes on.

Apologies to all those places, peoples and times
where women have been honored and respected . . .
for their intrinsic value to society.

Reprinted by permission of Cattryn I. Somers, 3653 E. Stanford Dr., Paradise Valley, AZ, 85253.

UNIT 6

UNIT

6

UNDERSTANDING THE PAST, CREATING THE FUTURE

An important human characteristic is our capacity to offer each generation an enriched set of experiences greater than the ones we ourselves received. Human language plays a key role in this regard because it allows us to speak about that which is not present, thus recording the past in order to transmit it to future generations. Although this desire to transmit collective and family histories manifests itself in different forms across cultures, it seems to be universal.

When young people know they have ancestors, that their own lives have been bequeathed to them by others who came before them, they develop a sense of belonging and well-being. This knowledge also supports their conscious development into adulthood. The more comfortable we are about our roots, the more at ease we are with ourselves and the better equipped we are to unlearn prejudice and address the biases around us. Therefore, strengthening young people's sense of identity both helps them individually and helps them better contribute to society.

Reflecting on our lives—the places, people, events, happy and sad moments—gives us the opportunity to develop greater self-understanding as well as greater compassion for ourselves. But strengthening a sense of self should never be misinterpreted as a license to encourage ethnocentrism. An ethnocentric viewpoint can arise from

Objectives

- To promote a better understanding of self by learning about the efforts of those who came before us and the family and community history we have inherited.
- To study the past in order to learn from its mistakes and build on its positive contributions.
- To strengthen the bond between children and their parents or caretakers by sharing family histories and nurturing a sense of continuity.
- To continue exploring the process of book authorship and the power of the written word.

157

Teachers	Students	Parents
Teachers are invited to: ■ Write a book about a childhood experience. ■ Read the book to their students and share with them any insights about the process of authorship. ■ Guide students in the process of writing a book about their lives. ■ Encourage meaningful communication at home and invite parent participation in the creation of books about their family history.	Students are invited to: ■ Create individual books about their lives or specific moments within their lives. ■ Collaborate in the creation of shared classroom books.	Parents or caretakers are invited to: ■ Engage in meaningful conversation with their children, sharing memories of the child's life, the parents' lives, and/or the lives of forebears. ■ Create, or collaborate in creating, books about their lives and their family history. ■ Provide sayings and proverbs to be included in a class book titled *From Yesterday to Today: Our Families' Sayings and Proverbs.*

ignorance or, worse, from a false sense of superiority. It is generally the case that a sense of superiority, whether individual or collective, is a way of covering up its opposite—that is, an unacknowledged sense of inferiority. The aim here is to encourage a healthy sense of identity and self-worth that is based on respect for all human beings.

❖ THE CREATIVE LITERACY PROCESS ❖

Invite students to read books that show how protagonists' experiences in the distant or recent past can help shed light on their present behavior. You will find a list of suggested titles in the appendix of recommended books. Make as many of these books as possible available to your students.

Next, select a text for engaging in the Creative Literacy Dialogue process. We have included here two selections by Alma Flor Ada for this purpose: *It Wasn't Me,* for primary students, and "The Rag Dolls" from *Where the Flame Trees Bloom,* for upper-elementary through high school students. Of course, you are welcome to select another book of your choice.

It can be helpful to introduce the reading by eliciting students' previous knowledge about the topic and inviting them to make predictions about the book. Once you have finished reading the book, use the corresponding questions to initiate the conversation. (If you have chosen your own book, you will need to spend some time designing thoughtful questions beforehand. See p. 42. For additional tips on facilitating dialogue, see pp. 44–48.)

It Wasn't Me
by Alma Flor Ada

This simple yet engaging story provides an opportunity for young students to share their own experiences. The book is particularly appealing in its Big Book format but will delight children even in a small-size book thanks to Vivi Escriva's charming illustrations. If you do not have a copy of the book, here is the story:

> The garden flowers have been trampled.
> Whose footprints are these? Who has trampled on the flowers?
> "It wasn't me. No, it wasn't me."
> The clean clothes on the clothesline are now covered with mud.
> Whose footprints are these? Who muddied the clothes?
> "It wasn't me. No, it wasn't me."
> There is mud all over the porch.
> Whose footprints are these? Who has dragged mud all over?
> "It wasn't me. No, it wasn't me."
> The flour is all scattered on the kitchen floor.
> Whose footprints are these? Who messed up the kitchen?
> "It wasn't me. No, it wasn't me."
> But Mom, it *is* me who loves you a lot.
> That's why I'm bringing you flowers and a cookie.
>
> But, whose prints were they?
> Have you ever seen a dog wearing two pairs of sneakers?

By putting shoes on the dog, the innocent protagonist initiates a series of incidents. It is hard for him to see his responsibility for the ensuing events. What *is* clear to everyone are his good intentions and his love for his mother.

This story, based on a real-life experience, invites students to discuss the consequences of our actions.

✤ QUESTIONS TO PROMOTE THE DIALOGUE ✤

 DESCRIPTIVE PHASE **To develop an understanding of the message of the book.**

1. How do you think the boy felt when his mother was asking him if he was the one who had created all the mischief?
2. Do you think the mother believed the little boy? Why or why not?

3. How do you think the dog ended up with shoes on his feet?
4. Why do you think the boy brought his mother flowers and a cookie?

 PERSONAL INTERPRETIVE PHASE **To encourage the expression of feelings and emotions in response to the book and to relate the book content to the reader's experiences.**

1. Has anyone ever blamed you for something you did not do? What was it? Were you able to explain what really happened?
2. When the boy put the shoes on the dog, he probably did not think that the dog would create so much mischief. Has that ever happened to you—have you ever done something that had unexpected and unplanned consequences? What did you do and what were the consequences?

 CRITICAL/MULTICULTURAL/ANTI-BIAS PHASE **To promote higher-thinking skills. To encourage reflection on the themes of equality, inclusion, respect, justice, and peace.**

1. The little boy did not step on the flowers, nor dirty the clothes, nor muddy the porch, nor spill the flour. But he had something to do with everything that happened because the dog did not put the shoes on his own paws. In what way is the little boy telling the truth when he says, "It wasn't me"? In what way is he not telling the whole truth?
2. How can someone be responsible for something without having done it? Can you think of other examples of situations when even though a person did not do something, he or she is still responsible for what happened?

 CREATIVE TRANSFORMATIVE PHASE **To encourage creative, constructive action leading to greater understanding and respect; to encourage taking responsibility for bringing about positive changes in our own reality.**

1. Is there someone to whom you would like to say, "I'm sorry"? How do you think you will feel once that person has forgiven you?
2. Is there someone to whom you would like to show your love or your friendship? What can you do to show that person how much you care about her or him?

The Rag Dolls
from Where the Flame Trees Bloom *by Alma Flor Ada*

My great grandmother Mina was tiny, as though time had not only wrinkled but had also shrunk her. She was not very much taller than the jasmine and the rose bushes she tended in her garden in the little house next to ours. Like the raisins she sprinkled generously in our *arroz con leche,* the rice pudding she made that smelled of cinnamon and cloves, her wrinkled form was filled with sweetness.

When she was not in the kitchen or in the garden, she would often sit in a rocking chair and sew. In her hands scraps of cloth became multicolored quilts of various sizes. The large ones were wedding gifts for her many granddaughters; the small ones, greeting gifts for new great-grandchildren.

Yet the best pieces of cloth she saved for her rag dolls. As the light left her eyes and they became covered with an opaque glaze, she spent less and less time in the kitchen and the garden. Unable to see, she could not stitch together the scraps and patches, so she stopped making quilts and took to crochet. But her blindness did not prevent her from making dolls. Her fingers, which had created dolls for so long, were able to give shape to the dolls' heads, to braid wool for their hair, to form their bodies and limbs.

Because she could not see the colors, I would help separate the greens and blues and reds that would become long skirts and bright red scarves. She would ask me: "This soft velvety piece, is it black? Can you find me a nice dark brown? A creamy chocolate? A toasted almond? A bright cinnamon?" And so the dolls would receive faces that resembled those of the neighborhood children.

Once a week her sister Genoveva came to visit from the other end of town, and on each doll she would embroider the dark round eyes, the lips, the two dots for a nose.

The dolls sat on the windowsill, four, five, six at a time. Little girls—some carrying cans full of water that their mothers needed to do the laundry, others loaded down with a bag of coal for cooking, and pulling a reluctant little brother or sister by the hand—would take a quick look to see whether the dolls had changed from the previous week. Or maybe, late in the afternoon, free of chores, skipping on one foot, jumping with a frayed rope, they would glance in the direction of the window and smile.

Whenever birthdays approached, mothers came knocking at Mina's door, in the hands an old handkerchief with coins tied up in a corner. "How much for the one with the red skirt?" they would ask. "And for the pretty one with the braids?"

Sunken in her rocking chair, my great-grandmother, sightless, knew. She knew when to say twenty-five cents, thirty, forty, to honor the woman's pride, to allow her the joy of giving. She also knew when to say: "I'd like so much for Marisa to have it. Seven she'll be, won't she?" and hand the doll to the woman saying, "Just save me some scraps, I'll make another one . . . "

At other times, a young mother, weathered down from long hours of laundering clothes under the hot sun, of cooking in a makeshift stove made of lard cans, would come to my great-grandmother's house saying only, "I've brought you a few oranges, or mangoes, or some watercress . . . " and my great-grandmother would close her sightless eyes a moment, concentrating, before saying, "Oh yes, Manuelita will be five very soon now, won't she? Isn't it time she had her own doll? Do you see any she would like?" The mother's hand would go up to her face, to cover a bashful smile. And the doll would leave its place on the front window, wrapped in the old newspaper that had previously held the golden, red, green offering.

❖ QUESTIONS TO INITIATE THE DIALOGUE ❖

 DESCRIPTIVE PHASE **To develop an understanding of the message of the book.**

1. What were the social conditions of the people around the great-grandmother's house? How can you tell?
2. Why do you think the great-grandmother felt that sometimes it was important for the mothers to pay something for the dolls? Why do you think that other times she charged nothing for the dolls?
3. What did some of the mothers who had no money do to obtain the dolls?

 PERSONAL INTERPRETIVE PHASE **To encourage the expression of feelings and emotions in response to the book and to relate the book content to the reader's experiences.**

1. The author has learned a great deal from her great-grandmother. Who are the eldest people in your family? What have you learned from them?
2. Have you ever wished for something you couldn't afford? How did that feel?
3. Have you ever been able to give someone something they wanted? How was that experience?

 CRITICAL/MULTICULTURAL/ANTI-BIAS PHASE **To promote higher-thinking skills. To encourage reflection on the themes of equality, inclusion, respect, justice, and peace.**

1. Why do you think that making dolls was important to the great-grandmother, besides the money she earned for them?
2. What do you think was the author's intent in writing this piece?

 CREATIVE TRANSFORMATIVE PHASE **To encourage creative, constructive action leading to greater understanding and respect; to encourage taking responsibility for bringing about positive changes in our own reality.**

1. What can you offer other people that can bring a smile to their faces?
2. What would you like to learn to make or do that you don't know how to make or do yet?
3. What things about people in your family do you want to remember forever?

❖ UNVEILING THE AUTHOR WITHIN ❖

TEACHERS AS AUTHORS

BOOK 26 **Creating the Teacher's Book:** *A Childhood Experience*

There are several ways to create a book of childhood experiences. You may want to use one of the following approaches, or a combination.

◆ *Reading books about childhood memories.* Because we learn to write by reading, it is usually a good idea to immerse ourselves in reading books of the same genre we want to explore in our writing. There are a number of excellent books of childhood memories, listed in the appendix of recommended books, that can serve as inspiration for writing one's own memoirs. Because of the richness of experience and the depth of emotion conveyed in its poetic brevity, we particularly recommend Lee Bennet Hopkins's *Been to Yesterdays.*

◆ *Telling one's story aloud.* Some writers find it useful to tell their memories aloud to someone in order to spark their creative process. For some people, speaking into a cassette recorder works well.

◆ *Exploring sense memories.* Some writers are surprised to discover the extent to which past memories can be accessed by focusing on the sensorial experiences (smells, taste of food, feeling of the clothes and shoes, sounds, shape and color of a specific object) that accompanied a given moment. When we are able to return to a given day or period in our mind's eye, we often remember many other specific details. Sometimes a photograph can serve as a useful trigger for one's memory.

Once you have decided which memory you wish to share, you can begin to describe it in writing and then decide on the best format for creating your book.

The richness of life is enhanced as we share it. Sometimes, even pain can be transcended as we draw lessons from it that can help others. Edward Cavanaugh, a teacher in San Francisco, wanted to write a book that could transform a challenging life experience into a useful learning experience for others. The result is *A Sweet Tale,* wonderfully illustrated by Left Hand.

In the summer, on hot, sunny days my brother and I would listen for the bells of the ice cream truck.

When we heard the jingle of the bells we would run outside with our saved allowance money. We always shared the ice cream and candy we bought.

4

A Sweet Tale
by Edward Cavanaugh

Reprinted by permission of Edward Cavanaugh, 1016 A Shotwell St., San Francisco, CA, 94110.

One day I began to not feel so well. I was very tired and extremely thirsty. I did not want to ride my bike or play ball. I wasn't even hungry for anything.
My Mom and Dad saw how I was feeling and they took me to see the doctor.

5

The doctor asked my parents and I many questions. He took blood from my arm and did lots of tests. He told us that I had diabetes. Later that night I went to the hospital and stayed for a week. I didn't even know what diabetes was. I was sad and afraid.

6

In the hospital the nurses and doctor helped me feel better and told me all about diabetes. I learned that my body had stopped being able to use the food I ate for energy. They told me that my pancreas stopped working. The pancreas is an organ that produces a hormone called insulin. Insulin breaks down the food we eat inside our bodies. This gives us the energy to be active and do fun things. I also learned that it is good to eat lots of fruit and vegetables. They are naturally sweet and good for you.

7

Third, to eat healthy foods. Eating good foods like fruits and vegetables help us to feel good. Remember, you are what you eat. Let's eat well!

10

A Sweet Tale   *by Edward Cavanaugh; illustrated by Left Hand*

As a young boy I was very active. I did lots of fun things with my sisters and brother. I loved to ride my bike, roller skate, play ball and swim. I really enjoyed doing these things.

I also loved to eat sweet stuff, like ice cream and chocolate. I especially loved the ice cream. I ate some almost every night after dinner. A big bowl with my favorite flavors of vanilla, chocolate and strawberry. Sometimes I even put chocolate syrup on top.

In the summer, on hot sunny days, my brother and I would listen for the bells of the ice cream truck. When we heard the jingle of the bells we would run outside with our saved allowance money. We always shared the ice cream and candy we bought.

One day I began to not feel so well. I was very tired and extremely thirsty. I did not want to ride my bike or play ball. I wasn't even hungry for anything. My Mom and Dad saw how I was feeling and they took me to see the doctor.

The doctor asked my parents and I many questions. He took blood from my arm and did lots of tests. He told us that I had diabetes. Later that night I went to the hospital and stayed for a week. I didn't even know what diabetes was. I was sad and afraid.

In the hospital the nurses and doctor helped me feel better and told me all about diabetes. I learned that my body had stopped being able to use the food I ate for energy. They told me that my pancreas stopped working. The pancreas is an organ that produces a hormone called insulin. Insulin breaks down the food we eat inside our bodies. This gives us the energy to be active and do fun things. I also learned that it is good to eat lots of fruits and vegetables. They are naturally sweet and good for you.

The nurses taught me how to give myself injections of insulin. They also taught me that reading about diabetes is the best way to educate myself. My doctor told me three things to do to take good care of my health. First, always take your insulin. Second, exercise regularly. It helps to breathe deeply and stay strong. Third, to eat healthy foods. Eating good foods like fruits and vegetables help us to feel good. Remember, you are what you eat. Let's eat well!

Being a diabetic is sometimes difficult. Occasionally, when I'm not feeling good I rely on my friends and family to help me. Diabetes has taught me that a healthy body helps you have a healthy mind. I have learned to respect and take good care of myself.

Reprinted by permission of Edward Cavanaugh, 1016 A Shotwell St., San Francisco, CA, 94110.

Students aren't the only ones to benefit from these books. Many teachers have discovered that their book of childhood memories is a wonderful gift for their own children and grandchildren, as well as for their parents, siblings, and other relatives.

STUDENTS AS PROTAGONISTS AND AUTHORS

BOOK 27 Creating a Collective Book: *On the Day We Were Born*

Many different kinds of collective books can be created once students have researched information about their lives. One possibility is a book titled *The Day We Were Born.*

To create this book, begin by brainstorming with students all the things they would like to know about the day they were born. Make a list of all their suggestions. You may want to include some of your own suggestions as well. The final list might include questions such as:

◆ What day of the week was it?
◆ Who was present?
◆ Where were the rest of the family members? What were they doing?

◆ Who was the first person to visit?

◆ What were the mother's first words, or thoughts, on seeing the baby?

After the class has decided on the questions, give each student a draft page on which they can write the answers provided by their family.

Once students have obtained the information, give them each a nicely prepared page for making their final copy. On each page, include spaces for the name of the student as well as the full date of birth. Once the pages have been completed and illustrated, they can be collated to create a class book. Use this opportunity to emphasize that although each person's birthday is a unique experience, we all share the sense that our birthday is an important date in our lives.

BOOK 28 Writing an Individual Book: *A Moment in My Life*

Help students explore a moment in their lives they want to write about and help them create their individual books. At Bell Middle School, in Miami-Dade, Florida, a group of teachers decided to involve their students in writing their life stories. The teachers initiated the activity by inviting students to read *Where the Flame Trees Bloom* (Atheneum, 1997) and *Under the Royal Palms* (Atheneum, 1999) by Alma Flor Ada. After analyzing the books together, the students realized that these books were not full-fledged biographies offering complete accounts of the author's entire life. Instead, the author had chosen a few salient moments and some significant people and offered a vignette about each. The teachers then suggested that students divide their lives into multiple chapters and describe the most salient experiences that have brought them to where they are today.

The students then embarked on writing their individual books. Each book was to have somewhere between six to ten chapters, and each chapter was to focus on a specific moment, a poignant memory, or a person who had a special significance in their life. Students wrote about their earliest memories, their first experiences with school, the death of a relative, the different places they had lived. Whenever students finished a draft of a chapter, they had the opportunity to share it with classmates for feedback. They wrote and rewrote. When they considered their chapters finished, they passed them on to their teacher for additional comments. Then they typed the chapters into the computer and saw the growth of their book. By the end of the semester, the students had written substantial accounts of their lives.

All of the books were impressive. Two in particular caught our attention because of their authenticity, sensitivity, attention to detail, and depth of feelings. ***Desde el balcón de mis recuerdos (From the Balcony of My Memory)*** is the account of the life of a young boy born in Cuba, Dayán Pérez, and is written with great sensitivity and a surprising richness of language. ***Un amanecer en el mar (Dawn at Sea)*** by Edgardo Vera Gallardo is a remarkable account of his young life (see p. 168). The book is divided into ten chapters: Introduction, Childhood Memories, School, Last Years in Colombia, The Trip, The American Dream, Changes, New York, Forever, With a Flame Torch in My Hand.

Mi familia paterna

7

Edgardo José
En pre-escolar

10

Un amanecer en el mar by Edgardo Vera Gallardo

Reprinted by permission of Edgardo Vera, 923 NW 123 Ave., Miami, FL, 33182.

"The American Dream" describes the difficult struggle Edgardo's single mother faced to survive and care for her son and his young cousin, who lived with them. How distant and unreachable the "American Dream" appears! This chapter also shows the solidarity and support the mother finds among other immigrants and how, with their help, life becomes bearable.

"Forever" deals with the loss of a grandfather. Although the young author has faced many challenges in his short life, this was the most difficult. At this point, the narrative style the author had been using no longer served his needs, so instead he created a poem to honor this man who was more than a father to him.

Given the opportunity and encouragement, students can create books of which they can be extraordinarily proud. After all, they themselves are the true protagonists of the most fascinating of all adventures—life!

Middle school and high school students are eager for the opportunity to reflect on their lives. When provided with a structure to follow, they can surprise us with the extent of their memories and the level of their reflections.

Students who have immigrated to this country often have rich experiences to share. When she worked as a classroom teacher, Peggy Laughlin would give her fifth-grade students specific questions to address in a four-part book:

◆ What was it like when you first came to this country?
◆ How do you feel about being bilingual?

◆ What are your dreams for your future?

◆ How will you contribute to changing the world?

PARENTS OR CARETAKERS AS TEACHERS AND AUTHORS

Home Conversations: Learning from Parents' Experiences

Encourage parents to share with their children information about the child's life. Parents can also be asked to share their own lives and their family history. Convey to parents the importance for their children of being aware of their personal and family histories. Remind parents that, as their child's first and most constant teachers, they have a wealth of information about their own personal and family histories, experiences, values, and beliefs that only they can convey. Demonstrate the value you place on this information by providing adequate space and time in the classroom to talk about, reflect on, and display the stories that parents share with their children.

Parents' Books

BOOK 29 **Parents' Individual Book:** *Things to Remember*

Invite parents to write or dictate their life stories. Sometimes it helps to provide parents with an initial structure consisting of pages with a space for writing, a space for illustration, and some headings. Some of the headings could be:

◆ Memories of My Childhood

◆ My Mother

◆ My Father

◆ What I Remember about My Grandparents

◆ Celebrations in My Family

◆ Our Most Difficult or Painful Experience as a Family

◆ A Joyful Experience as a Family

BOOK 30 **Parents' Collective Book:** *From Yesterday to Tomorrow:*
Our Families' Proverbs and Sayings

Teachers of all levels from elementary to high school have found this book a rewarding experience and a fairly simple one to complete. Each student collects from his or her relatives the most significant proverbs or sayings the family remembers. Next to each saying or proverb, students write the name of the family member who suggested it. Once brought to class, the sayings can be written on chart paper or sentence strips and organized in preparation for creating a book.

This process can turn into a simple research project. Because many of the sayings will be repeated, it can be fun for students to discover which are the most popular sayings. A more demanding exercise is to group the sayings by content. Bilingual students may want to find comparable sayings in other languages. An excellent multicultural activity is to find and contrast sayings from various cultures on similar topics: generosity, hard work, family, friends, and so on.

Frequently in our sessions with parents, we create this book by asking parents to dictate the sayings and proverbs they know and then write those sayings on a transparency. Later, we use the sayings to create a simple book to hand back to the parents. This is the preface we have created for books compiled in this fashion:

From Yesterday to Tomorrow: Proverbs and Sayings from Our Families

Preface

Our everyday speech is enriched by sayings and proverbs such as "the early bird gets the worm" or "he gives twice, who gives unasked." In most cases we don't know the origin of these words. They have been handed down to us by generations that used them before us. They reflect the wisdom of everyday people and the ability to say a great deal with very few words.

Now, these sayings and proverbs are the legacy we inherited from our culture. They please us with their familiarity. They create a bonding between speaker and listener when we realize we have something in common. Sometimes we do not even have to say the whole proverb. The first few words are enough: "a stitch in time . . ." or "dime con quien andas . . ."

When we pass on these sayings and proverbs to our children, we are familiarizing them with the richness of our culture. We do not always have to agree with the message of the saying. When that is the case, we can use the saying as an opportunity for reflection. In Spanish, for example, there are several sayings that are fatalistic. People say, "He who was born to be a tamale will have the corn husk fall to him from heaven" or "He who was born to be a potted plant will never leave the home hallway." If we believe that people can create their own destiny we will not agree with these sayings, but it is important to understand what people mean by them. And we can use these sayings as an opportunity to discuss our own values and beliefs with our children.

By collecting traditional proverbs and sayings in this book, we are sharing our legacy with our children. This is only a small sample of the wealth of knowledge that each one of us has in our home.

Creating Intergenerational Books

Parents and relatives are not the only ones who can create books with students. Tony Cox, a teacher at Greenway Elementary School in Beaverton, Oregon, carried out an extraordinary project during 1997. She invited the residents of a local senior living community to share their memories with the fourth- and fifth-grade students in her class. Some of the residents were the grandparents and elderly relatives of her students, but others did not share any family relationship.

The students and the senior citizens shared and wrote about different kinds of memories, including sad ones and funny ones. The teacher created nine different categories, inspired by the books *Wilfred Gordon McDonald Partridge* by Mem Fox and *I'll*

Love You Forever by Robert Munsch. She also suggested nine different kinds of writing for each of the nine chapters:

Chapter One
"A memory is something from a long time ago . . . "
interviews between students and seniors

Chapter Two
"A memory is something warm . . . "
writing about warm memories

Chapter Three
"A memory is something that makes you cry . . . "
"I Am" poems about sad memories

Chapter Four
"A memory is something that makes you laugh . . . "
writing about humorous memories

Chapter Five
"A memory is something as precious as gold . . . "
poems

Chapter Six
"My earliest memory . . . "
writing using similes

Chapter Seven
"Dear Teenager . . . "
acrostics that describe students as the teenagers they will be someday; imaginary
    letters that students may receive as teenagers

Chapter Eight
"When I'm an Adult . . . "
newspaper clippings from the future describing students' accomplishments as adults

Chapter Nine
"I Have a Dream . . . "
persuasive speeches about the world our children will inherit

In the introduction to his book ***Memories and Dreams,*** Tony Cox states:

Many friendships resulted from this experience, and many students became truly motivated to share their thoughts in a variety of written and artistic modes. I don't know what was more rewarding as a teacher: the academic improvements in writing which result from meaningful work and having an important audience, or the positive relationships that were created across generations.

We would love to be able to reproduce here for you all 154 pages of this amazing book. But as that is not possible, here are some excerpts from the second chapter. The theme of the chapter was warm memories and one student decided to focus on what his memories and those of his senior partner had in common.

Most in Common

I like Mrs. Torvend, because she is polite and nice. She doesn't worry about things that are true, like age. She was born in 1912, in Minnesota. . . . Her favorite memory was when her dad made an incline plane on top of the snow and put water all over it. It froze. She would get her sled and slide all the way to school. . . .

One of her jobs when she was little was to dust the attic. . . . She would get her mother's fur coat and wear it while she listened to music and read books. . . .

My warm feeling is when I first got my cat "Buster." . . . One night I happened to be sleeping in my living room. Buster was sleeping on my head. In the morning I felt funny but it's still a warm feeling. . . .

I think Mrs. Torvend and I have a little bit in common; . . . we're both talking about our families.

I can't wait until we are finished with our senior's book because I want to see what it is like when it is done. Maybe some people will want to read the book and meet the senior we met.

S. R., 10 years old

Reprinted by permission.

ADDITIONAL EXAMPLES OF BOOKS AUTHORED BY TEACHERS, STUDENTS, AND FAMILIES

Childhood memories can be approached from a variety of perspectives. Sometimes a narrative, a story, or something that happened that affected us is foremost in our memory. For others of us, what we remember most might be a feeling, an atmosphere, a way of being, that has left its mark and helped us become who we are today. Or it may have been the presence of a particular individual who made an indelible imprint on us.

Books by Teachers

Teachers who have been invited to write about their childhood memories have done so in a variety of ways. Here are some examples of their books.

Toys

A toy's significance may be enhanced by the relationship the receiver has with the person who offered that toy as a gift. In her book *Alis, Alyte, Ziuzione and Me,* Daiva Bienkowski from Brooklyn, New York, remembers her love for her Lithuanian grandfather, whom she calls Alis, a short form of Senelis. She is reminded of his love for her by two toys, a monkey, Ziuzione, and a doll, Alyte. Although worn down by over forty years of love and play, these two toys remain the author's most prized possessions. In her words, they are "the ones you grab when there's a fire." They transport her "back in time, to when my world was a simpler place. A world of unconditional love." (Used by permission of Daiva Bienkowski, 3875 Maplewood Dr., Seaford, NY, 11783.)

Immigrant Lives

The United States is a country of immigrants. Most of the population of this nation are the descendants of people born in other parts of the world. It is not surprising, then, that many people have childhood memories that reflect a dual or multiple heritage. We have seen some of these examples in the unit on transformation.

Iris M. Manners was born in the Dominican Republic. Like many other students who are immigrants, part of her childhood was spent without her mother, who had come first to the United States in search of better economic opportunities and had left her children in the care of their aunt. Although this experience was not too difficult for Iris, as she received a great deal of love from her aunt, for other children this separation can be very painful. ***The Rainbow of My Life (Mi vida de arco iris)*** is an evocative rendition of the life of a powerful woman.

Books by Parents

Every person has memories to share. It is all a matter of asking and of how we extend the invitation. When teachers begin by sharing their own memories, the process becomes easier. Asking specific questions can also help elicit more responses. For example, at the Even Start Program in Windsor, California, Spanish-speaking parents were asked to share their memories of how Christmas was celebrated in their hometown. The parents shared their memories orally, and the teachers wrote down what they said to produce the book ***Las celebraciones de Navidad de mi pueblo (How Christmas Was***

Las celebraciones de Navidad de mi pueblo **by Parents in the Even Start Program in Windsor, California**
Reprinted by permission.

Celebrated in My Hometown). Because the parents originated from different parts of Mexico, the customs and traditions varied in their accounts. Yet there was a common thread in their memories of pride in their childhood traditions, and the activity helped strengthen the sense of community among parents. Students participated by exploring the contrasts between different customs and illustrating the book, and they became inspired to ask their parents for additional details about their history and traditions.

A group of mothers at Suva Elementary School in Montebello, California, shared memories of their childhood. Their words were recorded and typed. Each mother provided a drawing to accompany her words. The memories vary, from fetching water from the river for a crippled grandmother to jumping rope, from school dances to riding in a father's truck. The memories were collected in the book *Cuando yo era niña ... (When I Was a Girl ...).* We have translated the following excerpts:

When I had my First Holy Communion my father owned a truck, as he sold bottled water. My sister and I had to ride in the back, sitting on the bottles of water, to get to church. And I was so happy.

Adelina L.

❖ ❖ ❖

I was born in Baja California, in the Valley. I remember when I went to elementary school. I loved it. We had to walk a long way from the "ranchito" where we lived. Since my parents were very poor, they decided that they could only afford to send the boys to school. I wanted to be a teacher. My older brothers were sent to school and now three of them are professionals.

María R.

U N I T 7

DISCOVERING OUR CAPACITIES AND STRENGTHS

Too often we do not recognize our own power to make decisions that can change the course of our lives. Many lives are lived according to tradition, custom, and habit, repeating the patterns set by others or following what the media or the world around us appears to dictate. In part, this may be the result of our experiences as children, when we were relatively helpless and dependent. In many cases, these early experiences can leave a feeling of insecurity, dependence, or weakness. Later, as we grow older, we may not easily outgrow the sense of helplessness. Therefore, it is particularly important for children and young people to have opportunities to discover that they have the ability to influence their own lives in positive and creative ways.

This unit encourages a process of self-discovery focused on one's own creative power. To this end, we have chosen an ongoing and long-term activity. In contrast to the activities in earlier units, in which a major objective was to complete a book, in this instance we recommend beginning a book and continuing to add to it for the rest of the academic year.

There are important reasons for including long-term activities in our curriculum. Young people in general have difficulty internalizing the idea of long-term planning, for understandable reasons. After all, their lives have been short. For an adult, however, a year may be one-thirtieth or one-fortieth of his

Objectives

- To identify and read books that explore the enormous capacity for creativity and action within each human being.
- To explore the capacity for creativity and action through dialogue.
- To continue developing the home–school interaction through the recognition of the potential and strength of the family.
- To create long-term books that celebrate human power and potential in teachers, students, and families.

PROCESS

Teachers	Students	Parents
Teachers are invited to: ■ Identify books for children or young adults that portray the power of human creativity. ■ Explore their own creative power. ■ Create a long-term *I Can* book by writing a page a day. ■ Share their writing with their students. ■ Guide students in creating their own *I Can* books. ■ Encourage students' parents to contribute to a collective book titled *Our Parents Can* as well as to create their own individual books.	Students are invited to: ■ Engage in the Creative Literacy Dialogue process with books that explore the power of human creativity. ■ Reflect every day for a few minutes on their own strengths and abilities. ■ Create a long-term *I Can* book.	Parents or caretakers are invited to: ■ Reflect with their children on their abilities and potential. ■ Make a contribution (orally or in writing) to a collective *Our Parents Can* book. ■ Create their own individual books.

or her life; for a young person, one year may be one-sixth, one-tenth, or one-fourteenth of his or her life.

The internalization of long-term planning is a slow process. Young people learn to do so, in part, by being immersed in environments in which adults talk and live in terms of long-term planning. It is easier for students to imagine themselves staying in school through high school and even going on to college if their home environments emphasize long-term goals.

Yet many students have not had the opportunity to experience long-term planning at home. Not all children have the opportunity to listen to parents speak of yearly salaries, long-term contracts, planning next year's vacation, or purchasing a house on a thirty-year mortgage. If parents are not paid by the year but by the hour, and there is no thirty-year mortgage but instead a monthly rent, it may be harder to envision long-term goals. Although this is by no means the only difficulty faced by students, the lack of opportunities for long-term planning is a situation in which teachers can make a difference.

Doing a yearlong school project will not change the social conditions that make it difficult or impossible for many children to continue their education. But including long-term projects in the curriculum can help students develop a greater sense of continuity and help them understand that bigger tasks can be accomplished one step at a time. Participating in a long-term project might even help a student begin to imagine the possibility of staying in school through high school, or even going on to college.

Just like learning, writing can be seen as a lifelong project. Writing a poem may take an hour, a day, or a lifetime. Writing a book of poems or a novel is something that can take place only over time. Providing writers the opportunity to work on a text for many days or weeks will help them discover the value of staying with an idea until it bears fruits. Thus, we see this unit as having two major goals: the discovery of one's own creative power, and experiencing the benefits of a long-term project.

❖ THE CREATIVE LITERACY PROCESS ❖

Invite students to read books that explore the enormous capacity for creativity and action within each human being. You will find a list of suggested titles in the section on recommended books at the end of this book. Next, choose a text for engaging in the Creative Literacy Dialogue process with your students. We have included two selections in this unit to serve this purpose: *In the Cow's Backyard,* for younger students, and *The Lizard and the Sun,* for older students, both by Alma Flor Ada.

It can be helpful to introduce the reading by eliciting students' previous knowledge about the topic and inviting them to make predictions about the book. Once you have finished reading the book, use the corresponding questions to initiate the conversation. (If you have chosen your own book, you will need to spend some time designing thoughtful questions beforehand. See p. 42. For additional tips on facilitating dialogue, see pp. 44–48.)

In the Cow's Backyard
by Alma Flor Ada

In this simple cumulative tale, whimsically illustrated by Vivi Escrivá and published by Alfaguara, various animals gather together on the hammock in the cow's backyard, enjoying the shade and taking pleasure in one another's company. Whenever a new animal approaches, the ant calls out: "Come join us! There's always room for one more." But when Mother Elephant appears, a major concern arises. Will the hammock break if she is invited to join them?

The fundamental theme of this book is inclusion. Once we are committed to inclusion, we can always find an appropriate way to reach our goal. And this is precisely what happens in the story. If the animals had asked the elephant to jump on the hammock, the most likely result would have been a torn hammock, broken tree branches, or even an uprooted tree. Instead, the animals set the hammock on top of the elephant's back and together head out for a stroll. The tale ends with a simple moral:

> When there's good will
> there's always a way
> for one more friend
> to join in and play.

❖ QUESTIONS TO INITIATE THE DIALOGUE ❖

 DESCRIPTIVE PHASE **To develop an understanding of the message of the book.**

1. What did you like most about the story?
2. What was the problem in the story?
3. How was the problem solved?

 PERSONAL INTERPRETIVE PHASE **To encourage the expression of thoughts, feelings, and emotions in response to the book, and to relate the book content to the reader's experiences.**

1. When do you like to share with others? What do you like to share? Who do you share things with?
2. When is it hard to share? Why is it hard to share at times?
3. Can you think of a problem that you solved? What was the problem and what solution did you find?

 CRITICAL/MULTICULTURAL/ANTI-BIAS PHASE **To promote higher-thinking skills. To encourage reflection on the themes of equality, inclusion, respect, justice, and peace.**

1. What do you think would have happened if the elephant had climbed onto the hammock?
2. How do you think the elephant would have felt if she had not been allowed to play? What do you think might have happened?
3. If the ant had decided not to invite the elephant, what might the other animals have done?

 CREATIVE TRANSFORMATIVE PHASE **To encourage creative, constructive action leading to greater understanding and respect; to encourage taking responsibility for bringing about positive changes in our own reality.**

1. Do you know someone who might like to join in your games? What can you do to include that person?
2. What can you do when you see that your friends don't want to let someone else play?

The Lizard and the Sun
by Alma Flor Ada

This Mexican legend has been illustrated by Felipe Dávalos and published by Dell. Drawing on his background as an archaeologist and his extensive knowledge of the ancient cultures of Mesoamerica, Dávalos created magnificent illustrations for this book. If you do not have access to a copy, invite your students to imagine all the extraordinary richness of the Aztec empire and share with them this summary of the story.

When the Sun disappeared from the sky, everyone was very worried since without the Sun there can be no life. The animals set out to look for the Sun, but not finding it anywhere, they all gave up—except for a little green lizard, who pursued her quest all the way into the desert. When she found a rock with a brilliant glow, the lizard went all the way to the majestic city of Tenochtitlán, built by a lake, to inform the emperor of her discovery. Unfortunately the emperor was so worried that he did not pay much attention to the little green lizard. He simply sent her back with orders to move the stone and see what was behind it.

Although she undertook the long journey back and tried to obey the emperor's wishes, the lizard was not able to make the rock move. When she returned to tell the emperor of her unsuccesful efforts, he was moved by her persistence and decided to accompany her to the desert. The emperor asked the woodpecker to travel along so he could peck at the rock with his hard beak. Inside the rock, cozily sleeping, was the Sun. Not finding any way to persuade the Sun to wake up, the emperor called all the musicians and dancers of the Aztec empire to play and dance. Their loud music finally woke up the Sun, who once more shone radiantly over everyone.

✤ QUESTIONS TO INITIATE THE DIALOGUE ✤

DESCRIPTIVE PHASE **To develop an understanding of the message of the book.**

1. What motivated the little lizard to keep looking for the sun?
2. Why did the emperor not pay much attention to the lizard the first time?
3. Why did he pay attention the second time?

PERSONAL INTERPRETIVE PHASE **To encourage the expression of thoughts, feelings, and emotions in response to the book, and to relate the book content to the reader's experiences.**

1. Have you ever seen pictures of the Aztec pyramids? Have you seen Mexican folkloric dances?

2. Have you ever had to do something that was so difficult that you felt like giving up?
3. Have you ever been able to finish something difficult by not giving up?
4. Have you ever seen your parents or someone in your family achieve something by not giving up?

 CRITICAL/MULTICULTURAL/ANTI-BIAS PHASE **To promote higher-thinking skills. To encourage reflection on the themes of equality, inclusion, respect, justice, and peace.**

1. In the Aztec empire, the emperor's words were the law and everyone had to obey. What are the consequences when only one person makes the decisions for everyone?
2. What would have been the consequences if the little lizard had given up like all the other animals?
3. What kept the little lizard going? In what circumstances is it important to not give up?

 CREATIVE TRANSFORMATIVE PHASE **To encourage creative, constructive action leading to greater understanding and respect; to encourage taking responsibility for bringing about positive changes in our own reality.**

1. Is there something in your life that requires perseverance? What can you do to help yourself not give up on that task?

✤ UNVEILING THE AUTHOR WITHIN ✤

TEACHERS AS AUTHORS

Preparation for Writing

In preparation for your ongoing book, you may want to complete each of the following sentences in ten different ways:

- ◆ To grow as a teacher, I can . . .
- ◆ To bring about greater harmony in my classroom, I can . . .
- ◆ To contribute to my students' lives, I can . . .

Most of the teachers with whom we work have experienced times when they felt limited by the constraints of school regulations and overwhelmed by administrative paperwork, disillusioned by the politics within their school district, and outraged by policies that victimize the students whom they are meant to serve.

Yet, although these frustrations are very real, all of us as teachers are very powerful when it comes to affecting our students' lives. We have the power to say the right word, or to be silent at moments when silence is a kindness. We have the power to choose how we look at our students, how we greet them, how we praise them, what tone of voice we use when we speak to them. We also have the power to ask thought-provoking questions, to encourage a diversity of answers, and to stimulate students' thinking.

Writing an *I Can* book often helps teachers reclaim the power they had previously neglected or forgotten. As a result, it can help make our teaching experiences richer and more satisfactory.

BOOK 31 **Creating the Teacher's Book:** *I Can*

Spend a few minutes each day creating a page for an ongoing *I Can* book. If you decide to write at the same time as your students, you will be modeling an author at work. After you and your students have finished writing your pages, share your writing with them. This can be a subtle but powerful lesson.

Some of your entries may be direct and geared to the physical actions you can do ("I can ride a bike," "I can swim"). These entries may include a description of why you enjoy that activity, where and when you first learned how to do it, with whom you share that activity, and if you have ever taught it to anyone else. You can illustrate each page with a photograph, illustration, or newspaper clipping.

Other entries might focus instead on what you can do intellectually ("I can enjoy reading a good book"). Still others, perhaps more significantly, will relate to what you can do as a teacher, as a committed human being, and as someone engaged in the process of facilitating transformation, as we explored in the preparatory activity.

As you share with your students entries on topics such as:

I can forgive those who have wronged me.

I can find something to be grateful about every day.

I can question authority when I am not convinced of what I'm being asked to do.

I can discover new strength in myself every day.

I can be little bit more patient today than I was yesterday.

I can choose to speak kindly about myself and others.

you will be giving them a lesson of hope. Of course, these statements are only offered as examples. Your own entries will be the product of your own reflections and feelings.

Cattryn Somers wrote her *I Can* book (shown on p. 182 and reprinted on p. 183) with a simple text of one sentence per page. But on occasion, she felt the need to add something more to the basic sentence. The freedom evidenced in her book is the invitation we would like to reiterate to you. It is your book: Design it as you see fit.

I Can by Cattryn Somers

Reprinted by permission of Cattryn I. Somers, 3653 E. Stanford Dr., Paradise Valley, AZ, 85253.

I Can . . . *Cattryn Somers*

I can write.
(and rewrite and rewrite)

❖ ❖ ❖

I can love.

❖ ❖ ❖

I can remember.

❖ ❖ ❖

I can dream.

❖ ❖ ❖

I can grow.
   Just keep pushing those edges.
     There are no boundaries.
       Always reflect.

❖ ❖ ❖

I can change.
   "Value questions more than answers."

❖ ❖ ❖

   "The question is not 'What is the right
   thing to do?' but 'What is the compassionate
   thing to do?' "

❖ ❖ ❖

   "Have the courage to face whatever life
   throws at 'me' without losing equanimity, and
   'love' the humility to treat every situation 'I'
   encounter as one from which 'I' can learn."

Reprinted by permission of Cattryn I. Somers, 3653 E. Stanford Dr., Paradise Valley, AZ, 85253.

STUDENTS AS PROTAGONISTS AND AUTHORS

BOOK 32 **Writing a Collective Book: *We Can***

As preparation for having students create their own individual books, you can begin by inviting students to participate in creating a collective ***We Can*** book. Remind students that everyone is to come up with an original statement, something that has not already been said. Then ask each of them to contribute one sentence describing something they can do. Write their words on the board or chart paper. Encourage them to come up with new ideas, and acknowledge their contributions. Later, ask each student to copy and illustrate his or her sentence. You may want to display the pages, before binding them into a book.

BOOK 33 Writing an Individual Book: *I Can*

Explain to students the nature of this ongoing activity. Let them know that this book is not one they will finish in just a few days, but one to which they will add new pages throughout the year. Decide whether your students will use a blank notebook for making this book, or whether they will write on loose pages that will later be bound. Set aside some time in the classroom for students to create beautiful covers for their *I Can* books as an art activity.

Take time on a regular basis, daily if possible, for students to reflect on and write about what they can do. From time to time, invite students to read what they have already written in order to help them think of new things. Also take time regularly to share your own entries with them.

This *I Can* book is a significant point in the process of transformation that we have been outlining over the previous six units. It offers the opportunity for teachers, students, and parents to develop greater understanding of their own power to initiate change, and to accept responsibility for that power. All of us can do many things in life, and each action we take has consequences for both ourselves and others. Reflecting on our own capacity for action, and facilitating that reflection in others, will help deepen our awareness of the great potential we have for transforming our reality.

Helpful Hints

If you see that students are focusing too much on physical activities and not sufficiently on other skills and abilities, you may want to say something like, "Today, let's write in our *I Can* book something we can do without using our hands or feet." Or you might suggest: "Today, let's write about something that we can do using words."

In any activity, some students may at times respond in an inappropriate manner. They might, for example, use the activity as an opportunity to express their anger by writing inappropriate statements. As a teacher, you are the best judge of how to respond if such a situation arises. Sometimes it can be enough to say, "Yes, you can do that, but I am more interested in knowing about something you can do that makes you feel proud of yourself. For example, I have noticed that you are very good at . . . "

PARENTS OR CARETAKERS AS TEACHERS AND AUTHORS

Home Conversations: Learning from Family Experiences

Encourage parents or caretakers to talk to their children about all the things their children can do. Invite parents to share with children how they have seen them develop, and how many things they are able to do today that they were not able to do before. Also, invite parents to talk with their children about things the parents can do, how they learned to do them, and the kinds of satisfaction they derive from their talents, gifts, and abilities.

BOOK 34 **Interactive Book:** *As Your Child's Teacher I Can/*
As Parents We Can

You can create an interactive book with the parents of your students. Plan for the book to have two parts. Use the following titles, or something similar, for each of the parts:

> *As Your Child's Teacher I Can*
> *As a Parent I Can/As Parents We Can*

Fill in your side of the book with four or five powerful statements of what you consider to be the most significant contributions you can make to your students' lives as their teacher. Then indicate the space where each parent or set of parents is to complete their statements. Send the materials home with the students, asking them to return the books by a certain date.

BOOK 35 **Parents' Collective Book:** *What Our Parents Can Do*

Invite each student to obtain from their parents or caretakers (orally or in writing) a sentence about something they feel proud of being able to do. This could be something they do with their hands, or it could be something in their minds and hearts. It can refer to a hobby, to their profession, to their work at home, or to the way they interact with other people. Have students explain to their parents that this sentence will be used to create a classroom book.

Ask each student to copy the statement and illustrate it in order to create a page for a collective book titled *What Our Parents Can Do.* Make a copy of the book for each family, or circulate the book among the families, as a way of continuing to build a sense of community among the parents and helping them get to know one another better.

BOOK 36 **Parents' and Children's Interactive Book**

Vicky Martínez from Colma, California, and her daughter Monica decided to write together the book *Yes! We Can!* (see p. 186). Vicky wrote a statement on the top of the page, and Monica replied with her own statement at the bottom of the page. Together, they chose the photos to illustrate each page.

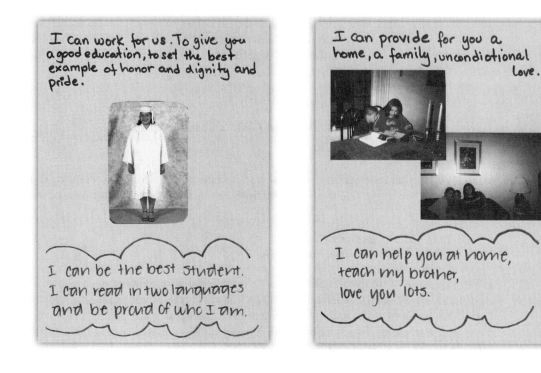

I can work for us. To give you a good education, to set the best example of honor and dignity and pride.

I can be the best student. I can read in two languages and be proud of who I am.

I can provide for you a home, a family, unconditional love.

I can help you at home, teach my brother, love you lots.

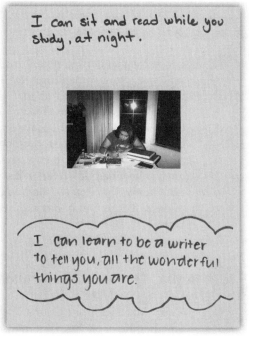

I can sit and read while you study, at night.

I can learn to be a writer to tell you, all the wonderful things you are.

***Yes! We Can!* by Vicky and Monica Martínez**

Reprinted by permission of Vicky and Monica Martínez, 411 C St., Colma, CA, 94014.

ADDITIONAL EXAMPLES OF BOOKS AUTHORED
BY TEACHERS, STUDENTS, AND FAMILIES

Teachers' Collective Books

Asked to think about what they can do as human beings, teachers respond in diverse ways. A group of teachers from District 15 in Brooklyn, New York, who participated enthusiastically in an Authors in the Classroom workshop wrote individual pages that were later compiled into a book. The first example is from Ted Slone, under whose leadership the course was offered. He wrote:

Para lo posible	For what is possible
puedo hacer lo imposible.	I can do what is impossible.
Para lo probable	For what is probable
haré la realidad.	I will create reality.
Y para los incrédulos	And for the unbelieving,
plantaré la semilla de lo posible.	I will plant the seed of what is possible.

Reprinted by permission.

Here is another example:

I can teach you as I learn,
   so let's learn together.
I can share my passion for the
   written word with you.
I can listen to you
   while you share yours.
I can point out that views belong
   to individuals: accept your own.
I can let you see how different people are
   and encourage you to realize
   how similar we really are.
I can feel your pain even when it tests
   my human weakness.
I can appreciate your innocence
   and nourish your growth.
I can teach you:
   you can teach me.
I can.

Australia Fernández

Students' Writing

At the end of the summer 1993 session of the Yo Puedo (I Can) Academy for migrant students, sponsored by the University of California at Santa Cruz, the participating students and staff produced a self-published book titled ***Nuestras memorias, ilusiones y pensamientos (Our Memories, Dreams and Thoughts).*** From this publication, we have translated a poem of reaffirmation by student Antonio Campos:

Thanks!   *by Antonio Campos*

Thanks, *Yo Puedo,* for all you have taught us.
Thanks for teaching us to be good leaders.
Thanks, *Yo Puedo,* for the confidence, respect, friendship, unity and communication
    we have developed.
Thanks, *Yo Puedo,* for giving us responsibility and an unforgettable experience.

Thanks, *Yo Puedo,* for teaching us to say:
I can study!
I can graduate!
I can go to college!
and above all:
I can be a leader and I can grow.

Who can? I can!

LEARNING
TO KNOW

Human beings are primarily beings of knowledge. Learning begins in the womb as the unborn child begins to recognize his or her mother's voice. This learning continues through the development of language abilities of surprising complexity and culminates in an ongoing and ever-deepening understanding of the world and of ourselves.

No human being has ever fully tapped the human ability to learn. Exploring our potential for learning is truly the next frontier for human beings. Consider for a moment the totality of knowledge accumulated throughout human history in all geographical areas, in all languages, in all disciplines. The knowledge of any single human being, even the most learned humanist or scientist, is very limited by comparison. Even the greatest genius would be in preschool when it comes to knowing all of the several thousand languages of the world and their literatures.

This is not to diminish our individual knowledge, nor to make us feel inferior. On the contrary, the intention is to enhance our vision of learning as an unending process. Although we are all constantly learning, we are not always aware of what we learn or of how we learn. Developing an awareness of the learning process can be a powerful experience for ourselves and our students. It has been posited that there is no single human intelligence but instead multiple intelligences (Gardner, 1993). Sometimes we learn through words:

Objectives

- To explore the learning process by reflecting on how we learn and how we teach.
- To reflect on our own goals as learners.
- To analyze the relationship between writing and learning, and explore the possibilities of writing to learn.
- To continue developing the expressive capacity.

Teachers	Students	Parents
Teachers are invited to: ■ Develop a book for self-reflection and to share with parents or other adults: ***My Goals as a Teacher.*** ■ Develop a book to share with their students: ***My Dreams for My Students.***	Students are invited to: ■ Dialogue with their teacher about various learning pathways. ■ Reflect on the multiple modalities of learning and explore some of the ways in they have learned in the past. ■ Reflect on any occasion they have helped someone else learn. ■ Participate in developing a collective book for the class by sharing their own individual goals: ***Our Goals for Today and for Tomorrow.*** ■ Create a long-term book: ***My Goals***	Parents or caretakers are invited to: ■ Reflect on their goals in life for themselves, their family, and their children. ■ Collaborate with the class in developing a class book: ***Our Parents' and Relatives' Dreams for Our Future.***

by listening, reading, discussing. Other times we learn by doing. We also learn through our body by means of kinesthetic intelligence, as well as by responding creatively through artistic media. Humans have a mechanical intelligence as well as an interpersonal intelligence.

It is important to remember that all human beings have the capacity to develop all of these forms of intelligence. A well-rounded education will ensure that everyone has opportunities to explore all of these realms. At the same time, individuals have their preferred modes through which they learn most easily, and everyone needs to be given the opportunity to excel in this area of strength. It is not always easy to create this balance—giving people an opportunity to learn through their preferred mode while also challenging them to explore other approaches. Of course, the teacher is also a human being, with a tendency to favor some learning styles over others, as well as a tendency to teach others in the same way he or she was taught.

The sooner that students become aware of their potential to learn in a variety of ways, the more likely it is they will develop multiple learning approaches. When multiple forms of learning are emphasized, teachers are less likely to persuade students to believe they can learn in only one way. And the more that students are involved in determining what they want to learn and how they can go about learning it, the greater likelihood there is that they will become independent and motivated lifelong learners.

❖ THE CREATIVE LITERACY PROCESS ❖

Invite students to read books that explore the experience of learning and discovering how one learns. You will find a list of suggested titles in the section on recommended books at the end of the book. Select a text for engaging in the Creative Literacy Dialogue process. We have included two texts in this unit to serve this purpose: for younger students, "Turkey for Thanksgiving Dinner?" "No, thanks!" by Alma Flor Ada, illustrated by Viví Escrivá; for older students, "The Teacher" from *Where the Flame Trees Bloom* by Alma Flor Ada. Of course, you may prefer to select other books of your choice.

It can be helpful to introduce the reading by eliciting students' previous knowledge about the topic and inviting them to make predictions about the book. Once you have finished reading the book, use the corresponding questions to initiate the conversation. (If you have chosen your own book, you will need to spend some time designing thoughtful questions beforehand. See p. 42. For additional tips on facilitating dialogue, see pp. 44–48.)

"Turkey for Thanksgiving Dinner?" "No Thanks!"
by Alma Flor Ada

If you have the book, or the book on tape, you may want to have your students listen to the story in its original version. If you do not have either the book or the tape, you can read them this excerpt:

It was a beautiful morning. After many days of rain, the sun had finally come out. Everyone in the chicken yard was busy scratching for worms in the moist earth. The one who was finding the most worms and gulping them down fastest was the turkey.

Gulping down one worm after another, the turkey wandered closer and closer to the farmhouse. He was very surprised when he overheard voices from the kitchen and realized they were talking about him.

"Take a look at that turkey! Isn't he nice and plump? I bet he'll taste good at Thanksgiving dinner!"

These words were very disturbing for the turkey. He forgot all about scratching for worms. The idea of eating other creatures had now become quite repulsive to him. With his head hung low, and his crest flopped over, he stood quietly under the large nut tree.

The turkey had been there for a long time when he heard a thin voice asking him: "What's the matter? Why are you so sad?"

The turkey looked up and saw a beautiful spiderweb upon which a few drops of dew still shone. Right in the middle of the spiderweb sat a tiny spider.

"If you only knew what I just overheard. It was enough to take anyone's appetite away."

"What did you hear?" the spider wanted to know.

"They were talking about me! They were saying I was nice and plump. That they like me well-roasted. That they want one of my drumsticks. One of MY drumsticks! Can you imagine?"

"Hummmm . . . " said the little spider. "How curious! How extraordinarily curious!"

"Curious? You call that curious? I call it horrible, terrible, abominable, frightening, scandalous . . . that's what I call it."

"It's just that it's such an interesting coincidence."

"Coincidence? What coincidence?"

"It just happens that I had a great-grandmother who used to tell me that her great-grandmother had a little pig for a friend and he also didn't want to get eaten."

"That doesn't seem like such an extraordinary coincidence to me. After all, who would like to get eaten?"

"The coincidence is that my great-grandmother told me that her great-grandmother managed to save the life of her friend Wilbur."

"She managed to save his life? Maybe your great-grandmother did have something interesting to say after all. How did she manage to save his life?"

The plot for the story has been set. The students may have guessed by now the name of the tiny spider's great-grandmother's great-grandmother. This may be a good place to have them recall the story of *Charlotte's Web*. Some students may also associate this story with that of *Babe*.

Invite students to imagine what this little spider might do to save the turkey's life. After students make their predictions, let them know that in this book the little spider sets out very specific goals. Her goal is to make the turkey less plump and juicy. She outlines a specific program of diet and exercise. By following it, the turkey becomes fitter and fitter every day. The spider has him jump higher and higher, using a branch as the desired goal.

When Thanksgiving day approaches and someone decides to grab the turkey to prepare him for dinner, the turkey sets off at top speed, flapping his wings with all his might:

And remembering that the fence was no higher than the lowest branch of the nut tree, he made a great leap and disappeared into the forest. He has lived there ever since, eating a vegetarian diet and exercising faithfully every day.

✤ QUESTIONS TO INITIATE THE DIALOGUE ✤

 DESCRIPTIVE PHASE **To promote understanding of the message of the book.**

1. The turkey's problem at the beginning of the story seemed to have no solution. How was he able to find a solution to his problem?
2. Why was the spider able to find a solution? What helped her?
3. Why did the turkey decide to become a vegetarian?

 PERSONAL INTERPRETIVE PHASE **To promote self-expression of feelings and emotions and to relate the book content to the reader's experiences.**

1. Have you ever had an opportunity to help someone?
2. Has someone ever helped you when you needed it?
3. The turkey set the goal of becoming trimmer. What are some of your goals?
4. The spider helped the turkey set his goals. Has anyone helped you discover your own goals?

 CRITICAL/MULTICULTURAL/ANTI-BIAS PHASE **To promote higher-thinking skills. To encourage reflection on equality, inclusion, respect, and justice leading to peace.**

1. The story told by the spider's great-grandmother about her great-grandmother proved to be very useful. Can you think of other situations in which it might be helpful to listen to the stories told by members of our family?
2. Our family members' stories are part of our family's inheritance. What can we do to make sure we don't lose them?
3. The turkey found a good solution to his problem with the help of the spider. Can you think of other things he might have done? What would have happened if he had not done anything?

 CREATIVE TRANSFORMATIVE PHASE **To lead to creative, constructive action leading to understanding and respect for others, and to become more responsible for bringing about positive change in our own reality.**

1. The turkey had a specific problem to solve. Is there anything you would like to improve in your life?
2. The turkey changed the way he treated worms after he thought about how sad it was to be eaten. Can you think of any way you could be kinder to others?

The Teacher
from Where the Flame Trees Bloom *by Alma Flor Ada*

This story is a chapter in the book of childhood memories *Where the Flame Trees Bloom.* If you do not have access to the book, you can read the following abridged version to your students:

My maternal grandmother, Lola, filled my early years with outdoor adventures, fun, and fascinating stories.

There are many stories in my family about this extraordinary woman. This is one of my favorites. Unlike many other family stories, which are often embellished or changed depending on the teller, I always heard this story told exactly the same way. This leads me to believe that this is exactly how it happened.

My grandmother had a school in the old house that she had inherited from her father. Lola loved to teach outdoors. The slightest pretext would serve to take the whole class out under the trees to conduct her lessons there.

Surrounded by her pupils, including her three older daughters, my grandmother was conducting a grammar lesson. Suddenly she interrupted herself. "Why is it," she asked her students, "that we don't often speak about the things that are truly important, such as our responsibility as human beings for those around us? Do we really know their feelings, their needs? And yet, we could all do so much for each other. . . ."

The students were silent, spellbound. They knew that their teacher sometimes strayed from the topic of the lesson in order to share with them her own reflections. And they also knew that those were some of her most important teachings. At times she could be funny and witty. Other times, she would touch their hearts. And so they listened.

"Look," continued my grandmother, as she pointed to the road that bordered the farm. The students saw a solitary man walking by. "Look at that old man. He is walking by us. In a few minutes he will be gone forever, and we will never have known who he is, where he is going, what may be important in his life."

The students watched the man, who by then was quite close. He was very thin, and a coarse guayabera hung loosely over his bent frame. His face, shaded by a straw hat, was weathered and wrinkled.

"Well," said my grandmother, "do we let him go away, forever unknown to us, or do you want to ask him if there is anything we can do for him?"

The students looked at one another. Finally one girl said: "Shall I ask him?" As my grandmother nodded, the girl got up and walked toward the road. A few of the other students followed her, my mother and my aunts among them.

Upon seeing them approach, the man stopped. "We would like to know who you are, and where are you going," said the student. "Is there anything we can do for you?" added my aunt Mireya.

The man was completely taken aback. "But who are *you*?" was all he could reply.

The girls then explained how their questions had come about. The old man looked at them. He explained he had no one to be with, that he had come a long way, hoping to find some distant relatives, but had been unable to locate them. "I'm nothing but an old man," he concluded, "looking for a place to lie down and die. As a matter of fact, I was heading towards that large ceiba." He pointed to a tree growing by the road not too far away. "I thought I would lie down in its shade to wait for my death."

"Please, don't leave," was all the girls could say. They rushed back to tell their teacher what they had learned from the old man.

"What do you think can be done?" my grandmother asked. The boys and girls came up with ideas: The old man could go to a home for old folks. Maybe he could be taken to the hospital. Or perhaps the police would know what to do. . . . "Is that what you would like to see happen, if it were you?" my grandmother asked.

Instead, the students took the man into the house. He was given a room. The students made the bed and cooked him some food. A doctor determined that there was nothing wrong with him except exhaustion and malnutrition. It took the old man several days to recuperate, but soon he was up and about. He stayed and lived with the family for many years, until one morning he was found to have died peacefully in his sleep. During all those years, he helped in the garden, fed the hens, or often sat on the back porch, whistling softly. But there was nothing he liked better than to sit in the back of the classroom, or under the trees, and listen to my grandmother teach.

❖ QUESTIONS TO INITIATE THE DIALOGUE ❖

 DESCRIPTIVE PHASE **To promote understanding of the message of the text.**

1. This teacher was dedicated to her students and wanted to enrich their minds with many ideas. What else did she want to achieve?
2. Make a list of Lola's goals as a teacher.

 PERSONAL INTERPRETIVE PHASE **To promote self-expression of feelings and emotions and to relate the book content to the reader's experiences.**

1. Meeting the students changed the old man's life, just as meeting the old man changed theirs. Often our lives are changed by an encounter with something or someone. What experiences have changed your life?
2. Teachers teach more than curriculum content. They also teach lessons about life. What are some of the important life lessons you have learned from your teachers?

 CRITICAL/MULTICULTURAL/ANTI-BIAS PHASE **To promote higher-thinking skills. To encourage reflection on equality, inclusion, respect, and justice leading to peace.**

1. It would have been easy for Lola and her students to not pay any attention to the old man. What might have happened then?
2. Could Lola have anticipated the consequences of her words for her students? What can we learn from this story about the power of words?

CREATIVE TRANSFORMATIVE PHASE **To lead to creative, constructive action leading to understanding and respect for others, and to become more responsible for bringing about positive change in our own reality.**

1. What do you think Lola meant when she said that we can all do more for one another? Is there something you could do for others?

"The Teacher" by Alma Flor Ada. Reprinted with the permission of Atheneum Books for Young Readers, an imprint of Simon & Schuster Children's Publishing Division from *Where the Flame Trees Bloom* by Alma Flor Ada. Text copyright © 1994 by Alma Flor Ada.

❖ UNVEILING THE AUTHOR WITHIN ❖

THE VALUE OF EXAMINING OUR PURPOSE AND GOALS

This unit is about learning and goal setting. By creating books that explore the purpose and goals we have as teachers, including both our own learning as well as our students' learning, we can invite students and parents to explore some of their own goals for learning and for life.

The vast majority of people who become teachers enter the profession filled with dreams and idealism. Our purpose seems very clear initially. Unfortunately, the everyday tasks and the many demands placed on teachers frequently wear us down and leave little time for reflection on the major values that inform our work.

Often we begin our workshops by inviting participants to share their sense of purpose and their goals as teachers. We find that teachers deeply appreciate this activity, for a number of reasons. To begin with, participants appreciate the opportunity to have a few moments of quiet reflection to contemplate the values that give meaning to their practice, and they appreciate the opportunity to share their reflections aloud with others. Participants also appreciate the sense of camaraderie generated by the recognition that many others share similar dreams. And last but not least, teachers are energized by the content of their reflections, by the sense of possibility, generosity, and idealism that is reawakened by their purpose and goal statements.

Here are some examples of the goals that teachers in a workshop in New York City discovered to be at the heart of their teaching practice:

To provide children with the opportunity to grow in an orderly, enriching, experiential universe.

To give parents a sense of their children's future as productive individuals.

To offer the community a positive view of the potential and promise found in America.

Nancy Tridlind

I want to give my students the knowledge and confidence that will help them realize that whatever they do or say is of value to society.

Olga Arguelles

For my students, my most sincere hope is that by the way my life touches theirs in this moment, and in the many moments we share, we will remember each other afterward, or see each other—and smile—and there will be a replay of the feeling of trust, of knowing that someone believes in them.

That they will feel good enough about themselves and their experiences to RISK new ones.

That by touching their creativity and finding themselves, they will be happy to be alive.

Sharon Bernard

In 1995, during the annual conference of the National Association for Bilingual Education in Phoenix, Arizona, we conducted an institute titled Teachers Becoming Authors/Teachers Becoming Publishers. After a conversation about values, purpose, and goals, we invited teachers to publish some of their thoughts onsite, with technological support from Apple Corporation. Here are some of the posters that teachers created as a synthesis of their goals and beliefs as teachers:

I am a marvelous creation. There isn't another like me. Then I look at you, and see another wonder.

Eva Williams

The children of today are the leaders of tomorrow.

Luisa V. Whelan

Trust in me for I believe in YOU!

Pilar Muñoz

My dream is to help children open their eyes to the millions of opportunities available to them!

Delphina J. Ávila

Trying and failing is better than failing to try.

Sylvia B. Stella

We all smile in the same language.

Pablo-Olga-María

Hablar un idioma es bueno; hablar dos, es mucho mejor.

To speak one language is good; to speak two is much better.

Rosa H. Rosa

Children are like flowers. Well tended, they bloom.
Not taken care of, they perish.

Los niños son como las flores. Si se cultivan, florecen.
Si se descuidan, perecen,

Miriam Miranda-Jurado

TEACHERS AS AUTHORS

BOOK 37 **A Teacher's Book for Self-Reflection and for Sharing with Parents:** *My Purpose and Goals as a Teacher*

In addition to the personal value to be gained from reflecting on one's goals, teachers can use their reflections to create a book to share with students' parents. By doing so, we open the door to a greater dialogue with parents.

Parents are the first and most constant teachers in their children's lives. For many parents, schools embody the hope that their children will be able to achieve more humane living conditions. Frequently, parents—especially those raised in other cultures—view teachers as professionals who hold the key to education and whose guidance must be followed without question. They send their children to school trusting that teachers have been trained how to best instruct and educate their children. Sadly, cultural minority parents' tendency to trust and defer to teachers is often misinterpreted as a lack of interest in their children's education.

Most parents want their children not only to receive knowledge, but also to develop the values and ethical principles that will enable them to live happy and successful lives. By creating a book about their goals for themselves, and sharing that book with parents, teachers can begin a dialogue about the need for an effective collaboration between home and school.

Our Goals for Our Students

In addition to exploring their goals for themselves as teachers, teachers can also explore the goals they have for their students. The following examples of teachers' dreams for their students are from Head Start teachers in San Diego who were invited to complete the following thought: "My dream for the children I serve is. . . ."

. . . to become the best they can be in life. I hope that they can accomplish anything they put their mind to, and overcome any obstacles they may face.
Petra Hurtado

. . . that they become thoughtful, delightful, and dedicated persons in their lives.
Susan Sueng

. . . that they may be able to give a little of themselves back in return to society . . . that they may lead happy lives and be able to help change the lives of those who are not so fortunate and make this a better world to live in.
Connie Garza

. . . to think positive even if they fail, and learn from it, and try again!
Antonia Gogue

. . . To be warm, loving, open individuals; . . . to communicate with great and vivid detail; . . . to be cognizant of what's happening in their lives, community, country, and world; . . . to be masters of their own lives, set high goals, and go for them.
Nini Quiñones

BOOK 38 **A Teacher's Book to Share with Students and Parents:**
My Dreams for My Students

Books need not always be typed nor printed on a computer. There can be strength and immediacy to free-flowing art and handwritten words. Kelly Hearn, from Sunnyslope Elementary School in Phoenix, Arizona, wrote the following book by hand. Using color crayons, she created bold, powerful images to illustrate the brief yet memorable text (pp. 200–201).

For My Students   *By Kelly Hearn*

Before you leave
there are a few things
I want you to take with you.

KNOWLEDGE
I'll give you all I can
and the resources to acquire more.

PURPOSE
I ask you this question so that you never grow complacent.
What do you want to accomplish in this life?

IDENTITY
I want you to know
and respect
who you are and
where you come from.

COMPASSION
I remind you to open your eyes and look beyond yourself
to recognize the needs of others.

PRIDE
Stand tall and believe in yourself.

MEMORIES
I give you all the good ones
and the bad ones.
The ones we have already created
and the ones we have yet to make.

Reprinted by permission.

For My Students
by Kelly Hearn
Reprinted by permission.

Lynn Gerardo, also from Sunnyslope Elementary School, created a bilingual book to share with her students' families. The text is printed on colored paper and illustrated with beautiful color photographs (see p. 202). Between each two pages of text, there are two pages of students' artwork. This is the English text:

I Wish for You/Deseo para ti   *by Lynn Gerardo; illustrated by the children of room 307, Sunnyslope Elementary School*

Dedicated to my precious students

I WISH FOR YOU . . .
a great wind that fills your sails as you explore life's infinite possibilities, but not so strong that it causes you to capsize.

I WISH FOR YOU . . .
magnificent trees, friends that will stay to strengthen you and protect you always.

I WISH FOR YOU . . .
mountains that you can climb so that you will develop a wider perspective.

I WISH FOR YOU . . .
bridges that help you cross difficult times and take you to new places.

I WISH FOR YOU . . .
rainy days so that you can listen to the music in your head and in your heart, and so that you will dance with joy for life.

I Wɪsʜ ғᴏʀ Yᴏᴜ . . .

sunny days that will illuminate your life so that you can appreciate your family, your health, and your blessings.

Reprinted by permission of Lynn Gerardo, Supai Middle School, 6720 E. Continental Dr., Scottsdale, AZ, 85257.

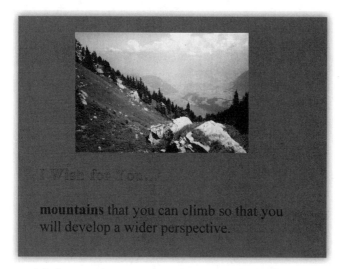

I Wish for You/Deseo para ti **by Lynn Gerardo**
Reprinted by permission of Lynn Gerardo, Supai Middle School, 6720 E. Continental Dr., Scottsdale, AZ, 85257.

STUDENTS AS PROTAGONISTS AND AUTHORS

Once you have shared your own book with students and parents, invite students to create their own books about their goals.

BOOK 39 Creating a Collective Book: *Our Goals for Today and for the Future*

Students can contribute individual pages about their goals and dreams for the future to create a class book. This process can help create or reaffirm a sense of community. By supporting one another, we can all achieve our goals more effectively.

In March 2000, the students in Class 3–227 from P.S. 140X in the Bronx, New York, wrote their book ***Our Goals:***

I go to school because I want to become a Kindergarten teacher when I grow up. I like children. I also would like to become a lawyer to help people in need.

J. Alexandra Duvergé

❖ ❖ ❖

I go to school because I want to become a doctor when I grow up. I like to help people when they get sick. I also would like to become a professional ice-skater.

Miguel Concepción

Instead of (or in addition to) creating a compilation of individual goals, you may want to help students create a collective book based on their shared goals for the classroom. Begin by inviting students to think about what kind of classroom they would like to create. Once students have generated a shared vision through dialogue, invite them to explore in writing how each of them might best contribute to realizing that vision. This kind of book can help students realize how greater power is achieved when individual strengths are brought together for the betterment of the larger group.

BOOK 40 Creating an Individual Book: *My Goals*

After students have created a collective book together, invite them to write and illustrate their own individual books about their goals. We have been delighted at the ability of even rather young students to write reflectively about their goals. For example, guided by their teacher Ms. Luna, students in Class 3-307, P.S. 161, New York, wrote the following:

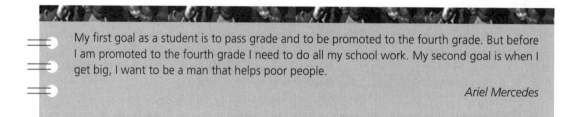

My main goal as a student is to learn. Another goal is to pass to fourth grade and pass all the way to college. My last goal is to become a veterinarian and help all kind of animals from different places.

Mirta Milanés

My first goal as a student is to pass grade and to be promoted to the fourth grade. But before I am promoted to the fourth grade I need to do all my school work. My second goal is when I get big, I want to be a man that helps poor people.

Ariel Mercedes

PARENTS OR CARETAKERS AS TEACHERS AND AUTHORS

The idea of making an interactive book of goals between teacher and parents is the brainstorm of Elba María Stell, a bilingual teacher in El Paso, Texas. Each year she introduces herself to the parents of her students with a book. In a few direct sentences, she states her goals for the students. Then she adds what she as the teacher can do for the children and invites parents to respond with additional goals they have as parents and what they can do to support these goals.

BOOK 41 **Creating an Interactive Book:** *Our Parents'*
and Relatives' Dreams and Wishes for Us

This interactively produced book is initiated by the teacher. Students' collaboration is essential for obtaining parents' contributions and for illustrating the book. The parents provide the text. One example of this type of book was developed by Cattryn Somers in Phoenix, Arizona. She produced the book bilingually so that all families would feel included and be able to read one another's contributions. When parents wrote in English, she translated the text into Spanish for the benefit of Spanish-speaking parents. When parents wrote in Spanish, she translated the text into English for the benefit of English-speaking parents. Many parents, English-speakers as well as Spanish-speakers, expressed how valued they felt by having their words translated into another language. They all showed immense satisfaction at being asked to share their dreams for their children with the extended classroom community.

The teacher took a photograph of each student outdoors against the same background. Each page of text contains parents' words, shown in both languages, alongside a color photograph of their child. The facing page is an illustration created by the

In the future we wish for our
daughter to succeed, prosper, have
lots of wisdom, knowledge and
understanding and be in perfect
health.

Gilbert and Emmeline,
   Sheenagh's parents

*En el futuro deseamos para nuestra hija
superacion, prosperidad, y que tenga
conocimientos y la sabiduria para estar
perfectamente sana.*

In the future I wish to see everybody
happy and smiling and singing and I
wish for Lavier to be happy forever
and ever. I wish for Lavier that all
her dreams come true and I wish the
same for my other kids, too. They
are Rene Elizabeth and Maurico.
I wish that Lavier could learn how to
fly a plane and be a happy girl.

Lavier's parents

*En el futuro espero que ver a todo el
mundo feliz y sonriente y cantando.
Deseo que Lavier sea feliz.
Quiero que Lavier se le realizen sus
sueños y tambien para mis otros niños.
Ellos son Rene Elizabeth y Maurico.
Deseo que Lavier pueda aprender a volar
un avion y que sea una niña feliz.*

In the Future/En el futuro by Parents in Room 507, Sunnyslope, Arizona

Reprinted by permission of Emmeline and Gilbert Stoney, P.O. Box 203, Rock Point, AZ, 86545; and Ruben Guevara, 5131 W. Diana Ave., Glendale, AZ, 85302.

same student. This beautiful book is titled ***In the Future: Our Parents' Dreams and Wishes for Us/En el futuro: Los sueños y deseos que nuestros padres tienen para nosotros,*** by the parents and children in room 507.

If you have a classroom of students whose families speak several languages, several options are possible. If parents are biliterate, you can ask them to offer their contributions in both their home language and in English and publish both versions. If parents are unable to translate, an older student or a person from the community may be able to help.

A more demanding but highly enriching activity would be to publish a multilingual book in which the parents' goals are translated into all of the languages represented in the classroom. This of course can be achieved more easily if parents' collective goals are first synthesized. This can be done in the classroom, with students helping to create a composite set of goals that includes and summarizes individual families' contributions. Afterward, different families can take responsibility for translating the synthesis into their own language. A book can then be created that includes all of the languages represented in the classroom.

Bilingual and multilingual books remind us of how deeply language and culture are interlinked. Even more importantly they offer a vivid portrayal of the rich social and cultural reality in which we live, and bring home the need to build bridges between all those who make up our communities.

ADDITIONAL EXAMPLES OF BOOKS AUTHORED
BY TEACHERS, STUDENTS, AND FAMILIES

Collective Books of Goals

While most of the collective books of teacher's goals in our archives have originated in our own workshops, the teachers at P.S. 48M, District 6 in New York decided to create a book about their goals under the leadership of Dinorah Peguero. They named it *My Goal as a Teacher* and printed it onto colored parchment. The pages are designed as small posters, suitable for framing in each individual classroom. Collectively, they represent a powerful statement of teachers' commitment to their students and their community.

Parallel Teachers' and Parents' Goals

Dinorah Peguero, who initiated the collective book just described, also invited the parents of her students to share their own goals. She then typed the parents' statements and printed them on the same paper she had used for the teachers' goals. In both cases, the books were bound by placing the pages inside a presentation binder. The similar paper, font, and binding used for both books communicated a powerful message of equality between the two sets of educators, those at home and those at school.

Collective Books by Parents

For the book *Metas para nuestros hijos (Goals for our children)* authored by parents of P.S. 161 in the Bronx, New York, each parent dictated his or her message in an interview with the teacher, Ivette R. Bayron. Afterward, Mrs. Bayron typed each statement and printed it on color paper. Here is a translation of one of the pages:

Lillian Rosario, mother of Jonathan Ríos.

My goals for my son are that he finishes his studies. I want him to finish school. He always tells me that he wants to be a pilot and I tell him that for that you need to study a lot. I ask God every night to give me a long life so that I am able to see my children educated and fulfilled. I hope they never get into drugs. I have four beautiful children and I know that one day, they will go far in this world.

Reprinted by permission.

Ms. Luna, another teacher in the same school, sent home an invitation to her students' parents to write about their goals for their children. Parents sent back their handwritten or typed pages, some in English, others in Spanish. Some of the pages were illustrated. The teacher collected the texts and typed them, using the same font and design to create a consistent pattern throughout the book. She printed the pages on colored paper of different shades, created a cover, and bound the pages with a spiral binding. The title page reads: ***Our Goals for Our Children/Nuestros objetivos para nuestros niños,*** written by the Parents of Class 3–307 P.S. 161. We have included one of the pages here. As we have seen on many occasions, when invited to share their goals for their children, parents often emphasize the importance of allowing their children to determine their own goals.

My Goals for Martha   *Evelyn Vélez*

My goals for Martha are many. I would like for you to be a doctor, a lawyer, or a teacher. But I think that, all those wonderful careers aside, my biggest goal for you is to see you as an independent, strong, hardworking and intelligent young woman. That will take you toward the goals you choose for yourself

Reprinted by permission.

A mother in Santa Clara, California, created a book of her goals to share with six-year-old Camille and four-year-old Jessica. Her reminder to share and enjoy the simple pleasures of life is of value to people of all ages. Trained as an artist, she illustrated her book with fine line drawings.

Teachers might worry about the possible risk of inviting parents' voices into the classroom. One need not agree with every statement made by a parent, yet all voices deserve to be respected. It is precisely this respect for a diversity of opinion that can preserve our schools as potential democratic arenas in which freedom of thought can be taught and practiced.

My Goals by Hannah Brooks

Reprinted by permission of Hannah Brooks, 1148 Pomeroy Ave., Santa Clara, CA, 95051.

Although most goals offered by parents will not be controversial, we may find parents with strong opinions worthy of respectful analysis. It is not our position to take sides, nor to decide whether the parent is right or wrong. But we can treat a parent's opinions as interesting and valuable reflections meriting our attention and thought.

Here is an example of a parents' contribution, translated from the Spanish, that could initiate an interesting dialogue in the classroom and possibly inspire a research project on nonviolent movements throughout the world.

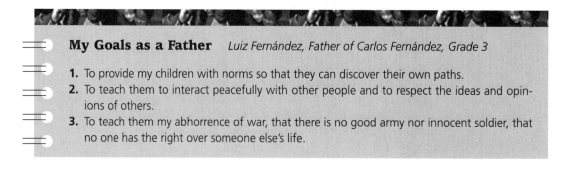

My Goals as a Father   *Luiz Fernández, Father of Carlos Fernández, Grade 3*

1. To provide my children with norms so that they can discover their own paths.
2. To teach them to interact peacefully with other people and to respect the ideas and opinions of others.
3. To teach them my abhorrence of war, that there is no good army nor innocent soldier, that no one has the right over someone else's life.

4. To let them know that one can always learn something new. The human brain does not fill up the way a computer hard disk does. A thirst for learning is the only worthwhile addiction.

5. To teach them that no one is perfect. It would be quite boring.

6. To teach them that God exists inside each person and that each of us can make him as great as we are willing and able. And that churches are simply large houses.

7. To teach them that it doesn't matter where their parents were born, nor even where they were born. Our nation is the whole planet and its name is EARTH.

DEVELOPING RELATIONSHIPS

Human life is deeply interwoven with the natural world. In addition, we are critically dependent on our relationships with other human beings. As humans we are essentially social beings. In contrast to many animals that can fend for themselves right after birth, human offspring require many years of support before they can survive on their own. For every human being who reaches adulthood, a great deal of effort has been made to keep that person alive. Yet mere survival is not what life is about, and thus children's well-being and human rights also involve nurturing and education.

Given the topic "an important person in my life," most of us are able to think of someone who has influenced the course of our life, who provided care, set an example, inspired us, or offered us support. In this unit, we invite you to continue the process of self-reflection by remembering and writing about a person who has been significant in your own development. You will be sharing this book with your students to offer them a model for their own reflection and authorship.

This biography can be about a person whom we have known, or it might be about someone whom we have never met but whose life has served as an inspiration. Writing the biography of someone who has been significant to us provides the opportunity for multiple levels of reflection:

Objectives

- To identify individuals who have been fundamental in the development of our character and our lives, as well as people who are significant in our immediate community.
- To reflect on the characteristics of a person that result in that person becoming significant for us.
- To honor the life of an unsung hero by recognizing and celebrating their values, virtues, and life accomplishments, as well as their influence on us.

Teachers	Students	Parents
Teachers are invited to: ■ Explore books for children or young adults in which the protagonists recognize the significant influence of other human beings on their own growth and development. ■ Dialogue with students about the influence of other people on our lives and the significance of recognizing and honoring them. ■ Create a book about a person who has been significant in their own lives. ■ Share their book with students as a way to deepen the dialogue and as a model for students' own writing.	Students are invited to: ■ Engage in the Creative Literacy Dialogue process to explore the role of other human beings in the protagonist's life. ■ Select a person who is special to them to research and write about. The research may be done through interviews. ■ Share orally what they have learned about the person they have chosen, with other students, the teacher, or the whole class. ■ Write and publish their books on a person who has made a difference in their lives.	Parents or caretakers are invited to: ■ Dialogue with their children about people who have been influential in their lives. ■ Write about a person who has been important in their lives, or share that story with their children orally so that students can create a book about significant people in their parents' lives.

- ◆ By honoring others, we recognize the values we want to encourage in ourselves and transmit to others.
- ◆ By understanding another person's journey, including their difficulties, challenges, and struggles, we gain a better understanding of human potential.
- ◆ By focusing on understanding one life, we can better comprehend the complexities of survival and success.
- ◆ Writing a life story or biography provides the opportunity for us and our students to do research on various aspects of a human life:
  - • A given time period and its historical significance
  - • Societal conditions of a particular era
  - • Specific jobs and occupations
  - • A geographic location and its particular characteristics

Writing about someone's life deepens our understanding of human nature and of the influence that circumstances can have on a person's development, from the immediate support provided by a family to the major historical events that shape a community. This exercise can bring extraordinary rewards, both emotionally and intellectually.

❖ THE CREATIVE LITERACY PROCESS ❖

Invite students to read books that show the significance of other human beings in the protagonist's life. You will find a list of suggested titles in the appendix of recommended books. Select a text for engaging in the Creative Literacy Dialogue process. We have included two selections in this unit to serve this purpose, both by Alma Flor Ada. *The Golden Cage* is appropriate for younger students, whereas for older ones we have included "Choices" a chapter from *Where the Flame Trees Bloom.* Alternatively, you may prefer to select another book of your choice.

Before you begin sharing the book, access the students' previous knowledge of the topic and invite them to make predictions about the book. Once you have finished reading the book, use the corresponding questions to initiate the conversation. (If you have chosen your own book, you will need to spend some time designing thoughtful questions beforehand. See p. 42. For additional tips on facilitating dialogue, see pp. 44–48.)

The Golden Cage
by Alma Flor Ada

This book is part of a collection, "Stories the Year 'Round," illustrated by Viví Escrivá and published by Alfaguara. If you have access to the book, offer students the opportunity to enjoy the illustrations. If not, you can share with them the abridged story presented here.

For Nicolás, the protagonist of the story, it is very upsetting to see his grandmother in a wheelchair. When he sees her watching the birds who come to feed at her windowsill, he decides to give her a beautiful birdcage for Christmas. Nicolás works hard running many errands to earn some money and saves every penny his father and uncles give him. Because he still does not have enough, he makes arrangements with the pet shop owner to pay the balance later. He feels extremely proud of having found the perfect gift, but when he asks his grandmother what birds she would like to keep in a cage, he discovers that what she enjoys about birds is their freedom. Nicolás realizes that the perfect gift needs to be something quite different, and trades in the birdcage for a little kitten.

✤ QUESTIONS TO INITIATE THE DIALOGUE ✤

 DESCRIPTIVE PHASE **To promote understanding of the message of the book.**

1. If you were to describe Nicolás, what are some of the things you could say about him?

2. When Nicolás decides that something is important, how does he behave?
3. How do you think he feels about his grandmother? Why do you think so?

 PERSONAL INTERPRETIVE PHASE **To promote self-expression of feelings and emotions and to relate the book content to the reader's experience.**

1. Do you have someone you love very much? Who is this person? What does this person mean to you?
2. Has someone you love ever been sick? How did you feel?
3. Have you ever been able to do something nice for someone? What happened? How did you feel?

 CRITICAL/MULTICULTURAL/ANTI-BIAS PHASE **To promote higher-thinking skills. To encourage reflection on equality, inclusion, respect, and justice in order to achieve peace.**

1. Why was it important for the grandmother to see the birds fly freely?
2. When Nicolás was able to listen to his grandmother, he learned some things about her. What was the most important thing he learned?
3. Once he found out how his grandmother felt, Nicolás had to change his plans. Why might it be difficult to change something one has worked hard to achieve?

 CREATIVE TRANSFORMATIVE PHASE **To lead to a creative, constructive action leading to understanding and respect for others, and to become more responsible for bringing about positive change in our own reality.**

1. When his grandmother talked to Nicolás about the birds she liked, she mentioned her own mother. What could Nicolás have asked in order to learn more about his great-grandmother? Why is it important to know things about our ancestors? Who can you talk to to learn more about your grandparents and your great-grandparents?
2. When Nicolás listened to his grandmother, he learned more about her feelings about freedom. He also learned about her as a person. Is there someone in your life you can learn more about?
3. Nicolás thought he understood his grandmother, but later he learned more about her by talking with her. What can you do to help others understand you better? To understand others better?

Choices
from Where the Flame Trees Bloom *by Alma Flor Ada*

This book is a collection of eleven vignettes of the author's childhood. Some are real-life stories she experienced; others are portraits of her relatives. If you do not have a copy of this book available, you can read this passage to your students.

My father's family and my mother's family were as different from each other as a quiet mountain stream and the vast ocean. My father's family was small in contrast to my mother's, with its many aunts, uncles, first and second cousins, great-aunts, and great-uncles. But not only was my mother's family large, it also was very lively, cheerful, and adventurous, while my father's father and brothers were quiet people who seldom spoke about anything personal.

We frequently spent our evenings together listening to stories of my mother's family. Through these stories, people whom I have never met seemed as familiar to me as those who lived nearby. It seemed as though I had heard their voices and taken part in their adventures. But it is a story told to me by my father's father that I would like to share with you now, a story that remains vivid in my memory and that has greatly shaped who I am today.

My grandfather Modesto would stop by my house every afternoon for a short visit, always with a cigarette between his yellowed fingers. He would pat me on the head or give me a formal kiss on the forehead, and then he would sit and talk with my parents about the political and social issues of the day. He sounded very knowledgeable to me, but also adult and remote. He was a large, formidable man, and although I listened in fascination to his words, I felt as though it would take many years before I would be able to share anything with him, or he with me.

One afternoon when he arrived, my parents had gone out and I was the only one at home. He sat to wait for them in the dining room, the coolest room in the city house where we lived at the time. The house was bathed in the quiet so prevalent in the tropics during the hottest part of the day. As usual, I was buried in a book. Then my grandfather Modesto called my name and motioned for me to sit on his lap. I was surprised by this gesture of warmth and affection since I was almost ten years old and especially since he never asked any of us to sit by him. Yet I welcomed the invitation to become closer to this man who seemed so remote and yet so wise. I never knew what prompted him to tell me the story that came next, but I have always treasured it.

"You probably know that I was once very wealthy," he began. As I nodded, he continued. "I was only twelve years old when I left Spain to come to Cuba. My father had died, and since my oldest brother was arrogant and mean, I decided to leave my home at La Coruña. I roamed the port until someone pointed out a ship that was about to sail, and I managed to hide aboard. A sailor discovered me shortly after the ship set sail, but the captain said I should sail with them, and when we arrived at Havana he helped me get ashore. I searched for work, and fortunately I was taken in by the owner of a hardware store. He worked me hard! I cleaned the store and helped with all kinds of odd jobs. I had to sleep in the storage room on some burlap sacks, but I learned the business well.

"One day a young American came into the store with a surprising machine that played music from round black disks. It was made in the United States and was called a gramophone. I was astonished and excited. Imagine a machine that could bring the great opera singer Enrique Caruso's voice into each home! I made arrangements with this man and set out to sell this new invention. Eventually I became the major representative in Cuba for RCA, the manufacturer, and traveled the island from end to end. I loved the land around Camagüey, and I saw how cattle could thrive on these fertile plains, so I bought some land. The land turned out to be even more valuable than I thought."

He paused. Even though I didn't know then the meaning of the word nostalgia, I know now that is exactly what I saw in his eyes. "The years passed," he continued. "I married your grandmother and we worked very hard. We had four sons and by now we were very wealthy. Then, she became ill. Since she was too ill to be moved, I had a doctor come to the hacienda. But although he did all he could, she did not improve.

"One evening, an exhausted horse and rider galloped up to the hacienda. The rider was my business manager in Havana. He'd ridden at top speed from the train station in Camagüey, and close up, I saw that it was not only exhaustion that marked his face, but panic. 'You must come to Havana immediately,' he urged me. 'There is a financial crisis and the economy is collapsing. The president of your bank sent me to warn you. It's urgent that you travel to the capital in person to withdraw all of your money or else it will be lost.' I considered this alarming news as the man looked at me impatiently, unable to understand why I wasn't ordering fresh horses to take us to the train. But was I going to leave your ill grandmother?"

He paused again and I saw that the look in his eyes had changed. This new feeling was one I recognized even as a child. My own eyes must have looked the same the day I found a bird, which only a short while ago had been alive, lying dead in our backyard.

My grandfather finished his story: "I did not return with him. Your grandmother did not get well, and the economy did collapse before I could get my money out of the bank. I was no longer a rich man. But I was there by your grandmother's side until the end, and I held her hand in mine as she passed away." I looked down at my grandfather's big hand, which was covering my own. And then I knew I would not have to wait until I grew up to understand my grandfather Modesto.

There is no one alive today who remembers María Rey Paz, the grandmother I never knew. And there are probably very few people living who remember my quiet but steadfast grandfather, Modesto. Yet, I am certain that these ancestors of mine live on in my children, who have known from a young age what choices to make when loved ones are concerned.

❖ QUESTIONS TO INITIATE THE DIALOGUE ❖

 DESCRIPTIVE PHASE. To promote understanding of the message of the book.

1. Why did the author begin by describing the contrast between her maternal and paternal families? How does that enhance the understanding of her grandfather?

2. The grandfather's story is told in the first person; that is, the author has presented the story in the grandfather's own voice. How does this affect the story?

3. For the author, it is important to look in her grandfather's eyes to understand his feelings. How did that influence you as a reader?

 PERSONAL INTERPRETIVE PHASE **To promote self-expression of feelings and emotions and to relate the book content to the reader's experience**

1. The grandfather was faced with a very difficult decision. Have you ever had to make a difficult decision? What helped you decide? How did you feel about the choice you made?

2. What has helped you live through the loss of a dear person or a beloved pet?

 CRITICAL/MULTICULTURAL/ANTI-BIAS PHASE **To promote higher-thinking skills. To encourage reflection on equality, inclusion, respect, and justice in order to achieve peace.**

1. Why do you think the author wrote this piece?

2. Why do you think the author chose to finish with a reference to her own children?

 CREATIVE TRANSFORMATIVE PHASE **To lead to a creative, constructive action leading to understanding and respect for others, and to become more responsible for bringing about positive change in our own reality.**

1. Think of someone to whom you would like to express your gratitude. How would that person feel if you wrote a piece about him or her?

2. Once your piece is finished, it will be a gift to many: to you, to the person you have written about, and to others. Who might appreciate reading your piece?

❖ UNVEILING THE AUTHOR WITHIN ❖

TEACHERS AS AUTHORS

 BOOK 42 **Creating the Teacher's Book: *A Person in My Life***

The nature of this book is highly personal. The person you choose to write about is someone only you can select. In addition, the relationships teachers write about vary greatly from one educator to another.

The books produced for this theme are the most numerous in our archives. They are also the most diverse and, in many cases, the most meaningful. We would like to offer you a few examples of the many books that have moved us deeply, although we will not be able to do justice to the many others we keep and treasure.

As with everything we have offered you in this book, these models are merely a point of departure. There are probably several individuals in everyone's life who merit our attention as writers and who would welcome a book written about them by us. Not surprisingly, after writing their first book about a person in their lives, many teachers have later authored several others.

Grandparents

Grandparents often play an important role in the lives of children, and many of our participants have created beautiful books to show their appreciation and special regard for a grandparent. One of the first books we received on this theme was created by María Teresa Campa. *Mi abuelita y el abrigo rojo que me regaló (My Grandmother and the Red Coat She Gave Me)* is a tribute to the author's paternal grandmother and the influence this small, quiet, but powerful woman had on her life. The pages are illustrated with striking black-and-white photographs of the grandmother and the author as a child. Recalling the stories her grandmother told her, her

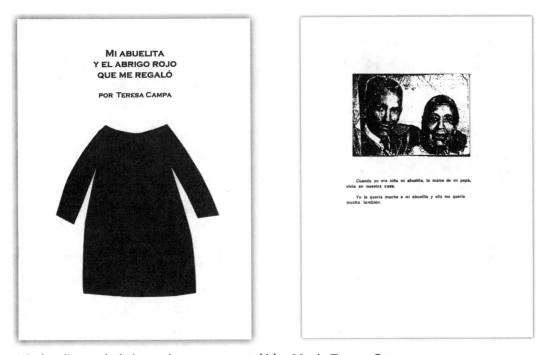

Mi abuelita y el abrigo rojo que me regaló by María Teresa Campa
Reprinted by permission.

Nonna carissima by Valerie Andriola

Reprinted by permission of Valerie Andriola Púrpura, P.O. Box 1574, Santa Teresa, NM, 88008.

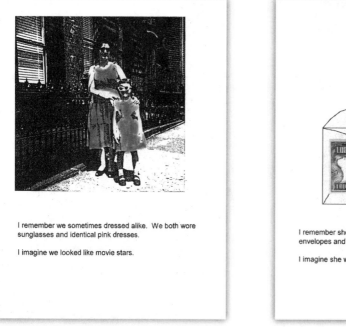

I remember we sometimes dressed alike. We both wore sunglasses and identical pink dresses.

I imagine we looked like movie stars.

I remember she wrote letters. She then put money in the envelopes and sat on them before she mailed them to Italy.

I imagine she was very generous.

All about Anna by Nina Montepagani

Reprinted by permission of Nina Montepagani, Enlarged City School District of Troy, Core Curriculum and Instruction, 1950 Burdett Ave., Troy, NY, 12180.

love of reading, and her willingness to let her grandchild comb her long hair, Terry Campa ends each page with the refrain, "I loved my grandmother very much and she loved me, too."

The last page concludes in a similar fashion. But after having read so many times "I loved my grandmother very much and she loved me, too" in the past tense, the reader is delightfully surprised to encounter: "I love my grandmother very much and she loves me, too." This grandmother, who died more than twenty years ago, is present before us through the evocative power of the written word.

Valerie Andriola tells the story of her grandmother in the form of a letter. Each page of the book, ***Nonna carissima (Beloved Grandma),*** presents one paragraph of the letter illustrated by a photograph. As Valerie's grandmother's life unfolds, the grandmother's love for her granddaughter becomes evident. To give the book a sense of permanence, Valerie pasted each page onto cardboard and laminated it. The use of lace paper doilies as background for the inner pages, and of real lace, rhinestones, and decorative pearls on the outside cover (see p. 218), are also expressions of how much her grandmother means to the author, and of Valerie's willingness to honor this connection.

Some of our memories are made up of small details, others of an overall feeling. How much did we understand as children about what went on in the lives of the adults around us? How much can a small granddaughter understand about the depths of her grandmother's experiences of forging a life in a new land and leaving part of her heart behind?

Nina Montepagani from Troy, New York, gives us an extraordinary portrait of her mother by combining the facts she remembers from the past with her current thoughts and feelings (shown on p. 218 and reprinted below).

All about Anna *By Nina Montepagani*

For Julia and Joseph,
that they may remember their grandmother
through their mother's memories

❖ ❖ ❖

I remember she wore turquoise.
I imagine she looked lovely,

❖ ❖ ❖

I remember we went to Coney Island and I wandered away. I sat in a room with the other "lost" children of the day. Mammima soon came.
I imagine she held me close.

❖ ❖ ❖

I remember sitting next to her at work. I played with a mountain of buttons as she sewed them on coats. It was a very hot and noisy place around the corner from home.
I imagine she was exhausted.

❖ ❖ ❖

I remember she wrote letters. She then put money in the envelopes and sat on them before she mailed them to Italy.
I imagine she was generous.

❖ ❖ ❖

I remember she knew a lot about the weather. One day, as she was ironing she taught me a poem that would make the rain disappear so I could go out to play.

  Piove, piove,
  Il bambino coglie un fiore.
  Goglie uno per Gesú,
  E poi, non piove piu!!

It worked!
I imagine she knew it was a sun shower.

❖ ❖ ❖

I remember we sometimes dressed alike. We both wore sunglasses and identical pink dresses.
I imagine we looked like movie stars.

❖ ❖ ❖

I remember she taught me to print my name. I wrote *Nina Americana*.
I imagine she laughed.

❖ ❖ ❖

I remember I was in kindergarten when I was told she had gone to prepare meals for God because she was such a good cook. I was given a rose to say good-bye.
I imagine I'll see her again.

Reprinted by permission of Nina Montepagani, Enlarged City School District of Troy, Core Curriculum and Instruction, 1950 Burdett Ave., Troy, NY, 12180.

Parents

Parents can be some of the most important influences in a person's life. When presented with the invitation to write about a person in their lives, teachers often respond by creating moving books about their parents.

While Laurie Wellman read her book *I Remember Sam* (shown on p. 221 and reprinted on p. 222) during a training workshop in Troy, New York, the audience listened spellbound. The dedication created a tone of mystery, which was not fully solved until the revealing ending.

He taught me how to swim and fish and how to write a song.
He carried me on his shoulders when the road became too long.

He read a hundred thousand books; wrote many of his own.
An English teacher all his life; the smartest man I've known.

We observed his latest birthday just a few short months ago.
He is with us but he's not, and what he's thinking we don't know.

We observed my father's birthday, blew out candles and went on.
But it's really not a party when the honored guest is gone.

ALZHEIMER'S ASSOCIATION

I Remember Sam by Laurie Wellman

Reprinted by permission of Dr. Laurie Wellman, 21 Linda Ln., Schenectady, NY, 12309.

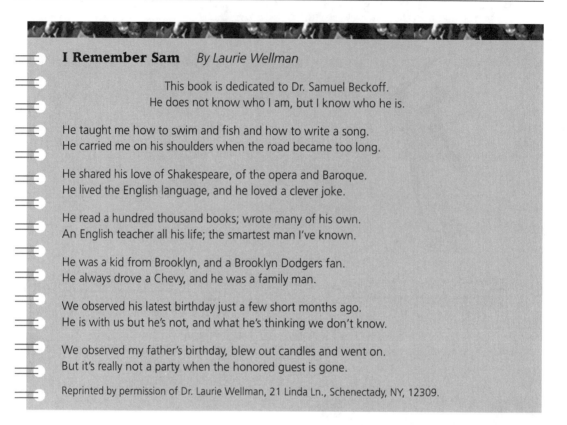

I Remember Sam   *By Laurie Wellman*

This book is dedicated to Dr. Samuel Beckoff.
He does not know who I am, but I know who he is.

He taught me how to swim and fish and how to write a song.
He carried me on his shoulders when the road became too long.

He shared his love of Shakespeare, of the opera and Baroque.
He lived the English language, and he loved a clever joke.

He read a hundred thousand books; wrote many of his own.
An English teacher all his life; the smartest man I've known.

He was a kid from Brooklyn, and a Brooklyn Dodgers fan.
He always drove a Chevy, and he was a family man.

We observed his latest birthday just a few short months ago.
He is with us but he's not, and what he's thinking we don't know.

We observed my father's birthday, blew out candles and went on.
But it's really not a party when the honored guest is gone.

Reprinted by permission of Dr. Laurie Wellman, 21 Linda Ln., Schenectady, NY, 12309.

On the last page, without any additional commentary, Laurie inserted the logo of the Alzheimer's Association.

Laurie Wellman has since shared with us that, shortly after creating this book, her father's battle with Alzheimer's disease came to an end. She also expressed how meaningful the book had been for her relatives in their grief over this outstanding man.

As a side note, we want to mention that this is one of the few instances we have seen in which clip art has been successfully incorporated to complement the text.

What a parent does for a living is not what determines our appreciation for or admiration of them. Instead, it is their love and nurturing, as well as the lessons about life we receive from them, that sustain us throughout our lives.

If parents' presence can be a source of well-being and support, their absence can be very difficult for children to bear. Dealing with her father's absence after a divorce is the topic of ***Always in My Heart*** by Kristina Hou (see p. 223). Written with great sensitivity and illustrated with delicate watercolors, the book conveys the special relationship between father and daughter by focusing on the simple details of everyday life. The child crawls into her father's empty closet the day he leaves to smell the scent of his clothes. She overcomes her sense of loss by treasuring her memories of simple things. Some of the memories she shares with us are of drawing faces on their hands

Always in My Heart by Kristina Hou

"so we could talk to each other in funny voices," and of sharing "long, lazy Sunday afternoons watching the football game together."

The final reflection will be important for the many children who have also experienced the pain of separation: "Now that I'm a grown-up, I realize a lot of things I didn't understand when I was a girl. I know my dad didn't mean to hurt me when he left, it was something he had to do. It wasn't because he didn't love me or because I was bad."

Children

The experience of bearing and raising children can awaken in parents the most tender feelings. Not surprisingly, their own children are often the subjects of teachers' books. Books can be a wonderful way to greet children who are just arriving in the world. Expectant mothers who have attended our courses have often begun writing a book to their unborn child as a welcoming gift.

Parenting also has its difficulties and challenges. It is hard to imagine greater pain than having a child die. The need to cope with this pain, and the possibility of finding solace in her memories, led Nancy Silver-Alvarez to create the book ***Blue Water/Agua azul,*** a poetic account of her son's death while river-rafting in the rain forest.

Siblings

The brothers and sisters with whom we shared our childhood can sometimes be significant influences on who we later become. Reflecting on their lives can serve as a mirror in which we see aspects of ourselves. In ***Mi hermana la electricista/My Sister the***

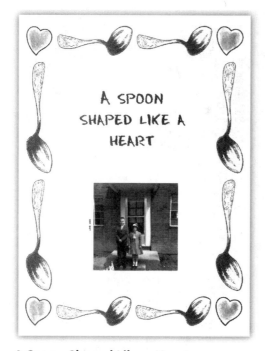

A Spoon Shaped Like a Heart
by Andrew L. Coffey

Reprinted by permission of Andrew Coffey, Pleasant
Valley Elementary School, Schenectady, NY, 12303.

Electrician by Miriam Parcel, the author describes how her sister chose a nontraditional career. Although the book is presented as a nonfiction description of the process of becoming an electrician, Miriam's admiration for her sister shines through each page.

A Spoon Shaped Like a Heart by Andrew L. Coffey tells us about the author's sister and a recent experience in her life. It also portrays the long process of two siblings forging a relationship in a large family of eight children, whose widowed mother struggled to make ends meet.

People Who Have Inspired Us

In life's adventure, there are no set rules. The protagonist of *Half Full* by Victoria Teshin-Anderson (shown on p. 225 and reprinted on pp. 225–226) would hardly be labeled a successful person by many people's standards. He did not distinguish himself by making money or by having a glamorous career. But this simple man, who struggled throughout his life to keep a menial job and a roof over his head, became an inspiration to the author as a result of his positive outlook on life.

A farm kid from north of Pittsburgh,

His education did not come from books.

Unemployment was not uncommon

But his conscience kept him from
working with crooks

Half Full by Victoria Teshin-Anderson

Reprinted by permission of Victoria Teshin-Anderson,
8 Chicory Ln., Huntington, NY, 11743.

Half Full   *told by Victoria Teshin-Anderson*

As sun was setting on the lake
And folks were gathering on their porches,
A slender shadow of a man emerged
Illumined by flickering torches.

How is it going, Howard?
Never had a bad day in my life.

A farm kid from north of Pittsburgh,
His education did not come from books.
Unemployment was not uncommon
But his conscience kept him
   from working with crooks.

How is it going, Howard?
Never had a bad day in my life.

We had heard some stories of his wife.
It was getting harder to keep her job.
He loved her so much, but to see such pain,
It would make a weaker man sob.

How is it going, Howard?
Never had a bad day in my life.

His only son had been to jail,
He confided to those on the lake.
The daughter-in-law left with his grandson
He was never to know his namesake.

How is it going, Howard?
Never had a bad day in my life.

Unpretentious and eloquent with a dry sense
    of humor
Like the day he thought he had died
His friends said he had a calm about him
Though he had to be screaming inside.

How is it going, Howard?
Never had a bad day in my life.

I remember the time I met Howard.
I was wallowing in my daily strife,
When I heard someone ask . . .

How is it going, Howard?
Never had a bad day in my life.

Reprinted by permission of Victoria-Teshin-Anderson, 8 Chicory Ln., Huntington, NY, 11743.

STUDENTS AS AUTHORS

Students' Individual Writing

Monica Martínez, a student in Colma, California, turned her admissions essay to Immaculate Conception Academy High School into a book (shown on p. 227). In a heartfelt narrative, Monica describes her admiration and love for her immigrant mother,

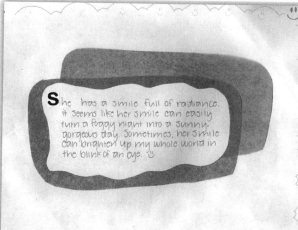

She has a smile full of radiance. It seems like her smile can easily turn a foggy night into a sunny, gorgeous day. Sometimes, her smile can brighten up my whole world in the blink of an eye. ☺

A Person in My Life
by Monica Martínez

Reprinted by permission of Vicky and Monica Martínez, 411 C St., Colma, CA, 94014.

who successfully overcame divorce and supported her family during a period of great hardship. Here is an excerpt from Monica's book:

A Person in My Life   *By Monica Martínez*

> To my mom and my family.
> They are always there for me.

She brought me into this world. Ever since, she has loved me in such a way that at times I ask myself how can someone love another being the way she loves me?

She is my light. Whenever I'm emotionally lost, she guides me and helps me find my way.

She has a kind and generous heart. No matter where she is or how she is feeling, she will always lend a helping hand.

She, the most important person in my life, is my mother. I don't know if you have noticed, but she means the world to me!

About the Author

Monica Martínez is 15 years old. She is currently a freshman in high school. She attends Immaculate Conception Academy in San Francisco. She likes to read and write. She also likes to play the guitar and enjoys watching soccer games on TV.

Reprinted by permission of Vicky and Monica Martínez, 411 C. St., Colma, CA, 94014.

BOOK 43 **Creating a Book: *A Person in My Life***

After sharing your book with your students, discuss with them the value of creating a book about someone who has been an influential person in their life. Then guide them in brainstorming some of the people they might write about. You may want to suggest that they make a list of names and write a sentence about each one before deciding who they would like to choose as the subject for their book.

You may also want to encourage dialogue among students as part of their preparation for writing. Once they have selected an individual, encourage them to make lists of:

◆ The qualities they remember about the person
◆ The significant memories they have about the person
◆ The facts they know about the person
◆ The specific ways in which the person has influenced their lives
◆ Anecdotes that would make the person come alive in the eyes of the reader

In some cases, it may be appropriate to interview the person they are choosing to write about, or to interview other members of the family who know or knew that person.

BOOK 44   Writing a Biography: *Someone I Admire*

As an alternative to writing about someone they know personally, older students might choose to write a biography about a historical figure. Invite them to pick someone who has contributed to the arts, science, or literature, or simply someone they admire. The person need not be famous and might be totally unknown, but the student must have a reason for choosing that person.

Even if students have chosen a living person, someone they know and are able to interview, this does not diminish the need to do research. Ask them to use more than one source in their research in order to explore the different ways in which a person can be portrayed by others. Even if they are writing about someone no one else has previously written about, they can still interview different people who know that person in order to explore a variety of perspectives.

Encourage students to do research in the following areas:

◆ *Historical times.* What were the most salient historical events throughout the life of this person during his or her childhood, youth, adulthood, and later years?

◆ *Geographical environments.* Where was this person born? Where did the person live during the different periods of his or her life? What kinds of environments did he or she encounter?

◆ *Social conditions.* What were the social conditions of the life of this person? Were the parents well-to-do, professionals, working class, rural workers? Did the family experience any economic hardship at any time? What effects did any of this have on this person?

◆ *Jobs, occupations.* What did this person do for a living? How did he or she arrive at that position? What kinds of responsibilities did that work entail?

Encourage students to focus on a particular event or sets of events, or a particular aspect of the personality of the individual, to make the biography focused and interesting. Remind them to include an explanation of why they chose to write about this particular individual.

STUDENTS AND PARENTS AS AUTHORS

Marilyn M. Pawlovich introduced us to a new perspective on this theme. An educational consultant and reader of children's books, Marilyn is also a devoted parent. As a parent helper in her daughter's first-grade class in Pleasanton, California, she asked her daughter's teacher for permission to conduct an activity in which the students in the class would write collectively the teacher's biography.

First, the students were guided in a brainstorming session to determine what they would like to know about their teacher. The students dictated questions that Mrs. Pawlovich wrote on chart paper. For the next session, the children worked in cooperative groups. Each group received a few questions, cut into sentence strips, one for each member of the group.

Each cooperative group had an interview session scheduled with the teacher over the next few days. Mrs. Pawlovich sat with the students and the teacher in each of the sessions. She tape-recorded the students' questions and the teacher's answers.

Two facing pages were created for each question. On one page, Mrs. Pawlovich transcribed the teacher's answers. That page was illustrated with photos provided by the teacher. On the facing page, the students wrote their teacher's answer as they had understood it, using their own words and illustrating the page with their own drawings.

Mrs. Pawlovich then scanned the pages to make a copy of the delightful book for each of the students' families. At the end of the book, she included two pages to describe the book's authors. Each participating child had a scanned photograph and a space to write something about himself or herself.

This collaboration between an experienced mother, a young teacher, and a whole class of students resulted in a delightful book. *Ms. Peters' Adventures,* featuring the names of all the student authors on the cover, is now a favorite of both students and parents. We suspect it will continue to be a favorite of Ms. Peters's for many years to come.

This kind of interview-biography can be developed in a variety of ways depending on the age and ability of the students. Each small group of students can write a list of questions about a specific area of their teacher's life, such as the teacher's favorite authors, books, films, sports, foods, activities, and friends. Students may also be interested in learning about the teacher's family, special occasions, funny anecdotes, memorable journeys, and moments of struggle, achievement, and success.

Students can also collaborate on the writing, design, and illustrations for the book. Although this project can be viewed from different angles, the most significant aspect is that it will provide opportunities for students to learn about their teacher as a human being and reflect on their teacher's life experiences.

ADDITIONAL EXAMPLES OF BOOKS AUTHORED BY TEACHERS, STUDENTS, AND FAMILIES

Books by Teachers

In addition to the many books previously mentioned, inspired by grandparents, parents, siblings, spouses, and children, educators have also found it fun to write books about other individuals, perhaps not so closely related, who have somehow inspired or intrigued them. One such book was written by Tracy Hefferman, who has researched the life of an educator from San Francisco, focusing on her experience as a child in the Japanese relocation camps during World War II. The book *Sansei Girl: The Nancy Yoshihara Mayeda Story* has gone through several revisions as Tracy has continued to research the topic, discovering more information. The first time she shared the book with Mrs. Yoshihara, Tracy discovered that her initial poetic rendition was perhaps more literary than the reality had been, and she became aware of the small nuances that may escape us when writing about people of another time or another culture.

In contrast to Tracy's efforts, Bobbi Kyle was free to take as much license as she wished because her book *With Nails and Cord and Leather* has only a very slight basis in real life and is more the product of her imagination. Because this book is an excellent model of how a life story can be told, and to show how the process of authorship can take many paths, we chose to include it here. Although Bobbi's Author's Note appears at the end of her book, we use it here to frame the story.

With Nails and Cord and Leather   *by Bobbi Kyle*

To my loving family, from Mom and Dad, Cindy,
Robyn, Mitch and the kids—all the way back
to William Whelple . . .
for always having the courage to dream.

❖ ❖ ❖

Author's Note

This story came about after I began researching my family's history. My mother's family can be traced back to the Whipple line, that came to New England in 1632 and settled Ispwich, Massachusetts. Looking back further, however, we have discovered an existing will for a William Whelple (a variation from Whipple). Filed in the Court of Hastings on 10 February 1385, his will reads:

The will of William Whelple, cordwainer, to be buried in
The church of St. Alban, in Wodstrete by Isabella his
Wife. Among other bequests, he leaves 8 doz. Pairs of best
Shoes to be given to the poor. If there be that number
In his house at the time of his decease; if not then so many
as are in his house at that time are to be distributed.

Curious about why a simple man could possess so many pairs of shoes when he was not a cobbler by trade led me to create this tale about having a dream and finding a way to help it come true.

Isabella walked alone through the streets of St. Albans. The wind from the North Sea blew hard as she gathered her scratchy wool wrap tightly around her shoulders. A basket of warm, sweet bread dangled from her arm. A dinner that would warm her belly, although her heart felt cold and empty.

Passing through the front door of her humble stone cottage, she glanced up at the black cotton swag draping the portal. "God rest ye, William," she sighed, her hot breath fogging in the night air.

Alice and Little Will jumped up at the sight of their mum, leaving their chores behind. Alice's broom made a loud crack as the wooden handle smacked against the stone floor. They ran to her, hugging her legs through her skirts. "Children, children," Isabella scolded, "it is only your poor mother." But she smiled and pulled them close. They had so little time, she mused sadly. So little time to learn to love their father as she did. So little time to understand all the good and hope in his frail, frail heart. She could see William in their eyes.

Her mind wandered back. How young and mischievious he had been, that glowing afternoon over ten years before when he had kissed her on the way home from chapel. "The world is mine, Isabella," he had screamed out to no one. "And I want you to see it with me. I want to walk and journey until my shoes wear thin as glass." But he was a poor cordwainer's son and the world seemed so far away. She remembered the light in his eyes, though, and she could see it still as she tucked Alice and Little Will beneath the downy quilt given to her on their wedding day.

"Finally, time to myself," she thought, lighting a candle which flickered in the cottage. She took up Alice's dress to mend, but even as her hands grew still, her mind raced with thoughts of her husband. She remembered the walks and the elaborate plans he had made for traveling across the sea to France and Rome and to Constantinople and the bazaars to smell the spices. She too could almost smell the saffron, the curry, the sweet cardamom. She hadn't even known what they smelled like, but like their names, she knew they would be foreign and exotic on her tongue. "Follow your bliss," he would say again and again, tightly squeezing her plump hand.

"He would have made it too," she thought, never letting her doubts steal the passion for travel from his heart. "He would have." But although filled with love and hope and passion, his heart grew weaker as his dreams grew stronger. It was almost as though his heart couldn't hold all that he could dream.

It was after his first bad spell and after the doctor had told him he would have to be happy to make St. Albans his world that she found him in the shed in the middle of the night. The cordwainer wanting to be cobbler. "What are you doing, William?" she had asked, pulling a blanket over his shoulders.

"Making shoes," he answered staring at the boot sole that sat on the bench before him.

"But we all have perfectly fine shoes," she replied confused.

"I know," he answered, slowly, thinking of the places where the shoes would go, the miles that would be walked, the places they would see.

Isabella took up her mending, almost believing that he was back in the shed that very evening, nailing and tying cords, and molding leather. Always a talented cordwainer, his skills were in building wagons and in working the ropes that held them together. But why shoes, she had wondered. Why now? And why did he need to stay away from her and away from the warmth of the fire? But every night he had sat by the dim light for hours, and each morning he had gone blurry-eyed to work to bring home food for his family.

She sobbed silently by the fire, remembering the tired eyes that sat above his never-ending smile. Eyes that knew he was getting sicker and sicker, but never complained, never said it was unfair.

On that last night when he finally made his way to their bed, he held her tight. She had awakened to feel his arms around her and had kissed his rough hand. "Were you dreaming?" he asked.

"Yes," she answered quietly, "of such great places and amazing things." He held her close to him and spoke to whoever was listening, "If you cannot follow your dreams . . ." and he fell into a deep and final sleep.

Isabella dried new tears on the corner of her apron. Stirring the last log as the embers burnt out, she felt comfort in the darkness. She stood at the back door, looking out at the shed, its shadow on the grass cast by the February moon. She smiled when she thought back to the words read aloud in the Court of Hastings only a week before. Words from her husband's will:

Among other bequests, he leaves 8 dozen pairs
of best shoes to be given to the poor.

The people in the court had looked puzzled and amazed. "William had 96 pairs of shoes?" With a shrug, Master Thomas Baker had continued. . . . But Isabella hadn't shrugged. She said then as she will always say when she crawls into her bed at night:

If you cannot follow your dream,
make it possible for others to do so.

Reprinted by permission of Roberta Kyle, 12 Davies Pl. #1, Poughkeepsie, NY, 12601.

10

FROM YESTERDAY TO TOMORROW

The exploration of self can take multiple routes: We can discover our qualities and strengths, rekindle our dreams, see ourselves in relationship to others, and acknowledge the significance of our actions. But our exploration will not be complete without a historical perspective. The person we are today originated in a specific environment, nourished by certain foods, surrounded by the words and examples of others.

In the first teaching unit of this book, we worked with Eloise Greenfield's poem "I Am" to inspire poems about identity. In a similar vein, Linda Christiansen has developed an activity based on the poem "Where I'm From" by George Ella Lyon to engage her high schools students in reflection. The description of the process, and the poems written by her students, were published in the teachers' newspaper *Rethinking Schools* and are now reproduced in her excellent book *Reading, Writing and Rising Up: Teaching about Social Justice and the Power of the Written Word* (Christiansen, 2000).

We were fortunate to participate in a demonstration of this activity offered by Ms. Christiansen in an anti-bias education seminar in Hungary, where we were also presenting. Since then we have incorporated this activity in our seminars with excellent results. With gratitude to Ms. Christiansen, we are pleased to share with you this powerful activity.

Objectives

- To further the process of self-discovery by revisiting childhood memories in search of a better understanding of our roots.
- To acknowledge our origin and accept our past as a point of departure for our present and future.
- To give words to experiences we may not have yet explored or expressed.

Teachers	Students	Parents
Teachers are invited to: ■ Visualize the places of their childhood and the people who influenced their childhood. ■ Follow the suggested model to create their own **"Where I Come From"** poem. ■ Use the poem to create a finished product in book form. ■ Share their book with students and parents and encourage them to write their own books on a similar theme. ■ Help students create their own poems.	Students are invited to: ■ Read and discuss **"Where I Come From"** poems. ■ Dialogue about the concepts of roots and immigration. ■ Write their own poems and share them with the class. ■ Illustrate their poem and expand on it by searching for photos of their childhood home and its surroundings, as well as for additional information about their childhood. ■ Share their process and their final product with their families and encourage their parents or caretakers to write a similar poem.	Parents or caretakers are invited to: ■ Receive and read a copy of the teacher's poem. ■ Dialogue with their children about the parents' childhoods, the places they lived, the everyday experiences they encountered, and the people who were significant in their youth. ■ Create their own *Where I Come From* books.

✤ UNVEILING THE AUTHOR WITHIN ✤

TEACHERS AS AUTHORS

Although they may take just a few minutes to write, the poems resulting from this activity can be exceptionally powerful. They bring to life the depth of feelings from childhood, feelings that often could not be fully understood or even accepted at that age. The process can move us deeply by awakening long-suppressed or forgotten memories, by evoking realities that no longer exist, and by enveloping the soul in nostalgia. It can also be powerfully reaffirming by allowing us to see clearly the wonderful person that the weak, frightened, or lonely child has become, the kind and generous person who follows a path created by others who have gone before, the courageous human being who never forgot the words said or the silent example.

This is Isabel's poem:

Where I Come From
F. Isabel Campoy

I come from a street that leads to the desert,
and from a house with balconies facing the sea.

I come from clothes drying under the sun,
and the smell of soap, of Mondays, of work.

I come from María and Diego,
peasants and poets, laborers of love.

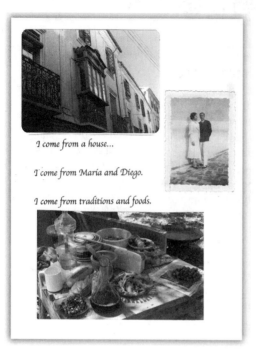

I come from a house...

I come from María and Diego.

I come from traditions and foods.

Where I Come From **by F. Isabel Campoy**
Reprinted by permission.

I come from jumping rope and playing marbles,
molding mud into cups and saucers, building castles in the sand.

I come from rice and fried chicken,
watermelon, tortillas y pan.

I come from "Be the best that you can be,"
from "Be proud of your origins" and "Never give up!"

I come from poverty and hard work,
from honor and pride.

I come from a country
that lost a war against itself and suffered
36 years of crime, of silence, of shame.

I come from the certainty of talking,
so that together we create new days of peace.

Full of compassion,
full of pride and pain,
I say:
    That is where I come from.

Reprinted by permission.

In the first stanza of her poem, Isabel goes back to the street where she lived as a child in Alicante, Spain, and remembers the whiteness of the chalklike earth in contrast to the blue Mediterranean Sea she could see from the balconies of her home. In the second stanza, she moves from the physical environment to the mood of the day and describes in a few words the unfolding of the daily routine.

Giving her mother's and father's names is important to Isabel. She wants them to be recognized as individuals. Then she manages to reveal a great deal of who they are through the image "laborers of love."

The next stanza, the fourth, is to remember the days of innocence—plays, games, handmade toys—and the dreams taking the form of castles in the sand. The fifth stanza tells about the meals served at the family table, offering an invitation to partake vicariously in their delight.

The words frequently said by her parents are still living truths for Isabel, and she shares them in the sixth stanza. This is followed by a stanza in which the author stands firmly upon the past, owns it with dignity, and finds her voice with pride.

The eighth and ninth stanzas address the social and political circumstances that surrounded her life; Isabel was born shortly after the Spanish Civil War and lived most of her youth under a dictatorship. She states her belief in the struggle to create a world of justice.

Isabel ends her poem with three words—*compassion, pride,* and *pain*—that the memories of the past have left within her heart and with one line of determination—the ownership of that past—as the starting point for what the future holds.

The poems teachers have written using this framework are as rich as their own diversity. We have heard and read poems about growing up in a concentration camp, about glorying in the beauty of a Micronesian island, about having no one to call mother or father, and about having been hurt by those who were so-called parents. We have seen poems so rich in flavorful food that the descriptions ate up most of the lines, as well as poems that made us want to laugh and play, but we have also shed silent tears along with those who have had the courage to share their pain.

Sometimes it has been hard for people to stand up and read aloud their own poems; in a few cases, their voices would break, and they had great difficulty finding the strength to read. But when they did, a new author was born and another life worth telling was revealed.

You will find several examples of these poems at the end of the chapter; here we would like to share four, the first three written the same day within the same class. That they differ so much speaks to the uniqueness of each human experience.

Where I'm From   *Peter Baird*

I am from sanctuaries bathed in dusty hues
From stain-glassed windows.
I am from church potlucks on Sunday afternoons,
Shepherd's Pie and Jell-o,

Ancient faces with ruby smiles.
I am from faith so as to move mountains
And bewilder young children.

I am from hell-raising rebellion generation
Make your own way or be swallowed.
I am from you can make a difference
But beware the warnings of Rap and Eldridge,
Malcolm and Franz—be no colonizer,
Destroy that part self/past.
I am from dreams lost with Jack, Martin and Bobby,
Even when imagined

I am from *quinceañeras* and Coyoacán,
Realismo mágico y el saber gozar la vida
I am from an emigrant's discovery of new worlds
And insight of the old.
I am bicultural, bilingual, bewildered
Stretched between worlds that offer par
Not whole, yet so much.

Reprinted by permission of Peter J. Baird, CSUS College of Education, 6000 J St., Sacramento, CA, 95819-6079.

Where I'm from There Was No Peace . . .   *Jon Bendich*

Where I'm from there was no peace
so I craved it
A middle child sometimes lost in the shuffle, I wanted to feel special
I yearned to find the place where I belonged
I'm still searching . . .

Where I'm from
only one person could be right
and everyone else was wrong
so I became contrary
always looking for another angle

I loved the sound of my grandparents' thick Jewish accent
I loved laughing with my father at Marx Brothers' movies
and at Lenny Bruce's records.
It transcended pop culture
so I knew it was real

I am from the house across the street from the hamburger stand
whose smoke my father hated
but whose hamburgers and milkshakes I loved
I hadn't yet learned how precious the veronicas and knishes were
that my grandmother used to bake

On the corner there was a laundry, and a liquor store around the block
my friend Barry Huey worked there with his family after school
whenever we would try and sneak some candy
Barry took delight in watching the fear on our faces
when their big German shepherd would jump up on the counter and snarl
I am from the era of innocence lost early
to drugs, sex, and rock 'n roll
'cept I liked r&b, soul, and afro-cuban
the sound of the drum called to me
and pulled at my soul like a spiritual magnet

I've spent my whole life trying to follow that rhythm
it spoke of a place I knew had to exist, somewhere
a place where I could be different and still accepted
I wonder if I'll ever find that place
where I'm from

Reprinted by permission.

I Come From   *Afriye Quamina*

I come from chocolate covered hearts that long existed in painful rejection and remembrances of soulless living as if life really counted.

I come from streets that toted dirty clothes on New Orleanean backs searching for a clothes line made of black children's sorrows.

I come from a house anointed by the parish priest (sacerdote), gre, gre ladies, and blessed by African cowboys wearing sidearms forged from metals found at the olduvai gorge.

I come from a house rich in scents blended by chef Justine mixed of high quality rice and beans, hot water cornbread, blackened catfish, stories of shrimp boat fiascos, and a kind of historical love that spanned the seasons.

I come from a people who rode tall in three window coupe pickups, drank rainwater under any reasonable condition, connected life to nature, searched for heaven in dreams, and knew richness and wealth were in the eyes of the children.

I come from the job of watching girls double dutch, tightly tucking that pure pearly marble between two fingers, climbing to the top of erector sets, turning checkers into chess and into spinners faster than string-pulled tops, and transforming pairs of brand new Wilson street skates into 2×4 nail scooters.

I come from food born of heaven's hands and kissed by the ten thousand mothers that miraculously heal external sores, tired feet, the monthly blues, kinky hair, straying husbands, bad debts, the lay away, ringworms, and the devil's winter ugliness.

I come from a mama's voice that says, "boy, don't let me call you by your middle name," and father's echo that reverberates, "as a man you got to cover the ground you walk on." And an auntie that recounts, "gimme some of that sweet sugar sugar pie," and an uncle that so wisely whispers, "here's a quarter, now don't go spending it all in one place. Be prudent." Black love ain't black at all. It's timeless and meant to embrace the heart and caress the soul.

I come from the wealth of spirit, the Knowledge that I am the reason for it all, and that black babies are made of God's literal best handiwork.

The next poem was written at a great geographical distance, in Guam. The realities it describes are very different than most of our experiences, and yet the significance of finding the voice to express one's roots is the same.

## Where I Come From	*By Silvina Taumomoc*

I come from an
    overhanging cliff
    a refuge from the overflowing river
    of Manñengon.

    I come from a canopy
    of open skies
    where bright stars
    are low enough to warm my heart
    because we could not light a fire.

    I come from the sunlit love
    of Pedro and Juanita,
    I am the seed,
    a little life growing
    in their warmth.

    Where I come from
    I did not learn to play
    before I learned to pray.

I come from where we live
on stinking fadang
provided by the grace of God
because without the fadang
I would starve.

I come from the desperate
Cries of Chamorro hearts
Saying over and over
"Santa Maria Nana Yuas
Tayuyuteham
Pago yan I oran,
¡finata mame!"

Where I come from
there surely is a heaven
for love, for hope,
one step away from death,
a minute from despair
one kiss away from hate.

I come from
the concentration camps.

Reprinted by permission.

The rich discussion that follows the presentation of books written by teachers becomes particularly meaningful because the protagonist is present and the topic is not only literary but also real. Issues of great formative value can be analyzed, creating a greater understanding of the world around us. When these teachers' books are taken home, the process of growth and reflection comes full circle.

 BOOK 45 **Creating the Poem and Book: *Where I Come From . . .***

Earlier in this chapter, we analyzed the way in which Isabel's poem was structured. You can create your own poem following this process. First, choose the phrase "I'm from. . . ." or "I come from . . ." You will use it to begin each stanza and give rhythm to the poem. Then, imagine yourself at a particular childhood age, perhaps six or seven, nine or ten, inside your home, and prepare to share what you see.

Now follow these prompts to create each stanza, always beginning with the chosen phrase:

1. List some of the most memorable items you see in your childhood home.
2. Now step outside. List what you see in your front yard, your sidewalk, the street, the neighborhood. This is your second stanza.
3. State the names of relatives, particularly those who link you to the past.

4. Write down any frequently-heard sayings and expressions. What are some of the phrases you heard again and again, those that would distinguish your family from others?

5. Name the foods and dishes that you recall from family gatherings, both daily meals and special treats.

6. Think of social, political, or educational ideas that were reinforced around you while you were growing up. Think of how these principles reflect in you as a person.

7. Name the place where your childhood memories are kept: either realistically (photo albums, diaries, boxes) or metaphorically (the branches of a particular tree, the shadow of a particular porch).

8. Think about the beginning and ending of your poem: where you are from, who you are, and where you are going.

After rereading your poem aloud, you will be able to make a final version to share with others. As mentioned earlier in this book, some teachers have preferred to create two versions of their poem, one to share with relatives and adult friends and a different one to share with their students.

Once the poem is created, it can be easily transformed into a book by selecting one line or stanza per page. The materials, size, binding, and illustration can all serve to support the message and help create a special atmosphere. Because the book is so personal, focusing on your own unique roots, it is difficult for clip art to do it justice. If the illustrations cannot add to the message, or do not help create the feeling the words suggest, it is better to do without them and to let the imagination of the reader or listener provide the images.

Alice Pickel, a teacher in Arizona, created her beautiful book using ripped-paper illustrations on colored paper. The illustrations are stylized, a mere suggestion, and work well in this case. We have included the text as well as reproductions of some of the pages so that you can admire the artwork.

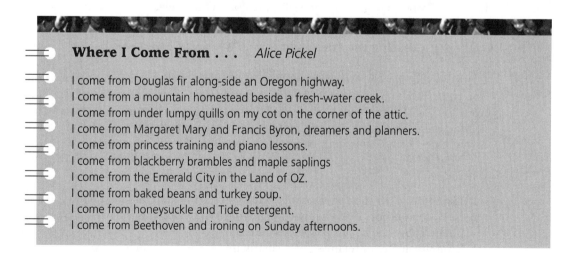

Where I Come From . . .   *Alice Pickel*

I come from Douglas fir along-side an Oregon highway.
I come from a mountain homestead beside a fresh-water creek.
I come from under lumpy quills on my cot on the corner of the attic.
I come from Margaret Mary and Francis Byron, dreamers and planners.
I come from princess training and piano lessons.
I come from blackberry brambles and maple saplings
I come from the Emerald City in the Land of OZ.
I come from baked beans and turkey soup.
I come from honeysuckle and Tide detergent.
I come from Beethoven and ironing on Sunday afternoons.

I come from Douglas fir along-side an Oregon highway.

I come from blackberry brambles and maple saplings.

I come from the promise that hard work and a good education will ensure the life I always dreamed of having.

ABOUT THE AUTHOR

Alice Pickel now lives in Phoenix, Arizona, where she teaches a multi-age bilingual class at Sunnyslope Elementary School. She is the mother of two successful children, and the wife to a wonderful husband. Alice is eagerly awaiting the arrival of her first grandchild early in 2000.

Alice loves to travel. Vacation pleasures find her swimming, snorkeling, shell hunting, and reading books.

***Where I Come From* by Alice Pickel**

Reprinted by permission of Alice Pickel, 9035 N. 37th Ave., Phoenix, AZ, 85051.

I come from callused hand and scholarly minds.

I come from the promise that hard work and a good education will ensure the life I always dreamed of having.

Reprinted by permission of Alice A. Pickel, 9035 N. 37th Ave., Phoenix, AZ, 85051.

Inspired by the idea of community building, a group of five teachers from New York decided to create a collective book using elements of the *I Am* and the *Where I Come From* activities. They called their book *The Common Thread* and decorated the cover and title page with photos of weavings. The inner pages are illustrated with photographs. This is the text:

The Common Thread

By Niria Álvarez, Shikha Dalal, Carole Keyes, Florence Pufothes, Lucía Rodríguez; We Five Publishing Co., *New York, June, 2000*

This book is dedicated to our students and their families

Shalom!   Éxito!

Mingalaba!   Om Shanti

❖ ❖ ❖

I am . . .

The temple bells
ringing peaceful tunes

A burning candle
that spreads aroma,
warmth and light

A dreamer,
a lover of God

The nurturing soul
of the universe

My mother's eyes

❖ ❖ ❖

I come from . . .

A dusty street laden with mango and flamboyán,
which leads to a rushing brook that meanders endlessly

a street that leads to the beach

I walk out of my apartment into an immense courtyard
filled with grass, swings and secret hiding places

a tree-lined street of hopscotch, stoop ball
and "brinca la tablita"

❖ ❖ ❖

I can still smell . . .

The fragrance of cooked rice and
warm spicy meat when I come home
from school on a rainy day

moro con bacalao, sancocho
y jalao de maní

matzoh ball soup,
    bagels and cigars

alcapurrias and steaming caldo gallego
and piping hot café negro

fish curry, mustard oil,
cumin and cardamon

❖ ❖ ❖

I was taught . . .

"Respect your elders.
Be modest."

"There are three advantages to being
orderly: it helps your memory,
it helps you not to waste time,
and it makes things last."

"It's just as easy to marry
a rich man as a poor man."

"Walk with your head high.
Be proud and compassionate."

"The test of steel is in the fire.
Women's lives are sheets of steel."

❖ ❖ ❖

Our lives are interwoven in an intricate and colorful tapestry in which the common thread that
binds us is our passion for the children.

Reprinted by permission.

STUDENTS AS PROTAGONISTS AND AUTHORS

BOOK 46 Creating in a Collective Setting the Poem:

Where I'm From . . .

After sharing your poem **"Where I Come From . . . "** and any of the examples provided that are appropriate for your students, explain to them that they also will create a similar poem. Prepare a quiet, safe atmosphere free of interruptions. If you wish, you can put on soft background music. You can also suggest that students close their eyes if the wish as you give each prompt.

Follow the prompts provided to scaffold the poem, as you did in writing your own. After each of the prompts, allow sufficient time for the students to write a line or a stanza before proceeding to the next prompt. At the end, offer time and space for the students to read their poems silently and to make revisions. At that point, you may want to share the prompts in writing, on an overhead or chart paper, to allow students to go back if they wish. Usually, spontaneity produces the most authentic images, but rewriting and polishing can help prepare the poem to be turned into a book.

Invite students to share their poems with a partner or in small groups. At an appropriate time, they will also be able to share them with the whole class. If possible, provide them with a microphone. Encourage positive comments from classmates after each reading. One way to prompt positive comments is for you to be the first to applaud. After the applause, ask the class: "Why did we enjoy this poem so much?" or "What was moving about this poem?" or "Which part of this poem did you enjoy the most?" or "How has this poem allowed us to get to know [the student] better?"

BOOK 47 Creating a Book Based on Reflections of One's Origins

Students can transform their **"Where I Come From . . . "** poems into books in a way similar to how Alice Pickel created her book. They can also use the poems as a starting point and focus on one aspect of particular significance to them.

Grace D. Meador, a ten-year-old student in Half Moon Bay, California, wrote a book titled *My Home* (shown on p. 247). Although it was not written following the format described above, it is a good example of how children can evoke memories. You will notice that Grace uses sensory experiences: sight, focusing on color; touch; sounds; and smells, all of which offer a vivid portrayal of her memories.

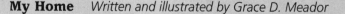

My Home   *Written and illustrated by Grace D. Meador*

This book is
dedicated to my mother
because she cares so much.

My Home
written and Illustrated
By Grace D. Meador

Grace Diana Meador is 10 years old. She likes to do Kuk-Sool-won, a martial art native to Korea.

This is her first book. She was born in Fridley Minnesota, lived there for three years then moved to California and still lives there. She is in fourth grade. Her favorite authors are Agatha Christie, JK Rowling, JRR. Tolkien and CS. Lewis. She enjoys writing and has fun in C7, Mrs Reno's English Language Arts class

My Home **by Grace D. Meador**

This book is also
dedicated to my father
because he helps her care.

Once I lived in a different home, in a different place, on a street called Beach Avenue. Maybe you know it, but I know it differently than you.

I used to live in a house as white as snow with purple plumlike wisteria and lavender daisies.

On the small red brick patio there was a picnic table and around the patio there was a cedar plank fence on which grew a yellow and white honeysuckle.

Sometimes we had tea there.

The swift night air closed in and brought fog. When there was fog it felt like being inside a cloud and smelled like there had just been a thunderstorm.

The language was of the calling birds, rocking waves, and the white foam breaking on the beach as the smell of pancakes tinted the air.

I heard the rain falling on the roof, the waves lapping up on the beach. Together, these melodies put me to sleep.

I smelled warm summer evenings and cool winter mornings.

I felt the rough carpet as I bumped down the stairs.

I remember tasting sweet as sugar honeysuckle and smelling the cool salty air that drifted out from the sea. I can still taste the sun sweet strawberries and vine riped tomatoes.

I recall the feel of the ocean air on my lips. Rushing past my hands and my head. We found small creatures at a beach nearby.

I remember the touch of the patio fence that was as bumpy as the back of a turtle's shell, the geckoes that stayed under the fallen leaves and the hidden toadstools.

When I see my street I remember all these wonderful and awe filled things.

And my old street is just a little place in the world.

Grace Diana Meador is 10 years old. She likes to do Kuk-Sool-Won, a martial art native to Korea. This is her first book. She was born in Fridley, Minnesota, lived there for three years then moved to California and still lives there. She is in fourth grade. Her favorite authors are Agatha Christie, J. K. Rowling, J. R. R. Tolkien and C. S. Lewis. She enjoys writing and has fun in C7, Mrs. Reno's English Language Arts class.

Reprinted by permission of the parents of Grace Diana Meador, 1121 Miramonts St., Half Moon Bay, CA, 94019.

PARENTS OR CARETAKERS AS EDUCATORS AND AUTHORS

Many teachers have chosen to include their poem alongside the poems written by the students in a *Where I Come From* anthology to be sent home to the families. Then they have asked the parents or caretakers to write similar poems to create a parents' anthology. Some teachers have chosen to make the anthology with contributions from all three sets of authors: teacher, students, and parents. In this way, the process has come full circle.

BOOK 48 *I Am on My Way*

As a sequel to the book *Where I Come From . . . ,* we have frequently suggested to teachers that they write and guide a book titled *I Am on My Way.* Because of the reflective nature of the process suggested by this book, it is essential that all aspects of time be recognized.

Some books, such as the *I Am* book, the acrostics, and the ABC book, are usually set in the present, grounded in the definition of "what is." Other books, such as *I Wasn't Always, A Person in My Life,* and *Childhood Memories,* are rooted in the past, exploring how the present came to be. Other books, such as *Our Goals and Our Dreams,* embody the nature of transformation, moving from what is today to what has yet to be. This movement forward can also be brought about after writing about *Where I Come From . . .* moving to *Where I Am Going. . . .*

Our students and their parents need to be invited to dream of a better tomorrow, to visualize the persons they want to become, and to set expectations for what they want to make happen. By sharing our life dreams, we build solidarity and take the first step toward making those dreams come true. Remembering Paulo Freire's words, "To say the right word is to change the World," we offer you this concluding poem. Let your mind soar and describe the future as the path upon which you are setting forth.

I Am on My Way
F. Isabel Campoy

I am on my way
and all that is unnecessary
must be left behind.

With me comes my inheritance
of parents, culture, language
and the right measure of pride.

I don't need to carry
anymore the guilt, fear, silence
that filled the pockets of my mind.

I am on my way to becoming
twenty, fifty, eighty,
knowing that life is precious, and is still mine.

I am on my way to tomorrow
holding hands with magic and its promises.

I am going there,
and not even I, will stop me.

Reprinted by permission.

EXTENDING AUTHORSHIP BEYOND THE CLASSROOM

✦ AUTHORS' FAIRS SHOWCASING THE WORK ✦ OF TEACHERS, STUDENTS, AND FAMILY MEMBERS

A group of teachers from Miami-Dade, Florida, who participated in a Summer Institute with us in 1996 decided that the significance of the authorship taking place in their classrooms deserved to be shared with the community. For several years now, they have been conducting authors' fairs showcasing the work of teachers, students, and family members.

To make the experience more meaningful, the teachers select a different school each month. At that school, the work of the students and their families is displayed, along with the work of the entire group of teachers, whether or not they teach in that school. By attending the fairs in one another's schools, the teachers lend support and add prestige to the event. Some children and families may also choose to attend a fair at another school, particularly if their teacher will be present.

The fairs are enriched by posters sporting proverbs and inspirational quotes that the teachers have created and illustrated. The posters have been laminated so they travel easily from school to school without getting damaged.

The teachers have also created profiles of themselves as authors, as well as a list of the book titles that they, their students, and the students' families have created. These profiles and lists are displayed prominently alongside the actual copies of the books.

The evening program includes readings of the authored books. Teachers read some of their own writing and some of the writing of their students, and students read some of their own writing as well as writing done by their relatives and their teachers. Or, alternatively, family members and students may read together. Each of these events is a true celebration of authorship and leadership.

✦ PUBLISHING OUTSIDE THE CLASSROOM ✦

Many teachers who have discovered the joy of writing and the power of words have approached us with questions about how to publish with a publishing house. If this is also something in which you are interested, there are many excellent books devoted to this process. Some are listed below for you to consult. In addition, we will gladly share a few thoughts with you.

◆ **First of all, follow your dream and don't give up.** You have already heard that it is difficult to publish. But although this is true, if you dream of being published, do not give up. There are many paths to reach your goal.

◆ **Understand the complexity involved in being a professional, published author.** Teachers often look at a published book and wonder: "Why is this book in print? My classroom-made book is much better than this one." And often this is true. But there is more to being a published author than writing a good book. The field of literature for children and adolescents is a complex world. Many people are involved in the decision to publish a book. Once the book is published, there are requirements and expectations on the part of the publisher, who expects authors to promote and support their writing. Authors belong to associations and writing groups; spend time at conferences and with editors; go to book fairs, bookstore, and library readings; visit schools and community organizations; and find many other ways of promoting their writing. It is a full-time job.

◆ **Protect your manuscript through copyright.** Many people have expressed concern about how to protect a manuscript and how to obtain a copyright. In order to copyright your materials you must send an original copy to the Library of Congress (check their address in any library) with a check. Be patient; sometimes it takes up to a year to receive a response.

◆ **Remember that there are many ways of getting published.** If you have written something that is important to you, find a way to get it published. There are various alternatives:

• **Self-publishing.** The ability today to design a book on the computer and print from a laser printer allows you to produce books at home or, with a little more expense, to find someone who can print it for you. There are many small presses and duplicating services that can produce multiple copies of your book. If you choose to illustrate the book with your own photographs or artwork you can produce striking results. If you decide to go this route, you will need to ascertain the cost per copy. You may want to begin with a few copies as Christmas gifts for relatives and friends, and later expand to more copies to sell among your colleagues and at professional events. If you plan to use photos of individuals, you need to obtain their permission.

One advantage of self-publishing is that you are not subject to the long waiting periods that are usually connected with submissions to publishers, nor to the possibility of rejection. You are in charge, so the whole process is in your hands. This may not be a bad proposition economically either. If you do your research carefully, you might be able to price your book so as to easily recuperate your investment. Once you publish your book, you can contact distributors to sell it for you.

• **Small-press publishing; school versus trade publishing.** If you are determined to publish with a commercial publisher, you need to have a clear understanding of the distinction between school and trade publishers. School publishers generally publish books for children destined for the school market. These books tend to be developed for their pedagogical value (the Wright Group and Rigby are examples of school publishers). Trade publishers publish trade books (books for sale at bookstores and to the general public; these are the kind of books usually found in libraries). Although these books may also be found in schools, they are published because of their literary and artistic value.

Although the distinction is clear for the publishers involved, the public may not always have the same understanding. Of course, the situation is compounded because some publishers have both a trade book line and a school line.

School publishers are often more willing to look at manuscripts from teachers. Among the trade publishers, you may want to take into account the size of the publisher. In general, small or middle-sized houses may be easier to approach than larger houses.

WHERE TO GET PUBLISHED

We are frequently asked, "Where can I go to become published?" Here are some resources.

1. The Big Publishers

Because of frequent mergers among publishing companies, there are fewer and fewer houses and more and more supercompanies. To learn more about who they are and how to contact them, as well as strategies for capturing the attention of an editor, you may want to read the following books.

Children's Writer Guide to 2002. Institute of Children's Literature. 93 Long Ridge Road, West Redding, CT 06896-0811.
This working writer's tool kit is 480 pages that cover the full range of juvenile markets, from picture books to young adults.

Writer's Market. Writers Digest Books by F&W Publications. 1507 Dana Avenue, Cincinnati, OH 45207.
Where and how to sell what you write: articles, books, short stories, novels, plays, scripts. This publisher specializes in books for writers and offers a vast selection of titles.

Poet's Market. Writers Digest Books by F&W Publications. (See above)
Specializes in poetry.

Writing Family Stories and Memoires by Kirk Polking. Betterway Books. 1507 Dana Avenue, Cincinnati, OH 45207.
Both a research guide and a manual on how to turn what you discover into a book.

The Insider's Guide to Getting Published by John Boswell. Doubleday. 1540 Broadway, New York, NY 10036.
The rare book for beginners that is neither preachy nor patronizing, it offers many useful and iconoclastic tips on everything from finding a marketable idea to selling it to a large publishing house.

2. The Small Press

Some small presses specialize in publishing for specific markets. Here our recommendation would be to attend conferences, visit exhibit halls, and talk to representatives personally. Many bring their books to conventions. Get a program from any conference and look at the exhibitor's page, which will provide addresses and the names of contact people. Some newsletters provide information about who these publishers are and even what kind of material they are looking for. These two are very useful:

Children's Writer. Newsletter of writing and publishing trends. 95 Long Ridge Road, West Redding, CT 06896-1124

Society of Children's Book Writers and Illustrators. 8271 Beverly Boulevard, Los Angeles, CA 90048.

3. Publish with Private or Personal Funding

A third way to get published is to seek financing from public or private institutions and contract personally with a printing company. Many also offer distribution of your book. Here are some sources that can offer price quotes:

Vantage Press, Inc. Subsidy Book Publishers. 516 W 34th Street, New York, NY 10001. Ph: (212) 736-1767.

Dorrance Publishing Co. 643 Smithfield Street, Pittsburg, PA 15222. Ph: (412) 288-4543.

Commonwealth Publications Inc. Acquisitions Department "D." 9764 45th Ave., Edmonton, Alberta, Canada T6E 5C5. Ph: (403) 467-7316.

First Books Library. A division of Advanced Marketing Technologies. 2511 West Third Street, Suite 1, Bloomington, IN 47404. Ph: (812) 339-6000.

Poets and Writers. 72 Spring Street, New York, NY 10012. Ph: (212) 226-3586.

4. Electronic Publishing

You may also want to consider electronic publishing, the fastest-growing market in the publishing field. There are many companies you can contact. Because of the volatility of this new field, we recommend that you contact your local library for the latest information.

5. Self-Publishing Hand-Made Books

Some of the most beautiful books are the ones people make with their own hands. Self-published books printed on a computer or at a print shop may lack the prestige provided by a publishing company, but as we often remind our students in the Authors in the Classroom course, they do not lack talent, creativity, or beauty. Don't get discouraged and don't wait. While you work your way out to the big world of publishing, produce your own books and distribute them on special occasions to family and friends. For wonderful ideas about how to go about it, try:

A Book of One's Own by Paul Johnson. Heineman Publishing, New Hampshire. 1990.

Making Your Own Book by Paul Johnson. Hodder and Stoughton, England. 1994.

Multicultural Books to Make and Share by Susan Gaylord Kapuscinski. Scholastic, New York. 1995.

RECOMMENDED BOOKS FOR CHILDREN AND YOUNG ADULTS

YOUNGER READERS

Ancona, George. (1998). *Barrio: Jose's neighborhood.* San Diego, CA: Harcourt Brace.

Eight-year-old Jose Luis introduces the Mission District in San Francisco as an active Latino community. The vibrant color photographs of Jose's home, food, games, customs, Day of the Dead, Carnaval, and daily life bring Jose close to the reader. Many issues are mentioned including illegal immigration, remembering a teacher who died of AIDS, and gangs. RL 7.0 IL 3–6

De Paola, Tomie. (1999). *26 Fairmount Avenue.* New York: Putnam.

In a romp of an autobiography, master storyteller Tomie De Paola lets us in on the secrets of his growing up in Meriden, Conecticut. Nana Upstairs, Nana Downstairs, Mom, Dad, Buddy, and all the characters that helped Tomie become who he is today come barreling in to delight and affirm a little boy's identity as part of a large, nurturing family.

Heide, Florence Parry, & Judith Heide Gilliland. (1990). *The day of Ahmed's secret.* Illustrated by Ted Lewin. New York: Lothrop, Lee & Shepard.

Ted Lewin reveals Ahmed's secret in scenes from Cairo's bustling sun-drenched markets. The sounds of the city include Ahmed's name and the "karink rink" of his full cart. He has stepped forward to assume the responsibility of working to help his family. Ahmed knows who he is and is proud of how he is becoming. When evening falls, he returns home to share his secret: He can write his name! RL 4.0 IL K–3

Hoffman, Mary. (1991). *Amazing Grace.* Illustrated by Caroline Binch. New York: Dial Books for Young Readers.

Grace loves to hear stories, read them, or create and act them out. When the teacher announces a class production of *Peter Pan,* Grace wants to play the lead. One classmate says she can't because she's a girl, another says she can't because she's black. Determined, Grace tries out and the children celebrate her talent as the best person for the part. A winning look at self-affirmation.

Kuskin, Karla. (2000). *I am me.* Illustrated by Dyanna Wolcott. New York: Simon & Schuster Books for Young Readers.

Everyone says she looks like other members of her family but a young girl states positively and absolutely that she is "NO ONE ELSE BUT ME." RL 2.5 IL K–3

Schick, Eleanor. (2002). *I am. I am a dancer.* New York: Marshall Cavendish.

Soft pastel illustrations and simple text suggest the many possibilities a young child can imagine and the joy of sharing the wonder of existence.

OLDER READERS

Beltrán-Hernández, Irene. (1989). *Across the great river.*

Suspense and danger follow Katarina Campos as she and her family cross the Rio Grande with her parents and baby brother. Katarina becomes aware of herself and others in this story of a strong young woman and her family.

Curtis, Christopher Paul. (1999). *Bud, not Buddy*. New York: Random House.

Bud runs away from a foster home carrying all the clues from his life before his mother died. He makes up hilarious rules to hold his precarious life together while looking for a jazz musician he thinks might be his father. His journey is filled with desperate humor and kind relief as he falls in with Steady Eddie, Doug the Thug, Dirty Deed Breed, and lovely Miss Thomas in a Depression-era jazz club where he finds a family to love. RL 5.6 IL 5–8

Jiménez, Francisco. *The circuit: Stories from the life of a migrant child.*

Twelve short, affirming stories about a loving Mexican family that has moved across the border. Panchito and his family work in the fields and move every few months with the harvest. Although Panchito begins school with no understanding of English, he achieves success by believing in himself and never losing hope. This is a semi-autobiographical account of Jiménez' life in California.

Hamilton, Virginia. (1993). *Plain City*. New York: Scholastic.

Buhlaire Sims' dad was missing in action. When things go missing from the house and Buhlaire finds her father hiding under a freeway, she pieces together her past and realizes her mother's love for her. This is a finely painted portrait of a young girl learning slowly to love herself and her complex family. RL 5.6

Yep, Laurence. (1977). *Child of the owl*. New York: Harper & Row.

Casey doesn't speak Chinese, but when she is sent against her will to live with her grandmother in San Francisco's Chinatown, she learns about her family and herself.

❖ UNIT 2: RECOGNIZING HUMAN QUALITIES ❖

YOUNGER READERS

Ada, Alma Flor, and F. Isabel Campoy. (2002). *Canvas and paper*. Miani, FL: Alfaguara (Gateways to the Sun).

Eleven paintings by artists from different Hispanic countries are accompanied by brief texts that invite reflection on the relationship between life and its representation on a canvas.

Adoff, Arnold. (1992). *Black is brown is tan*. New York: Harper & Row.

Free verse is used to create a portrait of an interracial family as they hug each other and the reader with the song of togetherness. RL 3.4 IL K–3

Bruchac, Joseph. (2000). *Crazy Horse's vision*. Illustrated by S. D. Nelson. New York: Lee & Low.

Beautifully recreated scenes of Crazy Horse's youth highlighting aspects of "Curly's" quiet nature, early leadership skills, and vision quest. Young Crazy Horse looks for divine inspiration after his tribe is invaded. His vision teaches him to "Keep nothing for yourself." That vision guided him throughout his life. RL 6.4 IL 3–6

Campoy, F. Isabel. (2002). *Rosa Raposa*. Illustrated by José Aruego and Ariane Dewey. San Diego, CA: Harcourt.

Jaguar, the sharp-toothed bully of the forest, wants nothing more than to eat Rosa Raposa. But in these three hilarious trickster tales set in South America, Jaguar ends up the biggest fool in the forest. Even pointy teeth are no match for a sharp imagination!

Cha, Dia. *Dia's story cloth*. Illustrated by Chue and Nhia Thao Cha. New York: Lee & Low.

The story cloth stitched by her aunt and uncle describes the author and her family in Laos and their coming to the United States. RL 3.4 IL K–3

Mochizuki, Ken. *Baseball saved us*. Illustrated by Dom Lee. New York: Lee & Low.

Shorty and his family are moved from their home to a barbed-wire–surrounded barracks in the desert. His father helps Shorty learn to play in the shadow of the guard tower. When they return home, he still hears insults and racist taunts—until he joins the team and hits a homer. He is able to channel the anger he feels to do his best. RL 4.2 IL K–3

Wood, Audrey. (1990). *Quick as a cricket*. Illustrated by Don Wood. New York: Child's Play.

A young boy describes himself using similes, comparing qualities in himself to those of animals using rhymes. RL 2.8 IL K–3

OLDER READERS

Bauer, Joan. (2000). *Hope was here*. New York: Putnam.

Sixteen-year-old Hope travels the country as a waitress, so she never gets to stay in one place for a long time. When she reluctantly moves to Wisconsin, she finds herself caught up in town politics and corruption. Wonderfully funny, this book is all about honor, trust, and the qualities that allow a person to remain true.

Cofer, Judith Ortiz. (1995). *An island like you: Stories of the barrio*. New York: Orchard Books.

These short stories about a group of young people from Puerto Rico negotiating their identities in a barrio in Paterson, New Jersey, are deftly written and perceptive.

Cole, Brock. (2001). *Larky Mavis*. New York: Farrar, Straus, Giroux.

A cloud-soft story of a "different" young woman who finds something in a peanut shell and cares for it. As it grows, she is more and more shunned and abused by the village people until her "heart's delight" lifts her from outcast to glorious. A monumental story about trust, caring, and responsibility. RL 3.2 IL K–Adult

English, Karen. (1999). *Francie*. New York: Farrar, Straus, Giroux.

Francie, the best student in her school, tutors a boy who is accused of murdering a white man. She gets in trouble when, out of courage and compassion, she offers him her friendship. RL 5.0 IL 5–8

Konigsburg, E. L. (1996). *The view from Saturday*. New York: Atheneum Books for Young Readers.

Four students who consider themselves outsiders tell their stories and develop a special friendship. They meet shyly on Saturdays for fun. Then, when their teacher notices their developing enthusiasm, she helps prepare them to represent their sixth grade class at the Academic Bowl competition. RL 4.8 IL 3–6

✦ UNIT 3: STRENGTHENING SELF-IDENTITY ✦

YOUNGER READERS

Aliki. (1998). *Marianthe's story*. New York: Greenwillow Books.

In Part 1 of this topsy-turvy book, Marianthe worriedly begins school in the United States without knowing any English. Her words are shared through her delightful artwork. She paints pictures of her family and her happiness. When a class bully repeatedly jeers at her she draws a picture to show how sad and wounded she is. At the end of Part 1, flip the book to hear Marianthe learning to understand spoken English and discovering her strength and self-confidence to tell of her journey from Greece to the United States through pictures and words. RL 3.5 IL K–3

Guback, Georgia. (1994). *Luka's quilt*. New York: Greenwillow Books.

Luka and her Hawaiian grandmother, Tutu, emerge from an argument about traditional quilt colors with greater understanding of each other—not in the roles they might occupy in a one-dimensional view of a family, but as real people with unique feelings and opinions. Luka now knows how she belongs in her family in a position of mutual respect. RL 2.3 IL K–3

Henkes, Kevin. (1991). *Chysanthemum*. New York: Greenwillow Books.

Her classmates' constant teasing makes Chrysanthemum feel uncomfortable with the name she used to love. Then the new music teacher they all admire reveals that her name is Delphinium and she is considering Chysanthemum as the name for the baby she is expecting. A delightful book, it brings awareness of the importance of one's own name.

Herrera, Juan Felipe. (2000). *The upside down boy/El niño de cabeza*. Illustrated by Elizabeth Gómez. San Francisco: Children's Book Press.

Juanito is upset in his new school and feels upside down. A kind teacher and his family help Juanito draw on his strengths of music, poetry, and art to help him achieve success. RL 3.5 IL K–3

Myers, Christopher. (2000). *Wings*. New York: Scholastic.

Icarus, a boy with wings who can fly on the playground, is taunted by the kids for being different. A young girl watches and sees the injustice. She hesitates to interfere but then steps forward to call out "Look at that amazing boy!" Photography, paint, and cut paper collage combine to make this city story resonate with the bravery of one girl's compassion and strength. RL 3.5 IL K–3

OLDER READERS

Ada, Alma Flor. (1993). *My name is María Isabel*. Illustrated by K. Dyble Thompson. New York: Atheneum Books for Young Readers.

María Isabel Salazar López is proud of her two last names. When her new teacher decides to call her "Mary Lopez," it becomes very difficult for María Isabel to recognize when she is being addressed. This book's message of pride in one's heritage is important for children in an increasingly multicultural nation.

DiCamillo, Kate. (2000). *Because of Winn-Dixie*. Cambridge, MA: Candlewick.

Motherless Opal Buloni and a big ugly stray dog find each other in the produce section of the Winn-Dixie supermarket. They give each other the courage to belong completely to the family and community who love them. RL 5.8 IL 3–6

Johnston, Tony. (2001). *Any small goodness: A novel of the barrio*. Illustrated by Raúl Colón. New York: Blue Sky.

When eleven-year-old Arturo Rodriguez' family moves to East Los Angeles and his teacher anglicizes his name, Abuelita encourages Arturo to hold onto his name and thereby keep his identity. The story is spiced with family celebrations and joyful meals at home. Recipes are included.

Na, An. (2001) *A step from heaven*. Asheville, NC: Front Street.

When four-year-old Young Ju and her parents emigrate from Korea to California, life proves to be far from heavenly for the family. The family must adjust to strange customs, a new language, government bureaucracy, and embarrassment. The author describes the pain and the small joys of home life for the young girl as she grows to adolescence. RL 5.5 IL 5–8

Nye, Naomi Shihab.(1997). *Habibi*. New York: Simon & Schuster Books for Young Readers.

Liyana's father moves her St. Louis family to Palestine to get to know his family while he takes a position at a hospital in Jerusalem. In the Arab side of the city, Liyana and her brother make friends with refugees, go to an Armenian school, and meet their Sitti—their grandmother. Liyana also meets Omer, a Jewish boy from the other side of the city. In this lyrical and complex setting, Liyana begins to realize that she has a double culture—American and Arab—and that she loves both her identities as well as the two countries that hold her heart.

Soto, Gary. (1991). *Taking sides*. San Diego, CA: Harcourt Brace.

Lincoln Mendoza and his mother have moved to the suburbs away from the Mission District barrio of San Francisco. Lincoln senses that he is discriminated against by his prejudiced basketball coach because he is Mexican American; he can't accept his mother's new white boyfriend; and, to top it off, his best friend in the barrio accuses him of getting soft. A basketball game with his old school makes him question where he fits. He comes to realize that life is not a matter of taking sides, but rather of recognizing the universal. RL 5.5 IL 5–8

White, Ruth. (1996). *Belle Prater's boy*. New York: Farrar, Straus, Giroux.

When Woodrow Prater's mama disappears, he tells a tale of her invisibility and possible return for him. He lives with his grandparents, right next door to his sixth-grade cousin Gypsy, who is intrigued by the story of his mother's absence. They become best friends. A classmate's cruel revelation of the truth of Gypsy's family and Woodrow's defense of Gypsy brings about the transformation of both Gypsy and Woodrow.

❖ UNIT 4: BUILDING COMMUNITIES ❖

YOUNGER READERS

Base, Graeme. (1986). *Animalia.* New York: Harry N. Abrams.

Climb right into this tapestry of fantasy and get lost for hours! Each page of Graeme Base's beautiful alphabet, *Animalia,* invites the reader deeper into the layers of picture that correspond to each letter. The book is enchanting and will have both little children and their favorite adults enthralled.

Ernst, Lisa Campbell. (1996). *The letters are lost.* New York: Penguin.

Everyone loves a good mystery. Once upon a time the letters on blocks were in a box. The game is afoot! It's your young one's turn to find out just where they have wandered. F is in the fishtank; Q curled up on a quilt; and S is in the sandbox. That's not all that's there! Detectives will find all the letters at the end of the mystery. Will the letters journey again to different parts of the house? Probably, but you will have your alphabet sleuth nearby to help solve the riddle. Elementary, my dear Watson!

Ford, Juwanda G. (1997). *K is for Kwanzaa: A Kwanzaa alphabet book.* Illustrated by Ken Wilson-Max. New York: Scholastic.

A is for Africa, B is for bendera, and C is for candle in Juwanda Ford and illustrator Ken Wilson-Max's colorful amble through the principles and language of Kwanzaa. Short definitions of Kwanzaa's seven principles help all readers get to know the customs, costumes, and language, right up to Z for "zawadi"—the presents! *K Is for Kwanzaa* is good for sharing in groups or one-on-one. A great book for seeing your holiday or understanding your neighbor's.

Johnson, Stephen T. (1995). *Alphabet City.* New York: Penguin.

By far, one of the best alphabets to come along in decades. *Alphabet City* invites the reader to find each letter in artfully created pictures. Johnson combines shadow and light to create a sequence of close observations of the city. Each page draws the reader to examine a bench, a bridge, a cornice, or a streetlight to find the shape of a letter as if it lingered there just so you would find it. The magnificent alphabet will encourage both young and older readers to con-

duct similar explorations of their own. The delight is in the details, the most wonderful of which is the medium. A Caldecott Honor Book.

MacDonald, Suse. (1986). *Alphabatics.* New York: Bradbury.

A is for ark. B is for balloon. The acrobatic characters in this tumbling show are the letters themselves as they roll and jump, soar, and finally transform. The best of alphabet books not only teach but invite creativity on the part of the young reader. This is an artist's delight as the reader is pulled in to twist, turn, and shape the letters to create animals, mustaches, and umbrellas that match the letter's sound. MacDonald's *Alphabatics* is an early way to play with the uses of the alphabet.

Martin, Bill Jr., & John Archambault. (1989). *Chicka Chicka Boom Boom.* Illustrated by Lois Ehlert. New York: Simon & Schuster.

This alphabet chant narrates what happens when the whole alphabet tries to scoot up a coconut tree!

Shannon, George. (1996). *Tomorrow's alphabet.* Illustrated by Donald Crews. New York: Greenwillow.

If you already know what an alphabet book can do, then become futurists with us as we explore the world of tomorrow. *Tomorrow's Alphabet* is about process and creation. Suspension of disbelief is a requirement as you read "A is for seed/tomorrow's apple and B is for Eggs/ tomorrow's birds." Get the concept? The left-hand page has the letter and today's challenge; the right-hand page has tomorrow's magic. This colorful book contains seeds of a game that can be clever and inventive and provide quite challenging riddles. Come along with George Shannon and Donald Crews as they make futurists of us all.

OLDER READERS

Ada, Alma Flor. (2001). *Gathering the sun. An alphabet in Spanich and English.* Illustrated by Simón Silva. Translated by Rosa Zubizarreta. New York: HarperCollins.

The extraordinary illustrations of Simón Silva, with bold colors reminiscent of the Mexican muralists, depict realistically the world of the migrant farmworkers he knows so well. The book honors the hard labor of those who bring food to our table and recognizes the dignity of their lives, their values, and their culture.

Bennett, Andrea T., & James H. Kessler (1996). *Apples, bubbles, and crystals: Your science ABCs.* Illustrated by Melody Sarecky. New York: Learning Triangle Press.

L is for lens and M is for magnet. This science activity book shows science fun. The last chapter explains the scientific facts for each activity in a straightforward, uncomplicated way.

Bryan, Ashley. (1997). *Ashley Bryan's ABC of African American poetry.* New York: Atheneum Books for Young Readers.

What a wonderful world of poetry Ashley Bryan shares in this alphabet book of themes from African American poets. Audre Lorde, James Weldon Johnson, Rita Dove, Paul Laurence Dunbar, Countee Cullen, and Lucille Clifton are among the many represented.

Chin-Lee, Cynthia. (1997). *A is for Asia.* Illustrated by Yumi Heo. New York: Orchard Books.

An alphabetical introduction to the diverse peoples, lands, and cultures of the world's largest continent. The Middle East, Siberia, East Asia, South Asia, and the Pacific Islands are included. A book of many cultures, climates and languages, *A Is for Asia* celebrates not only holidays but the everyday in Asia. RL 6.2 IL 3–6

Der Manuelian. (1995). *Hieroglyphs from A to Z: A rhyming book with ancient Egyptian stencils for kids* New York: Scholastic.

Each page has the English alphabet and ancient Egyptian hieroglyphs with explanations and a sample word to decorate your mummy or your Egypt report!

De Vicq de Cumptich, Roberto. (2000). *Bembo's zoo: An animal ABC book.* New York: Henry Holt.

This book uses the shape of letters in Bembo font to create animal pictures (M transforms to Monkey and I to Ibis). A website presents the same illustrations in animation. See www.bemboszoo.com. RL 1.2 IL K–Adult

Fisher, Leonard Everett. (1978). *Alphabet art: Thirteen ABCs from around the world.* New York: Four Winds Press.

Arabic, Cyrillic, Gaelic, Sanskrit, and Thai are a few of the thirteen alphabets illustrated by Fisher. *Alphabet Art* includes an overview of cuneiform, hieroglyphs, and the Sinai-Phoenician from which our English alphabet evolved. Each of the alphabets reflects the culture of the people who use it today. This well-written book will be appreciated by readers seeking a history of writing systems and calligraphy. The scratchboard art is striking in its simplicity. It is the kind of book you will enjoy going back to again and again for many years, long after the child has begun to gray at the temples.

Schwartz, David M. (1998). *G is for google.* Illustrated by Marissa Moss. Berkeley, CA: Tricycle Press.

Schwartz' math alphabet book explains the meaning of mathematical terms from abacus to Fibonacci and Googolplex to Rhombicosidodecahedron, all within the grasp of a curious fifth or sixth grader. The language is playful, but respectful of the reader and serious. The illustrations are cartoon-hip and clear. Schwartz' previous math concept picture books, *How Much Is a Million* and *If You Made a Million* earned him a well deserved place of honor with kids and teachers. This title continues to create a following and will inspire a whole new age group to read and understand math.

❖ UNIT 5: THE POWER OF TRANSFORMATION ❖

YOUNGER READERS

Bunting, Eve. (1994). *Smoky night.* Illustrated by David Díaz. San Diego, CA: Harcourt Brace.

When a riot starts in the neighborhood, young Daniel describes what he sees. Looters break

into a dry cleaner's and the scene is scary. When Daniel's own apartment is set ablaze, the people in the building learn the importance of mutual support and the need to bridge differences. RL 2.5 IL K–3

Choi, Sook Nyui. (1993). *Halmoni and the picnic*. Illustrated by Karen M. Dugan. Boston: Houghton Miffllin.

Halmoni, Yunmi's Korean grandmother, is having a rough time adjusting to life in the United States. She doesn't speak much English and she is homesick. Yunmi's friends ask her to have Halmoni chaperone a picnic in Central Park. Yunmi worries that her friends might make fun of Halmoni's rice and vegetable rolls and her traditional clothing. Happily, Halmoni enjoys Yunmi's friends and the picnic. Both Yunmi and Halmoni are transformed toward a greater understanding of each other and possibilities of the future. RL 4.5 IL K–3

Levy, Janice. (1999). *Abuelito eats with his fingers*. Illustrated by Layne Johnson. Austin, TX: Eakin Press.

English-speaking Tina says she doesn't like to visit her Spanish-speaking Abuelito, but her mother leaves her with him anyway while she goes out. Together they draw pictures that tell the story of Tina's grandmother. Abuelito gives Tina her grandmother's pearls. They make tortillas together and Tina discovers that she loves her Abuelito very much. A story of tenderness and youthful awakening to family. RL 2.8 IL K–3

Raschka, Chris. (1993). *Yo! Yes*. New York: Orchard Books.

Two sweet characters, one black and one white, meet on the street and have two-word exchanges. They become friends in this exuberant description of people making friends. A natural for acting out stories, understanding how to make friends, and the way one person can approach another to spread some joy. RL 1.2 IL K–3

OLDER READERS

Cushman, Karen. (1996). *The ballad of Lucy Whipple*. New York: Clarion.

Lucy Whipple is dragged along to the Golden State by her mother, who has always wanted to brave a rough-and-tough mining town. Lucy misses her quiet Massachusetts town and obstinately refuses to be lured into the excitement. But she does and transforms herself into a hardy pioneer who bravely decides to stay in California even after her mother remarries and moves to the Sandwich Islands. A rollicking good book with the right amount of tears, excitement, and inspiration. RL 5.5 IL 5–8

Hesse, Karen. (1996). *The music of dolphins*. New York: Scholastic.

A young girl is rescued from an island where she has been living with dolphins. She is brought to a hospital where she works with doctors who attempt to teach her speech and transform her into a person who can function in human society. RL 5.5 IL 5–8

Lowry, Lois. (1993). *The giver*. Boston: Houghton Mifflin.

In a distopian society, twelve-year-old Jonas gets his lifetime assignment at his coming of age ceremony. He will become the receiver of the memories of one other person in that society. He discovers the vast difference between his world and a world that can know joy and sorrow. RL 5.5 IL 5–8

MacLachlan, Patricia. (1993). *Baby*. New York: Delacorte.

A baby is left with Larkin's island family after the summer tourists leave. The note says the mother will be back. Larkin's family cares for the baby and loves her like their own, which transforms their lives after the death of their infant son. RL 4.5 IL 5–8

Mohr, Nicholasa. (1999). *Felita*. New York: Penguin Putnam Books for Young Readers.

The everyday experiences of an eight-year-old Puerto Rican girl growing up in a close-knit urban community. RL 5.0 IL 3–6

Sacher, Louis. (1998). *Holes*. New York: Farrar, Straus, Giroux.

Stanley Yelnats doesn't know whether he's coming or going. His self-esteem is pretty low already and then he's sent to Camp Green Lake—not a summer vacation, but a correctional institution in the Texas desert where he and the other kids dig holes from morning to night. Stanley finds true friendship and a new understanding of himself. RL 5.0 IL 3–6

Zubizarreta, Rosalma. (1991). *The woman who outshone the sun*. Illustrated by Fernado Olivera. San Francisco: Children's Book Press.

In this original story inspired by an old Oaxacan legend, the beautiful Lucía Zenteno is exiled from a mountain village because the villagers are jealous of her beauty and mistrust her unique ways. But when she is forced to leave, the neighboring river decides to follow her, leaving the village without water or fish.

❖ UNIT 6: UNDERSTANDING THE PAST, CREATING THE FUTURE ❖

YOUNGER READERS

Carling, Amelia Lau. (1998). *Mama & Papa have a store*. Illustrated by Amelia Lou Carling. New York: Dial Books for Young Readers.

Carling remembers with love her family's general store in Guatemala City. Her family had escaped from war in China and stock Chinese goods that the local Guatemalan, Mayan, and Chinese people love. Carling's watercolors introduce us to lottery tickets, tofu, the sounds of her father's abacus, the friends who stop in for a bite to eat, and her mother's chatting with customers in Spanish. A wonderful introduction to the many cultures in Guatemala.

Corpi, Lucha. (1997). *Where fireflies dance/Ahí donde bailan las luciérnagas*. Illustrated by Mira Reisberg. San Francisco: Children's Book Press.

Corpi recounts a young girl's story of home in Mexico with her mother, father, and brother; a haunted house adventure; an amazing jukebox; the warmth she left; and the destiny she chose. She dreams of Mexico now, in the flicker of firefly light in her dreams. Reisberg's thick, warm colors impart a close relationship to the family and their town and coax the reader to draw near to the memory.

Curtis, Jamie Lee. (1996). *Tell me again about the night I was born*. Illustrated by Laura Cornell. New York: Joanna Cotler Books.

A phone call brings the news in the middle of the night! The adoptive parents rush to the hospital by plane. The new dad cradles his baby in his arms and whispers sweet dreams of baseball. The new mom cries happy tears. This story, told by the parents to the child, reaffirms the love and belonging in their happy adoptive family. RL 3.9 IL K–3

Frasier, Debra. (1991). *On the day you were born*. San Diego, CA: Harcourt Brace.

The Earth celebrates the birth of a new being as animals whisper to each other about the new arrival; the moon promises a bright full face each month at the child's windowsill; and the world embraces the newborn.

Hearne, Betsey Gould. (1997). *Seven brave women*. New York: Greenwillow.

A girl reveals the stories of her courageous women forbearers who traveled by wooden boat and covered wagon, went to medical school, and raised children—all the tasks done by women that are rarely mentioned in history books.

Howard, Elizabeth Fitzgerald. (2000). *Virgie goes to school with us boys*. Illustrated by E. B. Lewis. New York: Simon & Schuster Books for Young Readers.

Virgie's determination to go to school to learn shines bravely as she quietly convinces her family that she can learn with her brothers in the Quaker school seven miles away. They walk through the fields and woods of Tennessee to Jonesborough where they stay the week at the Werner Institute, returning to tell Mama and Papa what they've learned. Lewis' warm, clear colors draw the reader in to the large green fields and forests of Tennessee and Virgie's quiet strength. RL 3.0 IL K–3

Say, Allen. (1991). *Tree of cranes*. Boston: Houghton Mifflin.

When a Japanese boy is feverish in bed, his mother goes out to their winter garden to dig up a pine tree. She brings it in and decorates it with silver origami cranes and tells him of her childhood in America and a holiday called called Christmas, when strangers smile at one another and arguments are stilled.

Sis, Peter. (1996). *Starry messenger: A book depicting the life of a famous scientist, mathematician, astronomer, philosopher, physicist*. New York: Frances Foster Books at Farrar, Straus, Giroux.

Spirals of Galileo's journal excerpts and Inquisition records swirl around the illustrations Sis has arrayed to convey the risk Galileo was willing to shoulder in order to share the truth. Sis's stellar panels convey the danger and the wonder of his conviction. After 350 years, Galileo's courage is still relevant in our world. RL 5.9 IL 2–5

OLDER READERS

Álvarez, Julia. (2002). *Before we were free*. New York: Alfred A. Knopf.

Anita's coming of age in the Dominican Republic in the 1960s is tainted by the horrors experienced by her family under the Trujillo dictatorship. When most of her relatives move to the United States or disappear from her everyday life, Anita begins to question what is happening in her country. She will eventually accept that the price of freedom is leaving behind all she loves.

Anaya, Rudolfo. (1999). *My land sings: Stories from the Rio Grande*. Illustrated by Amy Cordova. New York: Morrow.

This collection of ten original and traditional stories set in New Mexico, including "Lupe and La Llorona," "The Shepherd Who Knew the Language of Animals," and "Coyote and Raven," invite a confident knowledge of one's culture and respect for the past.

Bruchac, Joseph. (1998). *The arrow over the door*. Illustrated by James Watling. New York: Dial Books for Young Readers.

Fourteen-year-old Samuel, a Quaker, is questioning his family's belief in nonviolence. Stands Straight, also fourteen, and his small tribe of Abenaki are trying to decide whether to join the British. Their meeting, based on an actual historical event in 1777, will change them and their people forever. The connections between the two boys are told in alternating chapters and chronicle their growing up. Historical sources are given in an author's note.

Erdrich, Louise. (1999). *The birchbark house*. Illustrated by Louise Erdrich. New York: Hyperion Books for Children.

Louise Erdrich tells a lyrical story of Omakayas, an Ojibwa girl, her loving family, and the characters they cherish during the time when their lands were just beginning to see white people seep into the forested island in Lake Superior in the 1840s. When her brother Neewo is felled by smallpox, she is spared for a mysterious reason that is only revealed by Old Tallow. *The Birchbark House* is a brilliant account of four seasons in a family's life by an accomplished author. RL 5.6 IL 5–8

Hesse, Karen. (1995). *A time for angels*. New York: Hyperion Books for Children.

Influenza strikes a young Jewish girl in Boston during the epidemic of 1918 as she struggles to care for her two sisters. She is rescued by an elderly German man who reunites her with her family. RL 6.4 IL 5–8

✤ UNIT 7: DISCOVERING OUR CAPACITIES AND STRENGTHS ✤

YOUNGER READERS

Ada, Alma Flor, & F. Isabel Campoy. (2000). *Smiles*. Miami, FL: Alfaguara (Gateways to the Sun).

Ada, Alma Flor, & F. Isabel Campoy. (2000). *Voices*. Miami, FL: Alfaguara (Gateways to the Sun).

Each of these two books presents the lives of three important figures within the Hispanic culture, focusing on the challenges they had to face and overcome. *Smiles* includes the lives of Pablo Picasso, foremost artist of the 20th century; Gabriela Mistral, an uneducated rural child who went on to become a Nobel Prize winner; and Benito Juárez, an indigenous orphan boy who became one of the most important figures in the history of Mexico. *Voices* presents the lives of Luis Valdés, a migrant farm working child who grew up to found the Teatro Campesino and to become a recognized movie director; Judith Francisca Baca, extraordinary muralist; and Carlos J. Finlay, who discovered that yellow fever is transmitted by a species of mosquito. Ridiculed and ignored during his lifetime because he had a speech impediment and his discovery was too innovative, the credit for his discovery was given to Walter Reed.

Atkins, Jeanne. (1995). *Aani and the tree huggers*. Illustrated by Venantius J. Pinto. New York: Lee & Low.

This story is based on events in northern India. When developers came to chop all the trees down, the girls and women hugged the trees so they would not be destroyed. Now, each year new trees are planted. RL 4.2 IL 3–6

Castañeda, Omar. (1993). *Abuela's weave*. Illustrated by Enrique O. Sánchez. New York: Lee & Low.

Esperanza and her grandmother weave a beautiful tapestry to sell in the market in Guatemala. Because her grandmother has a birthmark, they are concerned that she might be scorned and be unable to sell the tapestry. Esperanza sells the tapestry and the two ride home with new understandings of each other. RL 4.0 IL 2–4

Isadora, Rachel. (1991). *Ben's trumpet*. New York: Mulberry.

A boy grows up playing his wonderfully imaginative trumpet as he listens to a jazz band from a nearby club. After school he watches the musicians as they practice. He plays and plays his imaginary trumpet until one musician helps him accomplish more. RL 3.6 IL K–3

Krull, Kathleen. (1996). *Wilma unlimited: How Wilma Rudolph became the world's fastest woman.* Illustrated by David Diaz. San Diego, CA: Harcourt Brace.

Contracting polio at the age of five, Wilma got around by hopping on her stronger leg while wearing a heavy steel brace. She focused on walking and then on basketball in high school and college. Eight years after giving up braces, she won three gold medals in the Olympics for track. Her triumph over adversity is an inspiration to all. RL 3.6 IL K–3

Smith, Cynthia Leitich. (2000). *Jingle dancer.* New York: Morrow Junior Books.

Contemporary Jenna wants to dance at the Powwow but she needs jingles to make her dress sing. She borrows just enough from four family members to give voice to her dress without stilling the voices of their dresses. She watches a video of Grandma to practice her bounce steps and carries on the tradition of her Muscogee (Creek) Nation and Ojibwa (Chippewa/Anishinabe) culture. RL 3.6 IL K–3

OLDER READERS

Ada, Alma Flor, and F. Isabel Campoy. (2000). *Paths.* Miami, FL: Alfaguara (Gateways to the Sun).

This book depicts the lives of three giant figures: poet and thinker José Martí, foremost figure in the struggle for Cuban independence from Spain; Frida Kahlo, a Mexican artist who overcame a lifetime of illness to become one of the most admired painters in the world; and César Chávez, leader of the nonviolent struggle of farmworkers seeking more humane working conditions.

Farmer, Nancy. (1996). *A girl named disaster.* New York: Orchard Books.

As eleven-year-old Nhamo flees the village and journeys to Zimbabwe, she must struggle to avoid drowning, dehydration, and delirium. A gripping tale of survival and search for family. RL 5.9 IL 5–8

George, Jean Craighead. (1988). *My side of the mountain.* New York: Dutton.

A young boy spends an adventurous year living alone in the Catskills struggling to survive. His dependence on nature, the animals he meets, and his realization that he needs the companionship of other people are wisely told. RL 6.7 IL 5–8

Levine, Gail Carson. (1999). *Dave at night.* New York: HarperCollins.

Orphan Dave gets sent to the Hebrew Home for Boys where he falls into constant trouble with mean Mr. Doom. He sneaks out at night and experiences the friendship and warmth of the people in the Harlem Renaissance music scene. RL 5.9 IL 5–8

Orlev, Uri. (1984). *The island on Bird Street.* Boston: Houghton Mifflin.

Trapped in a deserted ghetto in Warsaw, Poland, a young boy is left on his own for months in a ruined building. He learns to survive against all odds under the enormous shadow of the risk that he will be discovered and taken to a concentration camp. RL 6.3 IL 5–8.

Paulsen, Gary. (1989). *The voyage of the frog.* New York: Orchard Books.

Caught off-guard in a fierce storm as he is scattering his uncle's ashes, fourteen-year-old Owen must sail for nine days at sea. He finds courage and determination and learns to sail. A dynamic adventure of grit and understanding. RL 6.3 IL 5–8

✦ UNIT 8: LEARNING TO KNOW ✦

YOUNGER READERS

Curtis, Gavin. (1998). *The bat boy and his violin.* Illustrated by E. B. Lewis. New York: Simon & Schuster Books for Young Readers.

Reginald's father is the manager of the Dukes, the worst team in the Negro National League. When his father wants him to become bat boy for the team, Reginald protests that he needs the time to practice his violin. He winds up taking the violin with him to practice while the team is batting. Each time he plays, the team gets a hit. His father is transformed as he recognizes and admires his son's talent and dedication to his gift. RL 5.2 IL K–3

Delacre, Lulu. (1993). *Vejigantes masquerader.* New York: Scholastic.

In this bilingual book, Ramón sews his first vejigante costume. He saves his money from doing errands and is able to buy a mask. His courage and conviction pave the way for him to be in the parade for Carnival in Puerto Rico. RL 4.2 IL K–3

Gauch, Patricia Lee. (1994). *Tanya and Emily in a dance for two.* Illustrated by Satomi Ichikawa. New York: Philomel.

Tanya dances her joyful and passionate leaps and twirls. She loves ballet, even though she may not be the most conventional of the dancers. Emily joins the ballet class and does everything neatly and perfectly. The two become friends. Tanya teaches Emily to find inspiration to dance, and Emily teaches Tanya how to do a cabriole. RL 3.5 ILK–3

Hopkinson, Deborah. (1999). *A band of angels: A story inspired by the Jubilee Singers.* Illustrated by Raul Colon. New York: Atheneum Books for Young Readers.

This story is told in the voice of the great-great-granddaughter of one of the original Jubilee Singers from the Fisk School in Nashville, the nation's first school for emancipated slaves. Beth recounts the chorus's struggles to learn how to raise money to save their school. The singers traveled north to perform popular music; when they began to sing the jubilee or spiritual songs they gained popularity. As a result, they sang for Queen Victoria and President Grant. The money they earned helped to build Jubilee Hall and found Fisk University. RL 5.4 IL 3–6

London, Jonathan. (1995). *Froggy learns to swim.* New York: Viking.

When Froggy is slung from his swing into a pond, his mother reassures him that it's an OK situation because frogs are naturally great swimmers. Froggy's not too sure as he dons flippers, mask, and snorkle. But as soon as he's swimming around he doesn't want to leave the water! An enjoyable story for the younger set who will see themselves without any trouble! RL 2.0 IL K–3

Martin, Jacqueline Briggs. (1998). *Snowflake Bentley.* Illustrated by Mary Azarian. Boston: Houghton Mifflin.

Self-educated Wilson Bently wanted to study snowflakes, but could not save them to look at them for very long. When his mother gave him a microscope, he studied each of the crystals before it melted. He was the first person to find that no two are alike. With a combination of photography and etching, he made records of snowflakes we still use today as reference guides. Azarian's inspiring illustrations set the tone for high interest and respect for determination. RL 3.1 IL K–3

Nygaard, Elizabeth. (1998). *Snake Alley Band.* Illustrated by Betsy Lewin. New York: Doubleday Books for Young Readers.

After waking from a nap, Snake finds his snake band has hi-de-hoed out of Snake Alley. When his new pal Cricket chew-ups, Fish pop-pop-doo-wops, Turtle ta-toom ta-toom tooms, Frog cha-bop cha-bops, Snake shhh-booms, their new Snake Alley Band slips and slides the night away. The other snakes return and realize their own band is better when they include everyone! RL 3.5 IL K–3

Torres, Leyla. (1999). *Saturday sancocho.* New York: Farrar, Straus, Giroux.

Maria Lili's grandmother teaches her how to make a sancocho while strengthening the ties of community during a trading day at the market. The recipe is included. RL 3.5 IL K–3

OLDER READERS

Fine, Ann. (1995). *Flour babies.* New York: Bantam Doubleday Dell Books for Young Readers.

When his class is assigned to spend three long weeks taking care of flour sacks as if they were babies, Simon learns about himself and develops a new understanding of his relationship with his absent father. RL 6.2 IL 5–8

O'Dell, Scott (1988). *Black star, bright dawn.* Boston: Houghton Mifflin.

When her father is injured, eighteen-year-old Bright Dawn offers to run the Iditerod, the 1,179-mile sled dog race from Anchorage to Nome, in his place. Oteg, an older Eskimo who gives advice and reminds her of the folklore and wisdom of her people, helps prepare her for the harrowing race and natural dangers of the wild animals, ice and snow. RL 6.8 IL 5–8

Wilson, Diane Lee. (1998). *I rode a horse of milk white jade.* New York: Orchard Books.

Oyuna has a permanently injured foot. She must learn to ride a horse in nomadic Mongolia in 1285. She begins the story of how her father helps her buy a horse. Soldiers come and take all the family's horses and young men for the Great Khan's army. Oyuna disguises herself as a boy and rides with the soldiers to reach the goal of getting her beloved horse back. Her journey to meet with the Great Khan tests her courage and determination. RL 5.2 IL 4–7

Wolff, Virginia Euwer. (1993). *Make lemonade.* New York: Holt.

LaVaughn, fourteen years old and learning to babysit to make money, tries to earn enough to save for college tuition. LaVaughn babysits for Jolly, an abused, 17-year-old single parent who lives with her two children. LaVaughn's steady support helps Jolly to help herself and Jolly helps LaVaughn to understand her own values. The theme of learning and the value of education are explored in depth in this riveting story. RL 5.2 IL YA

Yolen, Jane, & Bruce Coville. (1998). *Armageddon summer.* New York: Harcourt Brace.

Marina and Jed meet on a mountaintop retreat where they are staying with their parents' religious group while they wait for the end of the world. The goal of saving their parents from cataclysmic devastation keeps the teens searching for courage and truth. RL 6.0 IL

❖ UNIT 9: DEVELOPING RELATIONSHIPS ❖

YOUNGER READERS

Anaya, Rudolfo. (1998). *Farolitos for Abuelo.* Illustrated by Edward Gonzáles. New York: Hyperion Books for Children.

Luz mourns her Abuelo's passing and honors him by tending their garden. At Christmas she puts farolitos around his grave. The community sees the warmth and love in the light of the farolitos and honor Luz and Abuelo by beginning a tradition. RL 4.5 IL K–3

Bercaw, Edna Coe. (2000). *Halmoni's day.* Illustrated by Robert Hunt. New York: Dial Books for Young Readers.

Jennifer is worried that her Korean grandmother will be an embarrassment on her school's Grandparents' Day. Halmoni more than surprises Jennifer as she is the hit of the day! Jennifer learns of the strength of her ties and her love for her family. RL 4.5 IL K–3

Mitchell, Margaree King. (1993). *Uncle Jed's barbershop.* Illustrated by James Ransome. New York: Simon & Schuster Books for Young Readers.

Uncle Jed is the sole black barber in the county and teaches his niece the value of patience, determination and belief in one's abilities. His determination to save enough money and open a barbershop is often blocked by obstacles, but his persistence leads to success. RL 4.5 IL K–3

Polacco, Patricia. (1998). *Thank you, Mr. Falker.* New York: Philomel Books.

Trisha loves school but has a hard time reading until a teacher believes in her and she learns to read. The story is Patricia Polacco's autobiographical account. RL 3.5 IL K–3

OLDER READERS

Ada, Alma Flor. (1994). *Where the flame trees bloom.* Illustrated by Antonio Martorell. New York: Atheneum Books for Young Readers.

Eleven vignettes tell the story of a childhood in Cuba, a country geographically very near, and yet culturally very different from, the United States.

Christensen, Bonnie, compiler. (2003). *In my grandmother's house. Award-winning authors tell stories about their grandmothers.* Illustrated by Bonnie Christensen. New York: Harper Collins.

Twelve authors—Cynthis L. Smith, Minfong Ho, Pat Cummings, Diane Stanley, Beverly Clearly, Gail C. Levine, Jean Craighead George, Beverly Naidoo, Bonnie Christensen, Ji-Li Jian, Joan Abelove and Alma Flor Ada—wrote original texts for this collection of memories about their grandmothers.

Jennings, Rchard W. (2001). *The great whale of Kansas.* Boston: Houghton Mifflin Company.

While digging a hole for a small pond in his backyard, a boy in Kansas unearths a fossil dinosaur. The state wants to claim the property and stop him from uncovering the rare specimen. With the knowledge and inspiration of his friend Tom White Cloud, the boy is able to realize his dream of finishing the project. RL 5.0 IL 4–6

Naidoo, Beverly. (2001). *The other side of truth*. New York: Harper Collins.

After their mother is murdered in Nigeria because of a newspaper article that their journalist father wrote, a young girl and her brother are sent to London to meet someone who will give them sanctuary. When they arrive, however, no one is there to help them and they must try to keep their courage and their honor as they struggle to stay out of Nigeria, not only for their own sakes, but also for their father's. RL 6.0 IL 6–8

Salisbury, Graham. (2001). *Lord of the deep*. New York: Delacorte.

Mikey works on his dearly loved stepdad's charter fishing boat in Hawaii. Mikey loves it until he sees his stepdad lie about a record catch to satisfy an obnoxious customer. A thought-provoking tale that will spark reflections on truth, honesty, and courage. RL 5.0 IL 4–7

Uchida, Yoshiko. (1983). *The best bad thing*. New York: Atheneum.

Rinko goes to stay with recently widowed Mrs. Hata and her two young sons in Oakland, California, in the 1930s. The Depression is raging and Mrs. Hata will lose her farm if the crop can't be picked in time to pay the bank. Just in time, the wise man who lives in the barn unexpectedly saves them all from disaster, even though he spoils his chances by helping. 5.0 IL 4–6

❖ UNIT 10: FROM YESTERDAY TO TOMORROW ❖

YOUNGER READERS

Ada, Alma Flor, and F. Isabel Campoy. (2003). *The quetzal's journey*. Illustrated by Felipe Dávalos, Fabricio Vanden Broeck, Orlando Cabañas, Alina Cabrera, and Bruno Gonzáles. Miami, FL: Alfaguara (Gateways to the Sun).

With lyric text and extraordinary illustrations, this book introduces the vastness and diversity of Latin America, focusing on the magnificent geography, the rich flora and fauna, the cultural legacies of its many civilizations, and its present-day promise.

Alarcón, Francisco X. (1997). *Laughing tomatoes and other spring poems/Jitomates risueños y otros poemas de primavera*. Illustrated by Maya Cristina Gonzales. San Francisco: Children's Book Press.

The laughing tomatoes turn their wire-framed bushes into Christmas trees in Spring. The poems in this collection are colorful, short, and lighthearted freeze-frames of life.

Huynh, Qyang Nhuong. (1997). *Water buffalo days: Growing up in Vietnam*. Illustrated by Jean and Mou-sien Tseng. New York: HarperCollins.

A young boy grows up with water buffaloes who protect him from a tiger and teach him the value of his close-knit home life in rural Vietnam. A beautiful autobiography of a boy learning about responsibility and courage.

Rockwell, Anne. (2000). *Only passing through: The story of Sojourner Truth*. New York: Alfred A. Knopf.

This well-told biography of Sojourner Truth takes the reader from her childhood as a slave called Isabella through her marriage and the loss of her child when he is sold, to her becoming a famous orator for the causes of real freedom for people of African descent and the voting rights of women.

OLDER READERS

Ada, Alma Flor. (1994). *Under the royal palms. A childhood in Cuba*. New York: Atheneum Books for Young Readers.

A companion to *Where the Flame Trees Bloom,* this collection of life stories—some humorous, some sad, but always truthful—encourages children to discover the stories in their own lives: stories that can help inform their own values and celebrate the joys and struggles we all share, no matter where or when we grew up.

Anaya, Rudolfo A. (1994). *Bless me, Ultima*. New York: Warner Books.

Told in flashback, this story tells the story of young Antonio as he is growing up in a small New Mexican village and a curandera comes to live with his family. Antonio learns to both understand and question the notions of good and evil with the help of Ultima, his spiritual mentor.

Erdrich, Louise. (1999). *The birchbark house.* Illustrated by the Louise Erdrich. New York: Hyperion Books for Children.

Louise Erdrich tells a lyrical story of Omakayas, an Ojibwa girl, her loving family, and the characters they cherish during the time when their lands were just beginning to see white people seep into the forested island in Lake Superior in the 1840s. When her brother Neewo is felled by smallpox, she is skipped for a mysterious reason that is only revealed by Old Tallow. *The Birchbark House* is a brilliant account of four seasons in a family's life by an accomplished author. RL 5.6 IL 5–8

Garrigue, Sheila. (1994). *The eternal spring of Mr. Ito.* New York: Maxwell Macmillan International.

The fate of a 200-year-old bonsai tree is decided by a young English girl who is living in British Columbia and an old Japanese Canadian gardener who resists being imprisoned in an internment camp after the bombing of Pearl Harbor. RL 6.9 IL 5–8

Hopkins, Lee Bennett. (1995). *Been to yesterdays. Poems of a life.* Illustrated by Charlene Rendeiro. Honesdale, PA: Wordsong-Boyds Mills Press.

This strong and rich collection of poems that paints bittersweet images of family life. Lee Bennett Hopkins presents a powerful and intense coming-of-age work that speaks to today's young readers.

Isaacs, Anne. (2000). *Torn thread.* New York: Scholastic.

In an attempt to save his daughter's life, a Jewish father sends her from Poland to Czechoslovakia to live in a labor camp during World War II. RL 6.0 IL 6–8

Magorian, Michelle. (1981). *Goodnight, Mr. Tom.* New York: Harper.

A child is sent from London to the countryside to escape the bombing during the war. He boards a train with other children and is assigned to spend the duration with a widower who doesn't want to participate in the project. After the boy leaves again for London, Mr. Tom realizes that he has come to love the little boy as a son. RL 6.0 IL 6–8

Santiago, Esmeralda. (1993). *When I was Puerto Rican.* Reading, MA: Addison-Wesley.

In this rich childhood memory frogs sing in mango groves and the rippled zinc roof plays music under the rain. At 13, being the oldest of eleven brothers and sisters, Esmeralda's world changes when her mother decides that the family is moving to New York.

REFERENCES AND SUGGESTED READINGS

Ada, A. F. (1987). Creative education for bilingual teachers. In M. Okazawa-Rey, J. Anderson, & R. Traver (Eds.), *Teachers: Teaching and teacher education*. Harvard Educational Review, Reprint Series No. 19.

Ada, A. F. (1988). The Pájaro Valley experience: Working with Spanish-speaking parents to develop children's reading and writing skills through the use of children's literature. In T. Skutnabb-Kangas & J. Cummins (Eds.), *Minority education: From shame to struggle*. Clevedon, England: Multilingual Matters.

Ada, A. F. (1991). Creative reading: A relevant methodology for language minority children. In C. Walsh (Ed.), *Literacy as praxis: Culture, language, and pedagogy*. Norwood, NJ: Ablex.

Ada, A. F. (1995). Fostering the home–school connection. In J. Frederickson (Ed.), *Reclaiming our voices: Bilingual education, critical pedagogy and praxis*. Los Angeles: California Association for Bilingual Education.

Ada, A. F. (1996b). A visionary look at Spanish language arts in the bilingual classroom. In C. Walsh (Ed.), *Education reform and social change: Multicultural voices, struggles and visions*. Mahwah, NJ: Lawrence Erlbaum Associates.

Ada, A. F. (1996a). The transformative language arts classroom. In L. Scott (Ed.), *Promising practices: Unbearably good, teacher-tested ideas*. San Diego: Greater San Diego Council of Teachers of English.

Ada, A. F. (1997a). Linguistic human rights and education. In E. Lee, D. Menkart, & M. Okazawa-Rey (Eds.), *Beyond heroes and holidays: A practical guide to K–12 anti-racist, multicultural education and staff-development*. Washington, DC: Network of Educators for the Americas.

Ada, Alma Flor (1997b). "Mother tongue literacy as a bridge between home and school cultures. In J. V. Tinajero & A. F. Ada (Eds.), *The power of two languages: Literacy and biliteracy for Spanish-speaking students*. New York: Macmillan/McGraw-Hill.

Ada, A. F. (2003). *A magical encounter: Latino children's literature in the classroom,* 2nd ed. Boston: Allyn & Bacon.

Ada, A. F., & Campoy, F. I. (1998a). *Comprehensive language arts*. Westlake, OH: Del Sol.

Ada, A. F., & Campoy, F. I. (1998b). *Effective English acquisition*. Westlake, OH: Del Sol.

Ada, A. F., & Campoy, F. I. (1998c). *Home–school interaction with cultural or language diverse families*. Westlake, OH: Del Sol.

Ada, A. F., & Campoy, F. I. (1999a). *Música amiga: Pedagogía creadora a través de la canción*. Westlake, OH: Del Sol.

Ada, A. F., & Campoy, F. I. (1999b). *Ayudando a nuestros hijos*. Westlake, OH: Del Sol.

Ada, A. F., Campoy, F. I., & Zubizarreta, R. (2001). Assessing our work with parents on behalf of children's literacy. In S. R. Hurley & J. V. Tinajero (Eds.), *Literacy assessment of second language learners*. Boston: Allyn & Bacon.

Ada, A. F., & Smith, N. J. (1998). Fostering the home–school connection for Latinos. In M. L. González, A. Huerta-Macías, & J. V. Tinajero (Eds.), *Educating Latino students. A guide to successful practices*. Lancaster, PA: Technomic Publishing.

Ada, A. F., & Zubizarreta, R. (2001). Parent narratives: The cultural bridge between Latino parents and their children. In M. L. Reyes & J. J. Halcón (Eds.), *The best for our children: Critical perspectives on literacy for Latino students*. New York: Teachers College Press.

Adorno, T. W., & Horkheimer, M. (1972). *Dialectics of enlightment* (Translated by John Cumming). New York: Seabury Press.

Anzaldúa, G. (1987). *Borderlands/La frontera: The new mestiza*. San Francisco: Aunt Lute Books.

Apple, M. W. (1993). *Official knowledge: Democratic education in a conservative age*. New York: Routledge.

Aronowitz, S., & Giroux, H. (1985). *Education under siege. The conservative, liberal and radical debate over schooling*. South Haley, MA: Bergin & Garvey.

Ashton-Warner, S. (1986). *Teacher*. New York: Simon & Schuster/Touchstone.

Auerbach, E. (1989). Towards a social-contextual approach to family literacy. *Harvard Educational Review, 59*(2), 165–181.

Auerbach, E. (1990). *Making meaning, making change: A guide to participatory curriculum development for adult ESL and family literacy.* Boston: University of Massachusetts Press.

Baird, P. (2001). *Children's song makers as messengers of hope: Participatory research with implications for teacher education.* Unpublished dissertation, University of San Francisco.

Baker, C. (1997). *Foundations of bilingual education and bilingualism.* Clevedon, England: Multilingual Matters.

Bakhtin, M. (1981). *The dialogic imagination.* Austin: University of Texas Press.

Barillas, M. R. (Nov. 2000). Literacy at home: Honoring parent voices through writing. *The Reading Teacher, 54*(3), 302–308.

Belenki, M. F., Clinchy B., Goldberger, N. R., & Tarule, J. M. (1986). *Women's ways of knowing: Development of self, voice and mind.* New York: Basic Books.

Bell, L. A. (1997). Theoretical foundations for social justice education. In M. Adams, L. A. Bell, & P. Griffin (Eds.), *Teaching for diversity and social justice: A sourcebook.* New York: Routledge

Berthoff, A. E. (1981). *The making of meaning— Metaphors, models and maxims for writing teachers.* Montclair, NJ: Boynton/Cook.

Bigelow, B., Christensen, L., Karp, S., Miner, B., & Peterson, B. (Eds.). (1994). *Rethinking our classrooms: Teaching for equity and justice.* Milwaukee, WI: Rethinking Schools.

Blumenfeld, W. (Ed.). (1992). *Homophobia: How we all pay the price.* Boston: Beacon Press.

Boal, A. (1979). *Theatre of the oppressed* (Translated by Charles A. and Maria-Odilia Leal McBride). New York: Urizan Books.

Brisk, M. E. (1998). *Bilingual education: From compensatory to quality schooling.* Mahwah, NJ: Lawrence Erlbaum Associates.

Brisk, M. E., & Harrington, N. M. (2000). *Literacy and bilingualism: A handbook for ALL teachers.* Mahwah, NJ: Lawrence Erlbaum Associates.

Carnoy, M. (1977). *Schooling in a corporate society: The political economy of education in America.* New York: David McCay.

Chomsky, N. (1989). *Necessary illusions: Thought control in democratic societies.* Boston: South End Press.

Christiansen, L. (2000). *Reading, writing and rising up: Teaching about social justice and the power of the written word.* Milwaukee, WI: Rethinking Schools.

Clemens, S. G. (1983). *The sun's not broken, A cloud's just in the way: On child-centered teaching.* Mt. Ranier, MD: Gryphon House.

Covey, S. R. (1997). *The seven habits of highly effective families: Building a beautiful family culture in a turbulent world.* New York: Golden Books.

Cummins, J. (1996). *Negotiating identities: Education for empowerment in a diverse society.* Ontario, CA: CABE.

Cummins, J. (1999). Beyond adversarial discourse: Searching for common ground in the education of bilingual students. In C. Ovando & P. McLaren (Eds.), *The politics of multiculturalism and bilingual education: Students and teachers caught in the crossfire.* Boston: McGraw-Hill.

Cummins, J. (2000). *Language, power and pedagogy: Bilingual children in the crossfire.* Clevedon, England: Multilingual Matters.

Cummins, J., & Sayers, D. (1995). *Brave new schools: Challenging cultural illiteracy through global learning networks.* New York: St. Martin's Press.

Delgado-Gaitán, C. (1994). Sociocultural change through literacy: Toward the empowerment of families. In B. M. Ferdman, R. M. Weber, & A. Ramírez (Eds.), *Literacy across languages and cultures* (pp. 143–170). Albany: State University of New York Press.

Delgado-Gaitán, C., & Trueba, H. (1991). *Crossing cultural borders: Education for immigrant families in America.* Bristol, PA: Falmer Press/Taylor and Francis.

Delpit, L. (1995). *Other people's children: Cultural conflict in the classroom.* New York: New Press.

Derman-Sparks, L., & the ABC Task Force. (1989). *Anti-bias curriculum tools for empowering young children.* Washington, DC: National Association for the Education of Young Children.

Derman-Sparks, L., & Phillops, C. B. (1997). *Teaching/learning anti-racism a developmental approach.* New York: Teachers College Press.

Fanon, F. (1967). *Black skin, white masks.* New York: Grove Press.

Ferreiro, E., & Gómez Palacio, M. (1986/1982). *Nuevas perspectivas sobre los procesos de lectura y escritura.* Mexico City: Siglo XXI Editores.

Fishman, J. A. (1972). *The sociology of language.* Rowley, MA: Newbury House.

Fishman, J. A. (1976). *Bilingual education: An international sociological perspective.* Rowley, MA: Newbury House.

Fishman, J. A. (1989). *Language and ethnicity in minority sociologuistic perspective.* Clevedon, England: Multilingual Matters.

Fishman, J. A. (1996). *In praise of the beloved language: A comparative view of positive ethnolinguistic consciousness.* Berlin: Mouton de Gruyter.

Frederickson, J. (Ed.). (1995). *Reclaiming our voices: Bilingual education and critical pedagogy & praxis.*

Ontario, CA: California Association for Bilingual Education.

Freinet, C. (1976/1974). *El método natural de lectura.* Barcelona, Spain: Editorial Laia.

Freinet, C. (1975/1973). *El texto libre.* Barcelona, Spain: Editorial Laia.

Freinet, C. (1986/1969). *Técnicas Freinet de la escuela moderna.* Mexico City: Siglo XXI Editores.

Freire, M. (1985). *A praixão de conhecer o mondo: Relatos de uma professora.* São Paolo, Brasil: Editora Paz e Terra.

Freire, P. (1970). *Pedagogy of the oppressed.* New York. Continuum.

Freire, P. (1982). *Education for critical consciousness.* New York: Continuum.

Freire, P. (1997). *Pedagogy of hope. Reliving pedagogy of the oppressed.* New York: Herder and Herder.

Freire, P., & Macedo, D. (1987). *Literacy: Reading the word and the world.* South Hadley, MA: Bergin & Garvey.

Frisbie, M. J. (1982). *The active writer.* New York: Macmillan.

Gardner, H. (1993). *Multiple intelligences.* New York: Basic Books.

Gilligan, C. (1982). *In a different voice: Psychological theory and woman's development.* Cambridge, MA: Harvard University Press.

Giroux, H. A. (1983). *Theory and resistance in education: A pedagogy for the opposition.* South Hadley, MA: Bergin & Garvey.

Giroux, H. A. (1988a). *Schooling and the struggle for public life: Critical pedagogy in the modern age.* Minneapolis: University of Minnesota Press.

Giroux, H. A. (1988b). *Teachers as intellectuals: Towards a critical pedagogy of learning.* Granby, MA: Bergin & Garvey.

Giroux, H. A., Simon, R. I., & contributors. (1989). *Popular culture, schooling, and everyday life.* New York: Bergin & Garvey.

González, M. L., Huerta-Macías, A., & Tinajero, J. V. (Eds.). (1998). *Educating Latino students: A guide to successful practices.* Lancaster, PA: Technomic Publishing.

Gordon, N. (1984). *Classroom experiences. The writing process in action.* Exeter, NH: Heinemann Educational Books.

Gramsci, A. (1971). *Selections from the prison notebooks* (Translated by Q. Hoare and G. N. Smith). New York: International Publishers.

Graves, D. (1982). *Children want to write . . .* Exeter, NH: Heinemann Educational Books.

Greene, M. (1995). *Releasing the imagination: Essays on education, the arts, and social change.* San Francisco: Jossey-Bass.

Greene, M. (1996). In search of a critical pedagogy. In L. Pepi, A. Woodrom, & S. A. Sherblom (Eds.). *Breaking free: The transformative power of critical pedagogy.* Harvard Educational Review, Reprint Series No. 27.

Greene, M. (1998). Introduction: Teaching for social justice. In W. Ayres, J. A. Hunt, & T. Quinn (Eds.), *Teaching for social justice.* New York: Teachers' College Press.

Gutiérrez, G. (1971). *Teología de la liberación: Perspectivas.* Lima, Perú: Editorial Universitaria.

Habermas, J. (1981). *The theory of communicative action: Reason and the rationalization of society.* Boston: Beacon Press.

Hewison, J., & Tizard, T. (1980). Parental involvement and reading attainment. *British Journal of Educational Psychology, 50,* 209–215.

Hoffman, E. (1989). *Lost in translation: A life in a new language.* New York: Penguin.

hooks, b. (1984). *Feminist theory: From margin to center.* Boston: South End Press.

hooks, b. (1989). *Talking back: Thinking feminist, thinking black.* Boston: South End Press.

hooks, b. (1994). *Teaching to transgress: Education as the practice of freedom.* New York: Routledge.

Horton, M., & Freire, P. (1990). *We make the road by walking: Conversations on education and social change.* Philadelphia: Temple University Press.

Hurley, S. R., & Tinajero, J. V. (2001). (Eds.). *Literacy assessment of second language learners.* Boston: Allyn & Bacon.

Igoa, C. (1995). *The inner world of the immigrant child.* New York. St. Martin's Press.

Johnson, D. M., & Roen, D. H. (1989). *Richness in writing—Empowering ESL students.* White Plains, NY: Longman.

Keis, R. (2002b). *Developing authorship in Latino parents.* Unpublished doctoral dissertation, University of San Francisco, San Francisco, CA.

Keis, R. (Producer) and Hogg, R. (Director). (1998). *Celebrating literacy: Reflections on literacy, language and culture* [Video]. (Available from the Libros y Familias Program, 150 S. 4th St., Independence, OR 97351.)

Kendall, F. E. (1996). *Diversity in the classroom: New approaches to the education of young children.* New York: Teachers College Press.

Knepper, S. (2001). *Educational philosophies of successful English teachers of adolescent female studies.* Unpublished dissertation, University of San Francisco.

Kozol, J. (1985). *Illiterate America.* New York: Anchor Press/Doubleday.

Kozol, J. (1991). *Savage inequalities: Children in America's schools.* New York: HarperPerennial.

Krashen, S. (1984). *Writing-research: Theory and applications*. Elmsford, NY: Pergamon Press.

Krashen, S. (1993). *The power of reading: Insights from the researcher*. New York: Libraries Unlimited.

Krashen, S. (1999). *Condemned without a trial: Bogus arguments against bilingual education*. Portsmouth, NH: Heinemann.

Kreisberg, S. (1992). *Transforming power: Domination, empowerment and education*. Albany: State University of New York Press.

Kridel, C. (1998). *Writing educational biography*. New York: Garland.

Lee, E., Menkhart, D., & Okazawa-Rey, M. (1997). *Beyond heroes and holidays: A practical guide to K–12 anti-racist, multicultural education and staff development*. Washington, DC: Network of Educators of the Americas.

Leistyna, P., Woodrom, A., & Sherblom, S. A. (1996). *Breaking free: The transformative power of critical pedagogy*. Harvard Educational Review, Reprint Series No. 27.

Levin, D. E. (1994). *Teaching young children in violent times: Building a peaceble classroom. A preschool–grade 3 violence prevention and conflict resolution guide*. Cambridge, MA: Educators for Social Responsibility.

Lorde, A. (1984). *Sister, outsider*. New York: Crossing Press.

Macedo, D. (1994). *Literacies of power: What Americans are not allowed to know*. Boulder, CO: Westview Press.

Marcuse, H. (1968). *An essay in liberation*. Boston: Beacon Press.

Marcuse, H. (1977). *The aesthetic dimension*. Boston: Beacon Press.

Marzán, J. (Ed.). (1997). *Luna, luna: Creative writing ideas from Spanish, Latin American and Latino literature*. New York: Teachers and Writers Collaborative.

Mayer, J. (1988). *The empowerment of ethnolinguistic minority students through an interactive pedagogy within an additive bilingual environment*. Unpublished doctoral dissertation. University of San Francisco.

McCaleb, S. P. (1994). *Building communities of learners*. New York. St. Martin's Press.

McLaren, P. (1986). *Schooling as a ritual performance*. London: Routledge and Kegan Paul.

Memmi, A. (1965). *The colonizer and the colonized*. Boston: Beacon Press.

Merchant, C. (1980). *The death of nature: Women, ecology and the scientific revolution*. San Francisco: Harper & Row.

Nieto, S. (1992). *Affirming diversity: The sociopolitical context of multicultural education*. New York: Longman.

Nieto, S. (1999). *The light in their eyes: Creating multicultural learning communities*. New York: Teachers College Press.

Okazawa-Rey, M., Anderson, J., & Traver, R. (Eds.). (1987). *Teachers. Teaching and teacher education*. Harvard Educational Review, Reprint Series No. 19.

Olsen, L. (1988). *Crossing the schoolhouse border-immigrant: Students and the California public schools*. San Francisco. California Tomorrow.

Paul, S. C. (1990). *Illuminations: Visions for change, growth and self-acceptance*. San Francisco: Harper.

Pérez, B., & Torres-Guzmán, M. E. (1992). *Learning in two worlds: An integrated Spanish/English biliteracy approach*. New York: Longman.

Pinkola-Estés, C. (1997). *Women who run with the wolves: Myths and stories of the wild woman archetype*. New York: Ballentine Books.

Ponsot, M., & Deen, R. (1982). *Beat not the poor desk–writing: What to teach, how to teach it, and why*. Montclair, NJ: Boynton/Cook.

Poplin, M., & Weeres, J. (1992). *Voices from the inside: A report on schooling from inside the classroom*. Claremont, CA: The Institute for Education in Transformation, Claremont Graduate School.

Ramos, J. (Ed.). (1994). *Compañeras: Latina lesbians*. New York: Routledge.

Reyes, M. L., & Halcón, J. J. (Eds.). (2001). *The best for our children: Critical perspectives on literacy for Latino students*. New York: Teachers College Press.

Reza, J. (2002). *Anti bias curriculum*. New York: Open Society Institute.

Rose, M. (1989). *Lives on the boundary. The struggles and achievements of America's underprepared*. London: Free Press.

Scott, L. (Ed.). (1996). *Promising practices: Unbearably good, teacher-tested ideas*. San Diego, CA: Greater San Diego Council of Teachers of English.

Shapiro, J. P. (1933). *No pity: People with disabilities forging a new civil rights movement*. New York: Random House.

Sherover-Marcuse, R. (1981). Towards a perspective on unlearning racism: Twelve working assumptions. *Issues in Cooperation and Power, 7,* 14–15.

Shor, I. (1980). *Critical teaching and everyday life*. Boston: South End Press.

Shor, I. (1992). *Empowering education: Critical thinking for social change*. Chicago: University of Chicago Press.

Shor, I., & Freire, P. (1987). *A pedagogy for liberation: Dialogues in transforming education*. South Hadley, MA: Bergin & Garvey.

Skutnabb-Kangas, T. (2000). *Linguistic genocide in education–or worldwide diversity and human rights.* Mahwah, NJ: Lawrence Erlbaum Associates.

Skutnabb-Kangas, T., & Cummins, J. (Eds.). (1988). *Minority education: From shame to struggle.* Clevedon, England: Multilingual Matters.

Skutnabb-Kangas, T., Phillipson, R., & Rannut, M. (Eds.). (1994). *Linguistics human rights: Overcoming linguistic discrimination.* New York: Mouton de Gruyter.

Smith, F. (1993). *Whose language? What power? A universal conflict in a South African setting.* New York: Teachers College Press.

Smith, F. (1995). *Between hope and havoc: Essays into human learning and education.* Portsmouth, NH: Heinemann.

Strachota, B. (1996). *On their side: Helping children take charge of their learning.* Greenfield, MA: Northeast Foundation for Children.

Takaki, R. (Ed.). (1987). *From different shores: Perspectives on race and ethnicity in America.* New York: Oxford University Press.

Takaki, R. (Ed.). (1990). *Iron cages: Race and culture in 19th century America.* New York: Oxford University Press.

Takaki, R. (1993). *A different mirror: A history of multicultural America.* Boston: Little, Brown.

Tatum, B. D. (1992). Talking about race, learning about racism: The application of racial identity development theory in the classroom. *Harvard Educational Review, 62*(1), 1–24.

Tatum, B. D. (1997). *"Why are all the black kids sitting together in the cafeteria?" and other conversations about race.* New York: Basic Books.

Tinajero, J. V., & Ada, A. F. (Eds.). (1997). *The power of two languages: Literacy and biliteracy for Spanish-speaking students.* New York. Macmillan/McGraw-Hill.

Torre, A., & Pesquera, B. M. (1993). *Building with our hands: New directions in Chicana studies.* Berkeley: University of California Press.

Vygotsky, L. (1962). *Thought and language.* Cambridge, MA: MIT Press.

Vygotsky, L. S. (1978). *Mind in society: The development of higher psychological process* (Trans. & Eds. M. Cole, V. John-Steiner, S. Scribner, & E. Souberman). Cambridge, MA: Harvard University Press.

Wallerstein, N. (1987). Problem-posing education. Freire's method of transformation. In I. Shor (Ed.), *Freire in the classroom: A source book.* Portsmouth, NH: Heinemann.

Walsh, C. E. (Ed.). (1991a). *Literacy as praxis: Culture, language and pedagogy.* Norwood, NJ: Ablex.

Walsh, C. E. (1991b). *Pedagogy and the struggle for voice: Issues of language, power and schooling for Puerto Ricans.* New York: Bergin & Garvey.

Walsh, C. E. (Ed.). (1996). *Education reform and social change.* Norwood, NJ: Ablex.

Wink, J. (1997). *Critical pedagogy: Notes from the real world.* Reading, MA: Longman.

Wong-Filmore, L. (1991). When learning a second language means losing the first. *Early Childhood Research Quarterly, 6,* 3223–346.

Zubizarreta, R. (1996). *Transformative family literacy: Engaging in meaningful dialogue with Spanish-speaking parents.* Westlake, OH: Del Sol.